Ira Progoff is the author of

THE CLOUD OF UNKNOWING (a modern rendering)

THE DEATH AND REBIRTH OF PSYCHOLOGY

DEPTH PSYCHOLOGY AND MODERN MAN

JUNG'S PSYCHOLOGY AND ITS SOCIAL MEANING

THE SYMBOLIC AND THE REAL

The Death & Rebirth of Psychology

An integrative evaluation of
Freud, Adler, Jung and Rank
and the impact of their insights
on modern man.

Ira Progoff

McGraw-Hill Book Company

New York • St. Louis • San Francisco • Düsseldorf

Mexico • Montreal • Panama • São Paulo • Toronto

150.19
Pr T

150. 19

The Death and Rebirth of Psychology

Library of Congress Catalog Card Number 56-12609

Design: Marshall Lee

Second printing, 1969

Reprinted by arrangement with The Julian Press, Inc.

First McGraw-Hill Paperback Edition, 1973

07-050890-9

1 2 3 4 5 6 7 8 9   MU   MU   7 9 8 7 6 5 4 3

A   s Note

T   cceptance which this book has received has in-
d   tifying, especially since it was originally con-
c   ecialized historical inquiry. Over the past dec-
a   nd ever wider use, especially in the universities.
I   rve the particular role of helping build a bridge
b   hology and the humanities. To enlarge the vistas
o   of man is one of the major tasks before us in the
present day. The broad perspective of holistic depth psychology provides a framework in which this can be done in an
integrative and unitary way.

The increasing use of this study of the historical unfoldment
of depth psychology may well have an additional significance.
It may be a sign of a shifting of directions that has been progressively taking place in the study of man over the past two
decades. Wherever the Freudian view of man has been dominant, it has led to a particular style of study in the humanities,
in social science, literary criticism, philosophy, and the history
of culture and religion. This style, centering itself on the repressed and pathological in man, has not at all been distinguished by the depth of its spiritual dimensions. It has felt the
glimmer of an aspiration, but it has been largely held back by
the heavy, nineteenth-century preconceptions with which
Freud began. This may well be why Freud himself in his later
years sought to reach out beyond his own framework of
thought.

On the other hand, a psychological conception of man as a
spiritually creative being, a being whose nature so requires
wholeness that he becomes ill for the lack of it, leads to a
much more open, in many ways much more profound approach to the humanities. In the past few years an increasing
number of major scholars in the field of social and philosophi-

cal studies have recognized this to be the case. One can mention many eminent names in this regard. Those of Arnold Toynbee, Mircea Eliade, and Paul Tillich are indicative.

We come then to an important question. When we recognize that a large, spiritually open, depth view of man is necessary to provide a new basis for studies in the social sciences and humanities, we have to ask specifically what style of psychological concepts will enable us to proceed in such a work. It was to begin to answer this question and to discover deep psychological working tools to be used in the unitary study of man that I undertook the researches which led to *The Death and Rebirth of Psychology*.

In this book the style of approach is historical. I wanted to see what conclusions the major authors in the field of depth psychology reached in their later years, feeling that this would give an indication of what fruitful next steps can be taken in the next generation. The result was an historical inquiry which seems to mark off a direction of thought that crystallized in the works of Freud, and primarily of Adler, Jung, and Otto Rank. It provides a starting point for other studies that have been conducted since then. Readers who wish to see how the lines of inquiry suggested in the last chapter of this book have been carried further since then may refer to *Depth Psychology and Modern Man*[1] for the systematic theoretical development; and to *The Symbolic and The Real*[2] for the practical psychological methodology and philosophical implications.

IRA PROGOFF

August 1969
New York City

[1] Julian Press, New York, 1959.
[2] Julian Press, New York, 1963.

Acknowledgments

The materials upon which this book is based have been drawn from diverse sources. For my knowledge of the life of Sigmund Freud I am greatly indebted to the writings of Ernest Jones whose monumental biography is in many ways a model of psychological honesty. We can hope that comparable studies will eventually be written about each of the other three great men whose works are examined in the following pages; but in the meanwhile I have undertaken to draw a balanced picture of the development of depth psychology from all their points of view using whatever materials have been available to me. In this way I have hoped to open a perspective with which we can chart our course for the future.

In the case of Alfred Adler, the biographical record compiled by Phyllis Bottome and supplemented by the interpretations of Lewis Way have been exceedingly helpful. Adler's personality, however, perhaps more than that of any of the other men under discussion, shines through his writings; and it is mainly upon his writings, in conjunction with the known historical facts, that I have based my study of his work.

Published material regarding Otto Rank has so far been severely limited, but I have had the benefit of the personal remembrances of several individuals who knew Dr. Rank when he lived in Paris and in New York. For the most part, however, I have relied on Rank's own books in interpreting the problems of his life and his personal struggles. Because of the intensity of his search for integrity as expresed in his psychological studies, Rank's writings reveal a great deal about the man himself.

C. G. Jung is the only one of the four authors whom I have been fortunate enough to know personally, and in his case the greatest variety of sources of information have been available to me, although I have not felt free to make use of all of them at this time. During the spring and summer of 1953 and again in the winter of 1955 I was privileged to spend many hours in conversation with Professor Jung regarding the advanced phases of his work and his views on the prospects of modern psychology in general. He was then living in semi-retirement at his home in Kusnacht, Switzerland, and I want to take this opportunity to express my appreciation of the many acts of cordiality, of intellectual openness, and of good will that he tendered me at that time.

For materials cited in the course of this inquiry, my great thanks are due to several publishing firms, particularly, Alfred Knopf, Basic Books, Pantheon Books, Liveright Publishers, Greenberg Publishers, Macmillan, Doubleday, Garden City

Publishing Company, Harcourt, Brace and Company, Routledge and Kegan Paul, Faber and Faber, G. P. Putnam, The University of Pennsylvania Press, and Rascher Verlag of Zurich.

I am particularly grateful to the Trustees of the Bollingen Foundation who have provided not only material support but personal support of the very highest order in the preparation of this work. I want to extend my sincere thanks to them, and to Mr. Fowler McCormick for his many patient acts of friendship.

None is so big as to be ashamed of being subject to the laws which control the normal and morbid actions with the same strictness.

We are concerned not with the possession of truth, but with the struggle for it.

ALFRED ADLER

The ever deeper descent into the unconscious suddenly becomes an illumination from above.

C. G. JUNG

The new type of humanity will only become possible when we have passed beyond this psychotherapeutic transitional stage.

OTTO RANK

Contents

THE DEATH AND REBIRTH OF PSYCHOLOGY

Psychology as a search for meaning

Although it began as part of the protest against religion, the net result of modern psychology has been to reaffirm man's experience of himself as a spiritual being. Despite its conscious intention, the discipline of psychology recalls the modern man to an awareness of his inner life, thus re-establishing the ancient religious knowledge that man's fundamental accomplishments began within himself. This is a paradoxical outcome of Freud's work, and it has the broadest implications for our time.

We are now in the midst of a transformation affecting the fundamental nature and spirit of psychological work. Depth psychology in particular, by which we mean all the varied theories interpreting the "unconscious depths" of man, has arrived at conclusions that reverse the major assumptions with which psychology began as a field of modern study. Its culminating insights suggest not only a new conception of human personality, but a new approach to art and religions as well as a change in the way we see ourselves in history. Our aim in the chapters that follow is to describe this transformation, its beginnings, its stages of growth, and its conclusions. We shall retrace its course of development, concentrating our attention on the progressive deepening of insight in the lives and works of Sigmund Freud, Alfred Adler, C. G. Jung, and Otto Rank. These are the four men who made the most fundamental and continuous contributions to depth psychology. We shall look into their personal experiences as far as the pertinent data are available to us. We shall present and interpret their writings, especially the advanced writings of their later years. And by integrating the disagreements and correspondences of their individual systems, we shall seek to crystallize the new view of man that emerges as the culmination of their collective endeavors.

In order to understand the development of depth psychology in perspective, we must think of it in relation to the changes in the tempo and structure of life that have accompanied the growth of modern industrial society. In the last hundred years the face of our civilization has been radically altered, and the consequences for human beings have often been sharp and severe. In history, whenever a fundamental social change takes place, at least one generation and sometimes two or three are pinned psychologically between the old and the new. Inevitably, the most painful burden falls on those individuals of the intermediary generation who are caught in the squeeze of transition. The recent surge of popular novels about Africa has familiarized us with the spiritual confusion that results when primitive tribesmen are converted into an economical "labor supply"; but that is no different in principle from the kind of social and psychological dislocation that has occurred in Europe and America at each step of the emergence of the modern mode of life.

In Europe, for example, before it was industrialized, just as in Africa before it was Europeanized, individuals experienced the meaning of their lives in terms of the local religious orthodoxies and the accustomed national or tribal ways of life. Wherever its impact was felt, however, the new technological culture disrupted the old patterns irrevocably. Often it came close to destroying them altogether, and it left only a void in their place. The traditional customs and beliefs had provided built-in psychic security for the individual.

They had protected him against losing his equilibrium—short of organic psychosis—as long as he could believe in the practices of the group and participate in them wholeheartedly. But when the old groups were physically broken up and their members were scattered in the factories of the cities, or when, for any of many reasons, the faith in their teachings was gone, the individual was left unprotected. He could no longer have recourse to the spiritual past of his people. He was isolated and cut adrift in life; and it is this situation of the lone individual no longer sustained by the cultural resources of his ancestors that is a main root of the psychological problems that have arisen in modern times.

There is considerable significance in the fact that neither pre-Freudian psychiatry nor psychoanalysis took this cultural background into account in studying the modern personality. They did not approach psychological problems with a social, historical perspective, but proceeded almost exclusively from a medical point of view; and inevitably, their orientation limited the kind of facts that they could see. Even Freud himself, who approached the psychology of neurotics with the open mind of a pioneer, was restricted in his vision because the habits and capacities to which his mind had been trained predisposed him to think medically in terms of pathology and diagnosis. The mental difficulties that late-nineteenth-century psychiatry was called upon to treat had a large historical background, since they were ultimately derived from the cultural transformations of the time; but only their medical aspects, the specific pathologic eruptions of personality, could be discussed and diagnosed in the clinics and consultation rooms. The larger aspects of the problem remained in the background and could be taken into account only later in the twentieth century when psychology began to widen its spiritual vistas.

Because the new era of technology began there, Europe was the first to feel the psychological effects of the modern way of life. Toward the end of the nineteenth century, in France and Germany and Austria, one could see throughout the population that the flux in social classes and the intense changes in the values of life were leaving their marks on the individual personality. It was becoming increasingly difficult for people to fulfill the requirements of family morality in the previously accepted ways. To do what had seemed natural in carrying out the traditional patterns of birth and marriage and death was becoming a matter of question, of tribulation, and often of severe moral conflict. The consequences of the social ferment of the time were felt with particular intimacy and with the greatest psychological force in the changes affecting the habits and desires of sexual contact. Individuals were torn between the traditional teachings they had received in their childhood and the new sexual vogues of modern city life. The changing attitudes toward sexual experience became the hub of the wide ranging transformation in European culture, for the question of sexual expression crystallized in a direct and personal way the larger issues of social freedom then coming to the fore of history.

The loosening of the old class system, the spiritual emancipation of women, the opening of higher education and the arts to large segments of the population were part of the cultural liberation taking place throughout nineteenth-century Europe. All the fixed social forms that hindered change were brought under heavy pressure, and particularly the rigid institution of the father-dominated family came under the heaviest attack. The temper of the time called the traditional structure of the family into question, weakened it at its core by doubt and disaffection, and led eventually to *the new tradition of the rebellion of the children* that has become in diverse forms the initiation of the modern personality to life. By the turn of the century in Europe, the relationship of children to parents lay under a heavy shadow of vague unconscious fears, largely because of the shifting sexual patterns. The confusions surrounding family life and the uncertainty regarding the social forms of sexual expression were at the center of the serious problems arising in an age of psychological transition. Practicing in Vienna, Sigmund Freud saw from the dreams of his patients how large a part sexual and family conflicts played in the neurotic disturbances he had to treat; and from those observations he generalized a theory that became the starting point for modern depth psychology.

The ultimate root of the personal problems that were brought to his consultation room was the historic upheaval at the foundations of European life; but a specific group of symptoms, the complex of family and sexual disturbances, formed a kind of psychological syndrome that Freud was able to study and eventually to treat in a medical way by means of psychoanalysis. The insights that Freud developed in this area remained the almost exclusive basis of therapeutic work in depth psychology for almost three decades. The theories developed by Adler and Jung dealing with these questions were little more than variations on Freud's fundamental themes. Of the three of them, however, Freud was the one who presented the most extreme formulation. He insisted on reducing the parent-child relationship to unconscious sexual drives, and he would admit neither compromise nor deviation. Adler also concentrated on the contact between the child and the parent, but he placed the problem in the context of the "family constellation" as a whole, and thereby minimized the specific sexual factor. Jung also accepted the parental situation as the central fact in psychology, but he interpreted the "mother" and "father" images in terms of complexes and, with other analytical embellishments, he combined the theories of Adler and Freud in terms of a conception of "psychological type." Each proceeded in terms of his own system with his special terminology and favorite points of emphasis; but all three of them "analyzed" their patients on the assumption that the parent-child relationship with its sexual overtones was fundamentally at the heart of the problem. In time, however, as the psychoanalytic point of view gained in popularity, new insights came with added experience, and the vistas of the work were gradually widened.

Adler was the first to enlarge the scope of depth psychology in a significant way. He perceived that, beyond the specific sexual and family factors, the question of the "meaning" of life to the individual has a prime importance in the functioning of the personality. The individual, Adler said, unconsciously constructs a system of "fictions" by which he finds a "meaning" for his life, at least in his own subjective terms. He does this, Adler maintained, because the nature of the human being is such that he inherently requires a frame of reference in order to be capable of functioning as a person. At this point in his work, as we will see more clearly when we discuss Adler's work in detail, Adler was interpreting the psychological significance of the "meaning" of life within the format of his earlier analytical theories. Later, however, he realized that a conception that was only psychological could do no more than hedge the fundamental issue. Adler then attempted the more difficult task of leading the individual psychologically toward an absolute meaning of life such as he himself had experienced via his religious sense of "social feeling." Here Adler achieved a limited success; but the problems he encountered were ultimate ones and their scope was larger than he was equipped to handle at the time. He had, however, embarked upon a new road for depth psychology.

Jung followed Adler's steps in this direction. Like Adler, he interpreted man's beliefs about the meaning of life as being "psychologically necessary" for the functioning of the organism. He came to this insight, in fact, rather early in his development, only a few years after Adler. As his lifework matured, Jung's point of view became more markedly historical, but in a way uniquely turned toward depth psychology. Increasingly, he turned his attention away from the personal and subjective factors in psychology, such as sexual and family influences, and concentrated on the objective, impersonal contents of the "psyche"—mostly symbolic beliefs and experiences—that pertain to the large collectivities of mankind or to the human species as a whole. Jung undertook to clarify man's search for the "meaning of life" by probing the obscure symbolism of the deep "collective unconscious." He identified a particular class of symbols as "archetypes," by which he meant that they represent "universal tendencies" towards types of "metaphysical" belief, and that they compise the psychological core of all the religions and mythologies throughout history. With this conception, Jung was attempting to mediate between the psychological and the spiritual, seeking to show the validity of the transcendent in man without violating the scientific spirit. It was a pioneering effort and exceedingly important for the later development of depth psychology, despite the occasional dogmatism and one-sidedness of Jung's bombastic style. In the end, however, Jung, like Adler, could not hide from himself the fact that his earlier theories had built a psychological hedge around the realities of man's creative and spiritual experiences. He recognized that a further step had to be taken. In his later years, therefore, Jung went to the very edges of psychology; and as he looked outward, his writings became learned, abstract demonstrations of the fact that the fulfillment of psychological work lies in a realm beyond psychology.[1]

In the briefer and more incisive writings of Otto Rank, we can see many of the implications of the later work both of Adler and of Jung drawn into sharper focus. Rank understood that the psychological problem of modern man can be fully appreciated only in historical perspective. He recognized, therefore, that the significance of psychoanalysis is to

[1] See, in particular, his *Answer to Job*. Routledge and Kegan Paul, London, 1954.

be found not in what it is in itself, but in the role that it is
playing in modern civilization. To evaluate psychoanalysis
properly, Rank pointed out, we have to see it in terms of what
it is unconsciously working to replace; and in this area Rank's
detailed analysis led him to the conclusion that psychoanalysis, both as a general conception of man and as a specific
method of therapy, is substituting its analytical interpretations
for traditional teachings of a fundamentally religious kind.

Freud's work treated the old moral problems that had
previously been experienced in spiritual terms, but he translated them into a language of psychological concepts. Ap-
pealing to an age that was on the verge of making science
its religion, this psychological language seemed particularly
"reasonable" and it carried a special aura of "truth." It
sounded convincing to those who were looking for such a
new framework of belief to replace the old spiritual concepts,
and it was accepted as a realistic version of the "truth" about
human nature especially because it was phrased in modern
scientific terms. Freud's rationalistic explanations of human
existence satisfied the new desire for an intellectual answer
to life's problems; but they could not solve man's problems
since man's life in the world inconveniently refuses to follow
rational patterns. Reluctantly, during the last two decades
of his life, Freud recognized this to be the case; and the fact
that it came as a serious disillusionment to him was a major
reason for the marked pessimism of his last years.

Since he had worked with Freud intimately through all the
critical years of psychoanalysis, Rank knew at first hand the
difficulties and disappointments Freud had faced. Gradually,
in the years after he left Freud, Rank drew the necessary inferences from those experiences, and he came finally to the
conclusion that man's existence can be comprehended only

from a point of view beyond rationalizing concepts. Because of the elusive, fateful, ultimately mythologic quality of man's life, Rank was convinced that all psychological theories that attempt to answer the problems of modern man in a rationalistic and analytical way must defeat themselves in the long run. After considering and reconsidering the experiences he had observed at first hand in Freud's life—and Rank studied Freud more closely and personally than a son studies his father—he concluded that the disillusionment of Freud's last years had been inevitable; and this was particularly so because the traditional religious views that psychoanalysis was replacing also had their foundation on a psychic level beyond rationality.

Underlying the search for a "scientific truth" in all psychological systems is the need of the modern person to reestablish a relationship with the creative sources of life. Analytical types of psychology may be aware of this need, but they cannot satisfy it. They can speak of it and offer their prescriptions; but the analytical method itself, because of the paradox of its rationality, cannot bring the necessary experience into existence. Analytical types of psychology cannot make the spontaneity of creative acts come to pass; and that spontaneity is the secret not only of works of art and religious faith but of meaningful experience in everyday life. This was the insight that Rank attained as the culmination of his work, an insight that marks a turning point in the development of psychology. It closes the period in which depth psychology was founded as a medical discipline; and it opens a new phase of development in which depth psychology comes to maturity with an affirmative orientation to the religious and artistic works of the creative personality.

In one form or another, camouflaged by a variety of

terminologies, this fundamental conclusion emerges from the work of all those who have followed Freud's theories to their ultimate consequences. Adler perceived it; Jung emphasized and expanded it; and Rank articulated its implications most candidly of all without reservation. The basic issue was succinctly stated in the pregnant title phrase of Jung's popular book, *Modern Man in Search of a Soul.* The search for a soul has been embodied in psychology wherever the old spiritual urges disguise themselves in scientific forms. And the most penetrating insight into the eventual outcome of this search was expressed by Rank in a phrase that epitomizes the new point of view. Psychotherapy will be able to have a lasting effect, he said, only when it brings the modern person *"a soul without psychology."* [2]

Between the early theories with which Freud laid the foundations of depth psychology and these later views of Jung and Rank, there lies an intricate and suggestive path of development. Out of it, emerging from the advanced writings of the four masters of depth psychology, a new conception of man has arisen, leading to a fundamental change in the nature of psychological work. In the chapters that follow, our aim is to describe the growth and deepening of insights that this transformation in psychology has involved. We want to see what its contents are, and what its implications may be. To do this we need a full historical perspective, and the one mode of procedure that is adequate for our purpose, therefore, is to follow the continuity of thought, and progressive reworking and reformulation of old problems in the light of new insights, as it appears in the

[2] Otto Rank, *Psychology and the Soul,* trans. Wm. D. Turner (Philadelphia: University of Pennsylvania Press, 1950), p. 32. See Chapter VII for the implications of this phrase.

work of the leading and most creative minds in depth psychology. The main core of this book is thus a descriptive history of the growth of depth psychology written with emphasis on its most basic concepts, and directed toward the special goal of clarifying the later, advanced work of Freud, Adler, Jung, and Rank. Our aim is to make possible a larger and fuller appreciation of the *culminating results* of their total lifeworks, for it is this that opens the door to the new directions in psychology.

The death and rebirth of psychology that is the theme of this book refers to the emergence of a new view of man that is fundamentally different from the conception with which psychoanalysis began. The contributions to this new view have come gradually, appearing bit by bit in the mature, reconsidered writings of the four men whose lifeworks have formed the pillars of modern depth psychology. We will not, however, find the new outlook stated explicitly in the writings of any one of them; but when we study the works of all together as part of the growth of depth psychology as a whole, a pattern of development and eventually of transformation reveals itself. Their individual writings and the various periods in their lifework then fall into place as integral phases of a cumulative unfoldment of knowledge in which the final result is radically different, virtually a new creation, when compared to the original starting point. The new view of man thus comes forth as an *emergent* of depth psychology in much the same way as a new species emerges out of the flux of nature. Something that is more than the sum of the individual parts comes forth, crystallized into a new form and living a new life.

Psychology began as an unconscious search for meaning in a civilization whose traditional meanings had been destroyed; but it itself was a victim of the nihilism it was called upon to heal. It was self-consciously rational, placing its faith in the principle of analysis. Increasingly, however, that has changed. Doors that seemed closed have opened from within. *Freud's conception of the unconscious has led beyond itself,* first on a psychological level in the later works both of Freud himself and of Jung; and then in the later writings of Adler, Jung, and especially Rank on a level beyond psychology where the new psychology begins. In its new version, psychology is engaged affirmatively in a search for meaning, not merely as a substitute for old beliefs, but as a creative encounter with reality in the knowledge that only an experience of the meaningful life can make man whole. Only at this late point in its development does depth psychology finally come into touch with the historical problem that first brought it into being. If psychology would fulfill its purpose in history, it must create with its own tools of analysis a practical means of transcending itself. Now it has come to a crossroads; but if we can judge from the mature, reconsidered works of its basic authors, the choice before it is clear. It must take the path that goes directly through the paradox underlying psychological work until, facing itself, it will ultimately fulfill itself by leading the "modern man in search of a soul" to a soul beyond psychology.

II

Sigmund Freud and the foundations
of depth psychology

I. DISAGREEMENT AND CONTINUITY

Psychoanalysis entered the world most modestly. When it began, it thought of itself as nothing more than a technique of therapy; but it became in time a full psychological point of view. Its influence has extended from the clinic to all branches of the humanities, from religion and art to the study of history and culture wherever it is necessary to look beneath the surface of men's minds. In his first studies, proceeding as a neurologist, Freud's main interest was to find a means of healing certain mental disorders then thought to be related to hysteria. His goal was specific and limited in its scope; but the hypotheses that he developed in the course of his work led far beyond medical therapy to a general conception of the human personality as a whole. It is here that we find Freud's greatest contribution. Far beyond the specific aims of his work or even his specific provable conclusions, Freud has been a fertile source of new conceptions and wide-ranging insights, not only for his "orthodox" followers but, more significantly, for those of his critics who have paid him the ultimate tribute of building upon his foundations.

In applying the suggestive hypotheses that Freud first developed, a number of schools of thought have emerged. Soon after his first works were published, Freud gathered around himself in Vienna a small group, composed mainly of medical doctors, with the purpose of stimulating research and discussion in his new science. Alfred Adler, then practicing as a Viennese physician, was an early member of this circle and he soon became one of its leaders, second only to Freud. After a few years, however, disagreements of which we will speak later led to a serious rift between the two men and Adler left to establish a separate center and develop his own point of view. A later addition to Freud's small circle was C. G. Jung, then just beginning to gain recognition as a psychiatrist in Zurich. Jung within a short period became one of the mainstays of the new movement, and Freud at one point was ready to delegate complete authority to him as president of the society and editor of its yearbook. Here, too, however, after a few years of an exceedingly close relationship, strong disagreements appeared. By 1913 Jung and Freud had met for the last time, and Jung's connection with Freudian psychoanalysis was at an end.

Throughout this period of growth and dissent, a young man, Otto Rank, not a medical doctor but a student of culture, was a favored disciple of Freud's. He was secretary for the group from its earliest days and exceedingly prolific in applying psychoanalytic theories in cultural areas beyond the immediate limits of psychotherapy. In 1924, however, Rank published *The Trauma of Birth* and it opened a breach between him and Freud that was too great to be healed. Rank then became the third major figure to leave the original Freudian circle and to work independently in the field of depth psychology. After Rank's departure, rifts and divergences continued to appear, and there are now several additional groups of greater or less significance. The increasing number of points of view has created an atmosphere of fluidity in the field and sometimes a certain confusion; but Adler, Jung, and Rank have retained their positions in the background as the giant figures who stand side by side with Freud as the creative pathfinders of psychoanalysis. By the originality and power of the conceptions they developed, they have been marked off as the four classic founders of modern depth psychology.

It may well be that there is something more than a coincidence in the fact that psychoanalysis, like international diplomacy, has had its "Big Four." Certainly, the comparison with foreign politics is not inappropriate when we consider that from time to time all four of them have given vent to antagonisms as basic and as bitter as though they were nations. And the rival schools have often behaved, as disciples tend to do, with greater partisanship than the masters themselves. None the less, despite the angry atmosphere that followed the great achievements during the early days of psychoanalysis, a unified development in a wide area of problems has taken place. At the same time, it must be kept in mind not only that the disagreements have concerned fundamental issues, but that the ultimate perspectives reached by men like Rank and Jung in their later years are virtually the opposite of the Freudian point of view with which they began. This change in orientation is part of the transformation taking place in psychological thought in our day, and it has to be understood as involving a broad range of divergence within the essentially unified context of depth psychology.

One of the confusing by-products of the history of depth psychology has been the multiplication of names to represent the various schools of thought that established separate positions within the psychoanalytical field. The name that Freud gave his new science when he founded it was "Psychoanalysis," and that has remained the generally recognized label identifying those who have continued along the lines originally laid out by Freud. To distinguish his group from Freud's, and to stress his conception of the "wholeness" of the human organism, Adler designated his point of view as "Individual Psychology," and that name has remained in use despite the paradox that in later years Adler stressed "*Social* interest" more than any other factor. Jung's school of thought was originally called "Komplex Psychologie" in German-speaking countries because one of Jung's most influential contributions to psychology has been his theory of the "autonomous complex." In English-speaking countries, however, the name "Analytical Psychology" has come into wider use as being more descriptive of Jung's basic system, his analysis of personality types, his dream interpretations, and his protracted analytical therapy. As in the case of Adler's "Individual Psychology," however, the name can be highly misleading since it describes only an early phase of Jung's thought. Although his school calls itself "Analytical Psychology," Jung's later theories have gone very far toward undercutting the analytical point of view in psychology. In Rank's case, no definitive name has emerged. His general standpoint is sometimes referred to as "Will Psychology" or "Relationship Psychology," and sometimes the term "therapy" is substituted for "psychology"; but none of these terms accurately describes the major contributions of Rank's later writings, as we will see.

The four groups have been marked off rather clearly as separate schools of thought distinct in their theories and in their approaches to therapy. The extent of their differences, however, has tended to be exaggerated by the fact that all four of the founders, Freud and Adler, Jung and Rank possess a system-maker's temperament, and since they have presented their theories in the dress of their own personally created terminologies, the ideas of each of them have seemed to be "unique"—especially to their loyal followers. Because of their special jargons they have often given the impression that they were discussing different problems, or that, if they were discussing the same problems, they were approaching them from opposite corners of the universe. In reality, however, even though their orientations have been markedly distinct, they have not only been talking about the same basic problems, but they have even arrived on many occasions at strikingly similar conclusions. And these conclusions, expressing different perspectives, have tended to complement one another and carry further the main line of investigation, thus achieving inadvertently a continuous and cumulative development in their young science.

When we consider the total lifeworks of Freud, Adler, Jung, and Rank within a single frame of reference as it is now beginning to be possible to do, it becomes clear that their final divergences are like branches of a tree. Each has grown in a different direction, but the root and source are the same. Though one branch may point north and another south, there is a single purpose behind their growth; and, in the end they all participate in the great scientific enterprise that gives their work its unifying meaning. One of the things that we will try to do in the pages that follow is to draw together and correlate some of the basic interpretations in which the common intentions of the "Big Four" of depth psychology reveal themselves. When the total lifeworks of Freud, Adler, Jung, and Rank are read together, a perspective emerges in which we can see their diverse outlook as integral parts of a continuous stream of development in modern thought. That a fundamental change in orientation can be discerned when we compare the first writings with the last is a sign not so much of disagreement as of a creative growth in insights and ideas with regard to the study of the human personality.

In his courageous essay, *Beyond the Pleasure Principle*, in which he called some of his basic postulates into question while admitting that he did not feel content with the new answers he had found, Freud wrote, "We must be patient and await fresh methods and occasions of research. We must be ready, too, to abandon a path that we have followed for a time, if it seems to be leading to no good end. Only believers, who demand that science shall be a substitute for the cathechism they have given up, will blame an investigator for developing or even transforming his views." [1]

This statement expresses the spirit of dedicated searching that dominated Freud's scientific life. It involved an intimate code of personal integrity, and we find it also in each of the

[1] Sigmund Freud, *Beyond the Pleasure Principle*, translated by James Strachey, The International Psychoanalytical Library, No. 4 (New York: Liveright, 1950), p. 88.

other three men who diverged from Freud's original theories in order to develop a point of view of their own. It was true of Adler when he altered his early biological outlook and sacrificed the advantage he then held in the field of medical therapy in order to present the social and pedagogic emphasis he felt to be required by the times. It was true also of Otto Rank when he overcame with great difficulty the inner struggle that pitted his personal dependence on Freud against his growing disagreement with Freud's theories; and it was true of Rank again when, having developed a social theory and a "will therapy" as correctives to Freud, he went beyond his own newly developed views to investigate the dimensions of experience that lie "beyond psychology." It was true also of the long peregrinations of C. G. Jung in the labyrinths of the psyche. Jung's researches into the psychological principles underlying man's experience of the timeless in himself have been the most delicate and the most difficult of all the studies that have derived from Freud's theory of the unconscious; and they have been the most vulnerable to attack because of their distance from conventional points of view. Despite many unfair personal attacks, however, Jung continued to follow his hunches with a stubborn devotion, following, often in inexplicable ways, the twists and turns of mind they made necessary for him. Jung's was the most uncertain search of all, and it was only in the 1950's after more than thirty years that the significance of his researches began to be recognized.

While it has been true of each of the four of them on the personal level, the integrity of which Freud spoke in the rejection of old ideas and the formulation of new ones has been expressed even more clearly in the aggregate. We can realize this if we think of the writings of Freud and Adler,

Rank and Jung as not merely the works of four individuals, but as the different aspects of a large and varied, ongoing intellectual development. Concentrating on the unity of their work as it has evolved in time, the divergences of opinion, the hypotheses and arguments that have come and gone fall into place, and we can see the old hopes and errors of psychoanalysis in the perspective of a still-unfolding depth conception of man. When we make allowances for the areas where they overlap, repeat each other, or say the same thing in different words, and when we balance out the personal facts that led to undue emphasis in one direction or another, there remains a fundamental consistency in the development of thought and practice from Freud and Adler through Rank and Jung. This is a unity of development that transcends any of the individuals involved in it, for it reaches beyond their particular schools of thought.

It is more than Freudian psychoanalysis or Adlerian individual psychology or Jungian analytical psychology, for all these special doctrines find their ultimate significance in the encompassing science to which they contribute. This science is depth psychology, by which we mean the study of man and all that pertains to him in terms of the magnitude of the human personality and the dimensions of experience that underlie and transcend consciousness. The lives and works of Freud and his great associates appear to us then as chapters in the establishment of depth psychology as a rounded science of the modern psyche, a science based not on the discoveries and personality of any one man, but on the juxtaposition and integration of several. Out of the creative contributions to theory and therapy and the critiques made by the various schools that derive from Freud's original work, a psychological science of depth has emerged at a stage now approaching maturity. In the chapters that follow our aim will be first to show the interrelations between the lives and the theories of the four founders of modern depth psychology in order that we may find the living core of the doctrine they developed; and while doing this, we will seek to follow the main lines of change and growth in their basic conceptions. In this way, by comparing the dead ends of the first period of analytical and reductive depth psychology with the more dynamic and constructive points of view that emerged in the later years, we will be able to perceive the transformation that has been taking place in the psychological approach to the human personality; and we will be able to chart the new directions that it indicates for depth psychology in the future.

2. THE FOUNDING OF A SCIENCE

As an approach to the study of man capable of being applied in the practical work of mental and physical healing, depth psychology can be dated only from the last decade of the nineteenth century. Its roots, however, reach back to ancient and oriental sources, and in this sense it may be said to have a long and profound history. The fact that human nature contains hidden levels beneath the surface of consciousness is much too fundamental a fact to be a new discovery. It was known by philosophers in the classic days of Greece as well as by European savants since the Renaissance. Particularly in the religious disciplines of the ancient Orient and in the practices of the mystery cults of Greece, the existence of "depths" in the personality was recognized as the basis of spiritual experience; and in modern thinkers from Erasmus and Montaigne to Schopenhauer and Nietzsche, the conception of the "unconscious" has provided a central insight into the nature of the human being.

In the case of ancient religious doctrines, especially those of the East, the application of the knowledge of the "depths" in man involved the development of spiritual exercises of various kinds, religious practices and disciplines designed to achieve the spiritual ends required by the particular doctrine. The varieties of Yoga and Zen Buddhist techniques are cases in point. In the East, the conception of the "depths" of the personality has been amplified in an eminently practical way, but its applications of course have always proceeded on the assumption that "reality" is to be found in terms of the Hindu-Buddhist view of the world.

For Europeans, on the other hand, the conception of the "unconscious" has served mainly as a tool of intellectual analysis. Following the temperamental bias of western civilization, the European mind up until our time has seldom conceived of the "unconscious" depths of the personality as a means of spiritual development, but has used the unconscious rather as a conceptual tool for explaining the phenomena of the psyche. Through the nineteenth century, however, even as an intellectual conception the idea of the "unconscious" seldom appeared in a significant way. Only with Freud did the European knowledge of the depth levels of the personality begin to be formulated in specific terms. Psychological facts that had previously been mentioned only in the most general terms in novels and literary essays were now observed and described in the light of sharply defined hypotheses. The philosophical formulations of Schopenhauer and Hartmann that had gained some currency at least in Germany could then be taken out of the realm of metaphysics and treated empirically. Mainly by the analysis of dreams, fantasies, and the symbols of mythology, what had been until Freud's time nothing more than a general notion of the unconscious was gradually crystallized into a definite concept that could be applied in the clinic and interpreted intellectually to clarify some of the confusions of the modern personality. That was the great accomplishment of Sigmund Freud. By means of his work, the philosophic conception of the unconscious was converted into a usable tool of knowledge that could be applied in the treatment of mental illness. It is for this that Freud stands out as the great pioneer whose genius created a science where none had been before. He provided a means of application for the age-old knowledge of the psychic depths in man, and it was this that initiated the growth in depth psychology that has transformed the perspectives of the modern mind.

Although the conception of the depths of the psyche had been found before his time mainly in books of religious wisdom and philosophy, Freud was a neurologist by profession and the primary purpose of his studies was to put the theory of the unconscious to medical use. It seems quite definite that Freud did not come to his discoveries by the road of philosophy but through clinical work and especially through his private practice with cases of "hysteria." In his remarkable record of Freud's life, Ernest Jones has shown that the guiding motive behind Freud's early researches was the hope of establishing a physiological foundation for the workings of the unconscious. There is great significance in the fact that Freud was never able to accomplish this, and that he was forced eventually to abandon the effort altogether. In the meanwhile, however, while he was carrying out his researches from a biological point of view, Freud developed the theories and methods that laid the basis for his later work; and, inevitably, these bore the imprint of his neurological interests. In point of fact, as Jones reports, the main stimulation for Freud's fundamental theories regarding wish fulfillment came not from his psychological researches, but from his medical work under Theodor Meynert, a man whose specialization had made him "the greatest brain anatomist of his time." "It was from the study," Jones writes, "of the disorder called 'Meynert's Amentia' (acute hallucinatory psychosis) that he obtained the vivid impression of the wish-fulfillment mechanism he was to apply so extensively in his later investigations of the unconscious." [2]

The framework of theory that Freud developed concerning the instincts and sexuality reflected the habits of mind of a medical man working with a neurological emphasis, and it was only under the impact of men who saw things from other standpoints—men like Adler and Jung—that Freud was impelled eventually to widen his psychological views. This enlargement of perspective did not take place, however, until after the first World War, particularly after 1920, about two decades after he had formulated his basic point of view, and these revisions were made mainly on an intellectual level. Freud's later theories were not nearly as intimately connected with the needs of his personality and his creative nature as were the original concepts with which he founded psychoanalysis. His earlier views had expressed fundamental aspects of his unconscious life, his intimate problems, his ambitions, and his underlying habits of mind. There can no longer be any doubt about the fact that the very tissue of psychoanalytical theory is closely and directly

---

[2] Ernest Jones, *The Life and Work of Sigmund Freud*, Vol. I (New York: Basic Books, 1953), p. 65.

related to the personality of Sigmund Freud. From the very beginning, the books in which he presented his hypotheses revealed this fact—for it was often his own dreams, his own forgetfulness and wish fulfillments that he analyzed—and the biographical material published in recent years documents it in detail.

Quite naturally, some of those who are ever eager to throw cold water on the psychoanalytical point of view have taken the fact that Freud's personal psychology was related to his psychological theories to mean that the theories were, therefore, not true. That is, of course, wishful thinking on their part. But the special nature of Freud's unconscious life is nevertheless exceedingly important for understanding his work and especially for judging its eventual significance and its areas of error.

The relationship between Freud's personality and his concepts turns out to be, on close scrutiny, rather uneven. At the best, it can be said that his personal life provided the occasion and the stimulus for him to study and recognize within himself psychic conditions that are present in other human beings as well. At the worst, it can be said that he constructed a general theory artificially by interpreting the psyches of others in terms of his own; or that, as Otto Rank intimates, he misread the symbols of some of his dreams—an error that is exceedingly common and easy to make in any school of thought even at this late date in analytical practice—and that he based his theory concerning the psychic significance of the father image on the foundation of this misinterpretation.

In between these two extremes there are several gradations. Ultimately the factual evidence on which the Freudian point of view must stand or fall is not the psyche of Freud himself but the psyches of countless others studied in the clinic and observed in the larger laboratory of society and history. The weaknesses we find expressed in Freud's life may well be understood as part of the price he had to pay for his discoveries. The great importance of understanding Freud's own personality is that it gives us hints as to where we ought to look to find the points where Freud's unconscious personal material may have led him inadvertently to prejudice his interpretations. The possibility of such errors is indicated on some fundamental issues involving the Oedipal relationship of mother and son, the image of the father as the primary psychological and social (also, for Freud, religious) fact, and the significance of sexuality in personal development.

In particular, we find that there are errors of a general and more fundamental nature that Freud seldom articulated, but which had far-reaching consequences in his work because they expressed unconsciously the inner structure of his thought. Errors of this type derived from deeply ingrained habits in Freud's mind, and it is, therefore, especially difficult to separate them from the man as a whole, from his approach to life, and his style of psychological interpretation. Freud's analytical self-consciousness is such a trait inherent in his personality, affecting the foundations of his work and coloring all his theories. It led him to seek "truth" and "understanding" by looking backward and reducing each situation to the one that went before. Because of emotional factors that the new biographical material discloses, Freud was never able to face the fact that to analyze the *origin* of a condition was not necessarily the best way to progress beyond it. But this was Freud's personal preconception, and it became a fundamental assumption of psychoanalysis as well.

It was not questioned because, being inherent in Freud's intimate mental mechanisms, it was taken for granted both by him and by his followers. Attention could be called to it only later on, after the main body of doctrine had been formulated and it was challenged from the outside, especially by Otto Rank.

The publication of Freud's revealing correspondence with Wilhelm Fliess, and the frank, though subdued, interpretation by Ernest Jones of that and similar relationships in Freud's life have revealed that the founder of psychoanalysis was indeed a complicated human being. It will be a long time before the last word has been written on Freud's private affairs, for depth psychologists will certainly be busy for many years to come studying the depths of the life of Freud in relation to his conception of human nature. Certain obvious parallels between his life situation and his theories have already become well known. Freud was the son of a young mother and a father twenty years her senior. He was his mother's first and most favored child, and he was much impressed by her abiding belief that great achievements would crown his life. It was as a mirror of his own experience that Freud wrote, "A man who has been the indisputable favorite of his mother keeps for life the feeling of a conqueror, that confidence of success that often induces real success." [3]

Freud's relationship with his mother was exceedingly close, and the emotional aura surrounding it was intensified by the unusual age situation in the family. In terms of years, Freud's mother was nearer to her son than to her husband. It was a family circumstance in which the son's fantasy of replacing the father by possessing the mother was not without some grounds in reality. Certainly Freud had much

[3] *Ibid.*, Vol. I, p. 5.

more reason than most youngsters have to be concerned with the relationships that he later described as the core of the Oedipal problem. We have several pieces of evidence of a possessive attachment to his mother in Freud's early years: his feelings of awe when as a child he first saw his mother naked (Jones tells us that in his forties Freud wrote of this event, but only in Latin;[4] his confusion at the pregnancy of his mother when the next child was born; his repressed jealousy toward his father; and various other emotional displays. There seems to be special significance in the fact that Freud was particularly impressed by a remark made to him at the age of nineteen to the effect that his immediate family really consisted of three and not two generations; that is, because of the age differences, his father should really have been his grandfather. Freud, Jones tells us, "found the remark illuminating. It evidently accorded with his own early feelings."[5] Obviously, if his father were his grandfather, as he might actually have been if the usual age patterns had prevailed, there would be room for the young Freud to move up into the position of being his mother's mate. The family constellation in Freud's life did indeed provide ample occasion for fantasies of wish fulfillment along Oedipal lines.

There was another condition in Freud's family that seems to have been reflected in his subsequent life experience. His father had had children in a previous marriage, and one of these sons had a son of his own, a boy a year older than Freud. Freud was thus the uncle of a boy older than himself, and this seems to have loomed before him as a confusing and upsetting problem throughout his youth. His nephew was his constant playmate, and Freud, being the younger,

[4] *Ibid.*, p. 13.   [5] *Ibid.*, p. 9.

seems to have considered himself to be the weaker one as well. Jones quotes some exceedingly interesting statements by Freud in connection with his nephew John, showing how Freud reflected on the meaning of the relationship for recurring situations in his later life. "Until the end of my third year," Freud wrote, "we had been inseparable; we had loved each other and fought each other, and as I have already hinted, this childish relation has determined all my later feelings in my intercourse with persons of my own age. My nephew John has since then had many incarnations, which have revivified first one and then another aspect of a character that is ineradicably fixed in my unconscious memory." "An intimate friend and a hated enemy have always been inseparable in my emotional life; I have always been able to create them anew, and not infrequently my childish ideal has been so closely approached that friend and enemy have coincided in the same person; but not simultaneously, of course, as was the case in my early childhood." [6]

Freud's life was indeed a succession of intense friendships that burned brightly, dwindled, and then, as they were about to die, turned to enmity. The instances are many. For twelve years he carried on an intimate friendship with Wilhelm Fliess, a medical doctor engaged in a questionable line of research in Berlin, and it was a relationship in which Freud was the weaker, the dependent individual. It appears from the record of the correspondence that when the break came it was Fliess who provoked it and Freud who sought to avoid it, even though Fliess was apparently far the inferior of the two both in capacities and in attainments. Freud bared his soul completely to Fliess, wrote him of his personal life

[6] *Ibid.*, pp. 8-9.

and of the development of all his basic ideas, since he corresponded with him during his most fertile period. The relationship was, as Freud certainly realized, a necessity for him emotionally, and its break-up seems to have come to him as a serious blow. He needed it, or some relationship that would be the equivalent of it, in order to have the energy with which to do his creative work. We need not undertake here to interpret the overtones of that relationship, except to note that Freud was apparently in need of a male muse, a condition not unknown among the ancient Greek philosophers. In his case, however, the termination of the relationship was always very negative, and left lingering antipathies and resentments on both sides.

In addition to Fliess, Freud had an exceedingly close friendship with Joseph Breuer, the doctor with whom he did his first researches on hysteria. This relationship does not seem to have been comparable in erotic overtones to the one with Fliess, but it did involve an exceedingly close collaboration. Once again Freud needed to have someone by his side to encourage him and stimulate him in order to do his best work. Like the Fliess episode too, the friendship with Breuer was intense while it lasted, at least on Freud's side, and the enmity that arose when it ended was equally intense.

Freud's relationships of this kind were carried over to those who worked with him, particularly as he gained in stature and fame, extending to those of his disciples whose own competence made them able to approach him as colleagues. Of these, Freud's relationship with C. G. Jung was certainly the strongest and the one with the greatest libidinal overtones. A transference based on a rather complex combination of factors was certainly involved in Freud's feeling for Jung. He was at one point emotionally so involved that he came very close to turning over the entire psychoanalytical movement to Jung's guardianship and control, even though Jung had already shown certain mental reservations regarding Freud's theories. Only the intervention of Freud's Vienna followers, motivated undoubtedly by quite understandable feelings of jealousy, caused Freud to alter his course.

Jones pertinently observes that Freud's relationship with Jung displayed a definite similarity to his previous involvement with Fliess. It was much shorter in duration and apparently it was not nearly as intimate; but it burned strongly while it lasted, and when it approached its end, Freud showed a marked reluctance to accept the facts. He became exceedingly negative about the whole affair. It was, however, an episode of the greatest significance in the lives of both men, and we will discuss it more fully a little further on.

3. A RIDDLE OF FATE AND PSYCHOLOGY

We must recognize an exceedingly profound psychological insight in Freud's remark that, after the years of his youth, his nephew John reappeared in his life in many different incarnations. It indicates the perspective in which Freud understood his personal situation; and it reveals one of his fundamental preconceptions, an unconscious assumption that was in the background of Freud's thought throughout his life though it came to the fore and was articulated clearly only in his later writings.

When he had reached the conclusion that the hedonistic "pleasure principle" upon which he had founded his original wish-fulfillment theories was not adequate for many problems in depth psychology, Freud began to look for alternate hypotheses. In his "Beyond the Pleasure Principle," he considered the possibility that "repetition" can be treated as a fundamental principle of psychic life, and there he developed some tentative hypotheses concerning it. In that book it can easily be seen (particularly if one knows that pattern of events of Freud's life) that Freud had something deeper, more far-reaching, and more elusive than "repetition" in the back of his mind. There was, to begin with, a simple fact of observation with which Freud seems to have been considerably impressed: the fact that individuals tend to relive the patterns of events they have experienced in the past, so that, in different settings and with different participants, there is a "recurrence of the same" in individual lives. Quite unconsciously, people behave in such a way that, even though they are in new situations with new people, the outcome of events follows the same lines as such situations in the past. It is as though a "fate" followed certain individuals, marking out a path for them and assigning a pattern of events to their lives, a pattern that repeats itself endlessly and inescapably.

We know that Freud was convinced from his earliest years that he was destined by fate for a life of great achievement. He was born with a covering of black hair over his body and this was interpreted as a sign of special favor according to traditional Jewish lore. An old woman fortuneteller informed his mother too, when he was still an infant that he was destined for great things; and his young mother, placing her dreams in her first-born son, did not neglect to tell him of these portents often during his childhood.[7] Freud spoke of these things as a skeptic, but there can be no doubt about the

[7] *Ibid.*, pp. 4, 5.

fact that they made a deep impression on him and that they became part of the intimate, unspoken beliefs he held about himself and the ultimate outcome of his life. Such a belief about personal fate could not, of course, be harmonized with his scientific attitude, particularly since Freud followed an exceedingly strict rationalistic point of view. On the conscious level, he could speak of it only in psychological terms, describing the psychological mechanisms by which "fate" makes herself felt in individual lives, but leaving the background of his thoughts unspoken.

One of the primary qualities of Freud's mind was a capacity for theorizing that enabled him to formulate large hypotheses on the basis of a few specific cases. That was part of his natural equipment for his work, and he felt himself drawn constantly to reconstruct the facts and feelings of his own experience in their universal aspects. His early, self-analytical books in particular are examples of this procedure. He would analyze himself, and then ask in what form what was true of him was also true of others. If a "fate" was operating in his life in some uncanny way that he could not accept consciously but did nevertheless accept unconsciously, such a "fate" must also be present in the lives of others, even if it were not leading them to lives of the same distinction that had been promised to him. By the last third of his life, Freud had already had many occasions on which to learn that his fate was not an altogether beneficent one. His destiny as a pioneer did not carry with it a life of ease and social acceptance. Freud understood that, however, and in the richer moments of his life when he was not torn by resentment and the shadowy sense of persecution that returned from time to time, he did not quarrel with it. As far as we can judge from his writings and behavior, he accepted the negative aspect of his fate as being as necessary and as inescapable as the affirmative side. He recognized that the "fate" of each person has its light side and its dark, and that neither can be avoided.

Such a point of view could certainly not be maintained scientifically, nor could it be defended on rational grounds. Freud could give it expression only indirectly, treating it not as a truth to be taken literally, but as a pattern of human events brought to pass for psychological reasons. That is what he did in his *Beyond the Pleasure Principle*. He spoke of people who give the impression that they are "being pursued by a malignant fate or possessed by some extraneous power." And he added with careful rational decorum, "But psychoanalysis has always taken the view that their fate is for the most part arranged by themselves and determined by early infantile influences."

Having translated "fate" into acceptable psychological terms, he then connected it directly with his hypothesis concerning "repetition." "The compulsion which is here in evidence," he said, "differs in no way from the compulsion to repeat which we have found in neurotics, even though the people we are now considering have never shown any signs of dealing with a neurotic conflict by producing symptoms." [8] In other words, he had been speaking of people who are not mentally ill, but whose actions led them time after time to unpleasant experiences that seemed always to repeat the past. Freud listed several examples of this, but the first two are particularly revealing. In them, under cover of anonymity Freud was describing his conception of his own life as we can now recognize it from his biography. "Thus," Freud wrote there, "we have come across people all of whose human

[8] Sigmund Freud, *Beyond the Pleasure Principle, op. cit.,* pp. 23-24.

relationships have the same outcome: such as the benefactor who is abandoned in anger after a time by each of his *protégés*, however much they may otherwise differ from one another, and who thus seems doomed to taste all the bitterness of ingratitude; or the man whose friendships all end in betrayal by his friend." [9]

He was speaking of himself and of the disciples and friends who had left him and had turned against him; and one feels in the tone of his words the self-pity of a man who is convinced that he has the inescapable destiny of suffering at the hands of others. Freud traced this unhappy fate to his ambivalent relationship with his nephew John, the boy he played with and fought with, his intimate friend and enemy. In both of these capacities John was always essential to him, and that was why, as Freud remarked in later years, John reappeared in many "incarnations" throughout the rest of his life. The series of men like Fliess and Breuer and Jung who were first Freud's intimate friends and collaborators, and then his foes, were each, with respect to Freud's recurring psychological pattern, incarnations of his childhood friend and foe.

That was the psychological explanation that Freud gave for the personal fate he felt to be governing his life; but his psychological understanding did not alter his underlying belief that his "fate" was inescapable and inexorable. Quite the contrary; his rational interpretations bolstered his irrational convictions. By tracing to their roots in childhood those patterns of behavior that become so fixed in the individual personality that they do in fact become his "fate," Freud was merely elaborating the "psychological mechanisms" by which, as his own experience had indicated, "fate" expreses itself in

[9] *Ibid.*, p. 24.

the individual. These reasonable explanations on the conscious level helped make it possible for him to retain on the deeper psychic level that intimate sense of destiny that seems to have sustained his personality in both its affirmative and negative aspects with its predictions of success and its unavoidable corollary of personal suffering. His analysis of the psychological origins of individual "fate" gave him a rational and scientific means of holding that irrational but emotionally persuasive conception of a personal destiny that had been sealed into his character by his mother's favor and loving faith in him as a very young lad.

Considering this, an odd but most significant observation suggests itself. Now that the facts of his life have been published and we are in a position to have a fuller view of Freud's personality, we can see several correspondences between him and the mythical figure of Oedipus. Curiously enough, it is precisely on those points where the similarity is most marked that Freud's interpretations are silent, even to the point of ignoring aspects of the Oedipus saga that are quite obvious and even of major importance to other scholars. The Oedipus story is underlain, for example, by a dark sense of fate moving uncannily in the background of events, and the spirit of this was not at all alien to the feelings that Freud had about his own existence, as we have seen. Nonetheless, in the case of Oedipus, Freud preferred not to concern himself with the question of fate directly, but to speak of fate rather as being forced upon defenseless man by means of relentless sexual urgings.

In his self-analysis, Freud wrote that he had recognized the fact that his great desire was not to become a doctor but rather to solve the "riddles of the world." "In my youth," he said, "I felt an overpowering need to understand something of the riddles of the world in which we live and perhaps even contribute something to their solution." [10] We are bound to recall then that the event directly leading Oedipus to his fateful marriage with his mother was his solving the riddle of the sphinx. The understanding of a dark mystery was thus the act that set the wheels of fate in motion; and when we follow the symbolism of Freud's unconscious mind as his writings and biography reveal it, we see that the act of achieving an understanding of hidden facts signified to him a step leading to union with his mother. There is thus a world of meaning condensed in the pregnant sentence of Ernest Jones when he says of Freud, "He had a veritable passion to *understand*." [11]

Jones's work has clearly shown that Freud's relentless quest for rational understanding was driven by a deeply irrational motivation. That fact is, by itself, altogether in accord with the fundamental insight of depth psychology that all human activity, creative as well as pathologic, derives from a source that is deeper than consciousness. The point that is important for us here, however, is that the particular kind of irrationality that governed Freud's psyche had an unbalancing effect on the underlying procedures he bequeathed to depth psychology. It led Freud, and those who studied under him, to an analytical point of view that glorified the use of intellectual reduction out of all proportion to its actual value in therapy. The mere fact of "analysis" had an emotional significance to Freud that was almost religious in its force. This was because analysis was for him the means of solving human riddles, and via the symbolism of his unconscious, solving riddles meant union with his mother. Freud's personal life

[10] Ernest Jones, *The Life and Work of Sigmund Freud, op. cit.,* Vol. I, p. 28.
[11] *Ibid.,* p. 14.

thus gave an analytical bias to the development of depth psychology, and since it was imbedded in Freud's basic conceptions, it had a profound influence that was exceedingly difficult to overcome. Only with the combined critiques of Adler, Jung, and Rank was headway made against it.

Despite his analytical bias, and beyond his personal difficulties and the occasional neurotic symptoms that he displayed, it seems obvious that Freud was essentially a creative type of person. As creative artists often do, he pursued his work by means of "hunches" and intuitions that shot ahead of his analytical mind. At one point, describing the workings of Freud's mind, Jones is moved to remark, "What a demonic intuition must have been at work!" And one can only agree with him.[12]

It is often the case with scientists that they reach their hypotheses by intuitive means and then retread their steps analytically, verifying their "hunches" with mathematical and laboratory data. Einstein, Henri Poincare, and other creative scientists have testified to inspirational experiences that crystallized their research and gave them new insights; and Freud must certainly be classed among them. In the case of Freud, however, there is one most important difference that sets him apart from the others, and this concerns an additional use to which he put the analytical method. When his intuition would open a new insight to him, Freud would delineate it analytically, check its inner logic, and verify it with the empirical data available to him. Thus far he would be following the procedure of other scientists. But Freud then continued and went a step further. He extended his use of analysis so that it became not merely an intellectual tool of study, but a method of psychic healing.

[12] *Ibid.*, pp. 53-54.

This additional step raises issues that are altogether separate from the more simple and fundamental principle involved in following an analytical point of view in scientific investigation. Freud's contention that to raise unconscious psychic contents to consciousness would have a healing effect on the personality leads to questions that are still unanswered; but for Freud it was something that he took for granted, as though it were a self-evident fact. He was completely committed to the belief that the understanding obtained by tracing events to their antecedents, that is, by reducing "effects" to their "causes," would have a healing result; and yet it seems quite clear that the basis and nature of this one-sided faith in analysis was something of which Freud himself was not conscious at all. It was simply a preconception of his, an unconscious habit of his mind, inclining him to regard analytical reasoning not merely as an intellectual mode of procedure but as a "higher" principle, a principle with curative and life-renewing powers.

This analytical approach to human experience was something that Freud could never surrender. It was too deeply ingrained in his mind. His analytical point of view remained at the very core of his writings and activities throughout his life, for it provided him with a criterion by which he could judge the "reality" of other people's words and deeds on the conscious level. In the depths of his unconscious psyche, this analytical attitude carried strong emotional overtones, so strong in fact that he often applied it with the fervor of a man with a religious dedication. Much more than an intellectual method or a psychological theory, it was a fundamental way of experiencing life that Freud described in the name he gave to his new science when he called it "psycho-*analysis.*"

In later years, after he had worked with Freud for more than two decades, Otto Rank came to the conclusion that this analytical attitude involved a specific kind of self-conscious mentality peculiar to what he called the "psychological era." Rank saw in Freud's work the epitome of the intellectual outlook in an age so weakened in its capacity for faith that it was reduced to brooding self-analytically over all its motives and acts. He recognized, undoubtedly from his own experience, that this was a spiritually paralyzing point of view, and he was impelled then, in the last years of his life, to seek a new road that would lead away from the analytical attitude and go "beyond psychology." At an earlier date, Adler and Jung had also perceived this weakness in Freud's orientation, but they had directed their attacks at only certain aspects of it. When they first developed their separate orientations, neither Adler nor Jung presented a fundamental alternative to Freud's approach. They had, rather, accepted it as their foundation and had been content to adapt it and modify it to meet the most pressing needs of their psychiatric practice. It was only later in their careers that they began to come to grips critically with Freud's fundamental assumptions and to question the basis of his analytical point of view.

All three of the men who made major additions to Freud's work eventually discarded his compulsively analytical emphasis. In each case, however, they could readjust their modes of procedure only very slowly and with the greatest difficulty. As disciples of Freud, they had naturally absorbed his habitual style of thinking, and on a level below consciousness, it had become their own. As a result, Freud's analytical and reductive approach was deeply imbedded not only in the tissue of the psychoanalytical doctrines with which they had worked, but also in the concepts that Adler,

Jung, and Rank themselves developed when they emerged from the Freudian cocoon and undertook their individual flights.

We find in each case that the ideas that first made them famous—the theory of "organ inferiority" and the "family constellation" in the case of Adler, the theory of "psychological types" and the "collective unconscious" in the case of Jung, and the conception of the "birth trauma" and the "analytical situation" in the case of Rank—were all expressions of Freud's analytical habits of thought. The significant fact, however, is that despite the heavy commitment and attachment that their years of training had laid upon them, they all took gradual but clearly perceptible steps away from Freud's analytical orientation. And in their later years, after their reputations and positions had been secured, they each made increasingly bold strides in the direction of a non-analytical depth psychology. We see this in Adler's effort to communicate "social feeling" as a humanistic religious experience; in Jung's transcendent sense of the "self" as well as his conception of the creative power of archetypes; and in Rank's impassioned drive to reach the irrational ground of artistic and religious experience. In their mature works, each of them showed a clear realization that the analytical and reductive point of view leads to a dead end for depth psychology, and each in his own way undertook to go beyond it. Interestingly enough, there are even signs that in the last two decades of his life, Freud himself would have wished to accompany them in this direction, if he had only been able.

The last writings of Freud, Adler, Jung, and Rank contain the seeds of a fundamental transformation in the spirit of psychological work. Most significantly, the new view of their later years tends toward agreement on a much deeper level than the conflicting theories of earlier days that led to personal recriminations among their respective "schools." At the furthest reaches of their thought, the lines converge. A new outlook on life then suggests itself, radically different from the self-conscious psychologism with which Freud and his followers began. It opens a larger perspective than psychology had had in the past, and we now turn to retrace the steps by which it has emerged to see what it involves and what its ultimate consequences may be.

III

Alfred Adler and the wholeness of man

I. THE FIRST DEFECTION FROM FREUD

At the time that he became interested in Freud's work, Alfred Adler was engaged in medical studies regarding the effects of inferiorities in the organs of the body. He had come to the conclusion that the human organism tends to compensate for its bodily weakness psychologically, or physiologically by overdeveloping another part of the body. When he came into contact with Freud, Adler had not yet formed the theories for which he later became famous; but he seems already to have embarked upon his special line of investigation. He did not have a conception of the unconscious comparable to Freud's, but it is probably correct to say that at no point in his life did Adler share Freud's view of the "unconscious." On the basis of his clinical material, however, and adapting for his purposes some of the theories of the French psychiatrists, notably Pierre Janet, Adler came independently to his view that the process of compensating for organ inferiorities takes place below the threshold of consciousness. It was this general conception, roughly analogous to Freud's theory of the unconscious, that was the basis of Adler's sympathy with Freud's point of view. During the years that they worked together their underlying conceptions were similar, but by no means identical.

When Freud's first major book, "The Interpretation of Dreams," was published, Adler was a young physician practicing in Vienna. "That man has something to say to us," he is reported to have said when he read the book.[1] Soon afterward the book was strongly attacked in the Vienna press, and Adler wrote in its defense, thus calling himself to Freud's attention. Freud invited him to join the small psychoanalytical circle in Vienna, and though he seems to have had some misgivings about doing so, Adler accepted the invitation. He worked closely with Freud, soon becoming a leading figure in the group, second only to Freud himself; and this is remarkable when we consider that Adler and Freud seem never to have shared a fundamental agreement as to the nature of the unconscious portions of the psyche.

Through all the years that Freud and Adler worked together, their underlying conceptions remained markedly distinct. It was more a working relationship than a union of minds, and the rupture that came with such bitter recriminations in 1911 seems to have been inevitable because of the objective differences of their points of view. It has often been said that personal feelings, jealousy, and ambition were the

[1] Phyllis Bottome, *Alfred Adler: A Biography* (New York: Putnam, 1939), pp. 56 ff.

cause of the rift between Freud and Adler; but the animosities that came seem to have been a result of the separation rather than the cause of it. There was much wounded vanity on all sides. In later years, for example, Freud referred to Adler as an ungrateful disciple who could not bear to stay in second place; and Adler replied that he had never been a student of Freud's but that "Freud and his followers are uncommonly fond of describing me in an unmistakably boastful way as one of his disciples, because I had many an argument with him in a psychological group." [2]

Both these attitudes are one-sided. Adler for his part seems really to have developed his insights independently of Freud, although the similarities were strong enough to provide much common ground and a basis for co-operation in their studies. On the other hand, it must also be said that Adler's contact with Freud was a tremendous catalyst for his maturing creative powers and brought him a degree of prominence that might otherwise have been difficult to attain. Adler seems to have arrived at a full realization of his abilities during his relationship with Freud, for proximity to greatness often has the effect of drawing the latent strength of an individual to the fore. Adler's capacities developed wonderfully during his years with Freud, and when his researches came to fruition his personal stature as well as his point of view made it necessary that he travel a separate road.

In their mature years, Freud and Adler displayed a marked difference in temperament; and this difference was reflected at fundamental levels of their psychological work. Freud was primarily a searcher for "truth." He thought of himself as being, before all else, a discoverer, an explorer of new realms

[2] Alfred Adler, *Social Interest: A Challenge to Mankind* (London: Faber & Faber, 1938), p. 254.

of science. He desired naturally that his discoveries would be of practical value to other people, but his desire for the acquisition of knowledge came first. Writing in his autobiography about the time when he had had to choose a profession, Freud said, "Neither at that time, nor indeed in my later life, did I feel any particular predilection for the career of a physician. I was moved, rather, by a sort of curiosity, which was, however, directed more towards human concerns that toward natural objects." [3]

While Freud was moved by curiosity and his urge to solve the "riddles" of life, Adler was impelled by an intense desire to be of help to people. In this sense, Adler was primarily a physician, a practitioner of the art of healing; and his "science" of individual psychology can be understood as the tool that he developed when he realized that he would be able to help human beings only when he had a knowledge of the body and mind, and the encompassing unity of the wholeness of man.

Because of his dominant interest in helping and healing, Adler was not content with Freud's laborious method of tracing the roots of a neurosis back to early sexual experiences. To do this, he felt, turned the attention of the individual still further away from the problems at hand and tended to encourage the wish to escape from reality that is the neurotic's main difficulty. The neurotic, Adler said, cannot face the problems of his daily life, and so retreats into an unreal world of fantasy, or he becomes physically ill so that he will not be called upon to meet the demands of life. The problem of the "present moment" that cannot be faced is the one, Adler held, that brings the patient into the doctor's office. The job of the therapist is, then, so to

[3] Freud, *An Autobiographical Study*, p. 13.

strengthen the individual that he will be able to look his present situation squarely in the eye and come to grips with it. To turn back self-consciously to the events of the past encourages the tendency to retreat from life that has already become a pattern for the patient and is the hallmark of his illness. Particularly is this true if the analysis of the past is more than a brief excursion and lasts for several years as psychoanalytical therapy tends to do. Such probings may be exceedingly interesting in the psychic material they produce, and also in the self-knowledge they bring both to the patient and to the therapist; but they do not meet the primary requirement of healing the person sufficiently to help him meet the pressing problems of his existence. This was a criticism of Freud with which C. G. Jung concurred; and it was echoed even more dramatically a decade later by Otto Rank.

Adler's basic objection involved his general orientation to the personality; but his specific objection was directed against Freud's tendency to reduce neurosis to sexual terms. Adler was by no means inclined to undervalue the importance of sexuality in the development of the personality; but his point was that by concentrating on libidinal drives, Freud lost the larger perspective and failed to consider the individual as a whole. Every individual, Adler said, has a particular point of view from which he interprets the events and circumstances that comprise his life. A great many factors come into the individual's orbit to be judged by him and to be given a personal meaning in terms of what Adler called the "style of life"; and of these many things, sex is one.

Adler's view countering Freud's did not minimize the force of the sexual urge, nor its role in the personality; but

Adler insisted that sexual life can be understood only in the context of the individual's total pattern of experience. He insisted that Freud's theory that the character traits of the whole person are determined by sexual factors is true only of certain types of persons. In cases where sexuality is the primary element, he said, that very fact has to be interpreted as a sign of the one-sidedness of the personality and as an indication that something of a more fundamental nature than sex is disturbed in the individual. As Adler saw the problem before him, therefore, he required a principle of interpretation with which he would be able to study the personality as a whole and place sexuality as well as the other components of the psyche in their proper perspective.

2. EVOLUTION AND THE DYNAMICS OF INFERIORITY

In approaching this problem, Adler followed the biological point of view to which he was accustomed. He began by considering the human being as an organism that has appeared at a late date in the scheme of evolution, and he set out to see how far he could understand man's mental development against that background. He then made an elementary observation that had the greatest significance for him. He noted the fact that the human species is markedly inferior when it is judged by the criteria that determine whether a species is fit to survive in the struggle of evolution. "Imagine a man alone, and without an instrument of culture, in a primitive forest!" Adler wrote. "He would be more inadequate than any other living organism. He has not the speed nor the power of other animals. He has not the teeth of the carnivore, nor the sense of hearing, nor the sharp eyes, which are necessary in the battle for existence." [4] From a physiological point of view the human species could not possibly hold its own in the competition of primal life. "Man," Adler concludes, "seen from the standpoint of nature, is an inferior organism." [5]

With this negative beginning, Adler's line of thought quickly took an affirmative turn. It was quite possible, he noted, that man's weakness could have resulted in his extinction. That has certainly been the fate of countless other unfortunate species. The human species, however, was able to survive, and the reason is to be found in its ability to respond to its natural inferiority by developing other capacities. In particular, Homo sapiens compensated for his physical weakness by developing mental abilities, and these carried him from the rudimentary state of primal consciousness to the high degree of mental life that man has achieved in civilization. Adler's point then is that the inferiority with which human existence began in nature has had a most affirmative result: it has led to the development of the human psyche.

Inferiority has acted upon man, Adler says, as a "stimulus to the discovery of a better way and a finer technique in adapting himself to nature. This stimulus forces him to seek situations in which the disadvantages of the human status in the scheme of life will be obviated and minimized." [6] But in order to achieve this, it was necessary to have "a psychic organ" capable of conceiving and carrying out the many plans and stratagems that would make so insecure a species

[4] Alfred Adler, *Understanding Human Nature*, trans. by W. B. Wolfe (Garden City: Garden City Publishing Co., 1927), p. 28.
[5] *Ibid.*, p. 29.
[6] *Ibid.*, p. 29.

able to survive. Adler comments, "It would have been much harder to have made an organism out of the primitive and original man-animal which would be capable of fighting nature to a standstill, by the addition of anatomic defenses such as horns, claws, or teeth. The psychic organ alone could render first-aid quickly, and compensate for the organic deficiencies of man. The very stimulation growing from an uninterrupted feeling in inadequacy developed foresight and precaution in man, and caused his soul to develop to its present state, an organ of thinking, feeling, and acting." [7]

If man's inferiority has resulted in the development of his psyche, it has also made of him a social being. "Darwin long ago drew attention to the fact that one never found weak animals living alone." [8] And Adler adds the observation that, "No human being ever appeared except in a community of human beings." But, he pointed out, "This is very easily explained; the whole animal kingdom demonstrates the fundamental law that species whose members are incapable of facing the battle for self-preservation, gather new strength through herd life." Because of his weakness compared to other species, man has had to "supplement his feeble body with many artificial machines in order to continue his existence upon this planet." "Social life became a necessity because through the community and the division of labor in which every individual subordinated himself to the group, the species was enabled to continue its existence." [9]

The development of man's psyche and his inherently social way of life thus are bound to each other. Both are the affirmative results of the poor physical equipment with which the human species emerged in the process of evolution. To survive, man needed to use resources other than those avail-

[7] *Ibid.,* pp. 29, 30.   [8] *Ibid.,* p. 28.   [9] *Ibid.,* p. 28.

able to the individual organism alone. He needed to band together in groups; and he needed to use his mental powers in
turning his environment to account. Both of these go together, psyche and society; neither is possible without the
other, and each bears the marks of the other through and
through. In his all too infrequent theoretical passages, Adler
points out that the relationship between the development of
the mind with its special patterns of operation and man's
social existence involves an indissoluble unity that is now
ingrained in the permanent nature of man. "Since society
has played an essential role in the process of adaptation," he
says, "the psychic organ must reckon from the very beginning with the conditions of communal life. All its faculties
are developed upon an identical base: the logic of communal
life." [10]

There is in this statement of the inherent unity of the
psyche and society a theoretical pronouncement of the greatest importance, but Adler, unfortunately, developed it only
to a limited degree. In his conception of "social feeling," of
which we shall speak shortly, he treated the social nature of
the psyche only in relation to the therapeutic requirements
of his individual psychology, and he devoted hardly any attention at all to its historical and cultural aspects. It is interesting to note in this respect that C. G. Jung began his
work with a conception very similar to Adler's regarding the
social nature of man and the exceedingly close relationship
between the psyche and society; and in his case, because of
his wide-ranging hypothesis concerning the historical nature
of the unconscious, it has had some profound and highly suggestive elaborations reaching beyond the scope of Adler's

[10] *Ibid.*, p. 30.

work. Particularly in his later writings, too, Otto Rank worked with a social conception of man and the psyche comparable to Adler's, and he developed it in a highly original way in charting the outlines for a depth social psychology.[11] All three, Adler, Jung, and Rank are thus significantly ranged against Freud on this question, for they base their work on a social conception of the psyche in contrast to Freud's insistence, derived from his connection with eighteenth century romanticism, on the fundamental conflict between the individual psyche and civilization.[12]

The conception of evolution on which Adler based his psychological theories was a working combination of the views of Darwin and Lamarck. Fundamentally Adler accepted the Darwinian principle of the "survival of the fittest"; but he had to modify it by adapting Lamarck's hypothesis in order to support his special theory that it is not only the least fit species that very often survives, but that such species often become superior when they are able to adapt themselves and transmit their acquired traits. That has been the pattern by which the human species has been able not only to survive but to build imposing civilizations upon the limitations of nature. Man began with an inherent organic inferiority that might well have eliminated him from competition in the animal kingdom had his psyche not developed with sufficient strength to undertake co-operative social living and overcome the physical inferiorities of the species. That is Adler's meaning when he says, "Imperfect organs and functions are subject to constant stimulation from without, and it is when such stimulation bears fruit, i.e.

[11] See Chapter VII, Sections 3 and 4.
[12] See Ira Progoff, *Jung's Psychology and Its Social Meaning*, pp. 39-48.

when the organ or function adapts itself to the outside world, that evolution takes a step forward." [13]

On the basis of this pragmatic interpretation of the evolutionary process, Adler came to the conclusion that there is a "fundamental law of life" expressed in the development of the species as a whole and in the psychology of individuals. It is, he said, a law of "overcoming" based on the deep insecurity, the "psychical agitation," that the organism feels as a result of its weakness. In the rough-and-tumble of evolution, the organism that does not overcome its inferiority falls by the wayside, for it has failed to prove itself fit to survive. In the advanced condition of human life the individual is protected by civilization and he does not feel the impact of the struggle for self-preservation in the same stark physical terms. The overtones of the primal insecurity remain, however, and they are felt as part of the situation. Because of the sense of inferiority ingrained in the psyche from evolutionary days, man feels that his "mental equilibrium is constantly threatened." Always he "feels his incapacity before the goal of perfection"; there is ever something more that he must do, something more he must become in order to subdue his basic sense of insecurity in the face of nature.

Man is driven from within himself, as by a blind teleology, ever striving toward goals he cannot see, seeking to overcome his inferiority by reaching toward perfection. "It is only when he feels that he has reached a satisfying stage in his upward struggle that he has the sense of rest, of value, and of happiness." But even such sensations of fulfillment are fleeting. They are brushed aside by a renewed realization of weakness and an urge to overcome it. "In the next moment his goal draws him farther on, so that it becomes clear *that*

[13] Alfred Adler, *Social Interest, op. cit.,* p. 69.

to be a human being means the possession of a feeling of inferiority that is constantly pressing on towards its own conquest. The paths of victory are as different in a thousand ways as the chosen goals of perfection. The stronger the feeling of inferiority that has been experienced, the more powerful is the urge to conquest, and the more violent the emotional agitation." [14]

It is inherent in man's nature, this "law of overcoming:" and it is for Adler the guiding principle behind his psychological theories. The insights that led to the famous doctrine of the "inferiority complex" derive from this, and Adler's psychological point of view depends on a conception of inferiority that is much more than psychological. It is, on the intellectual side, an evolutionary conception of the human organism as a whole, with a theory of how the psyche compensates for physical weakness. But for Adler personally it was more than an intellectual conception. To him at least, as we can judge from his practical work, it was a continuing experience of the teleology at work in the human being, guided by his sense of the inner rhythm of psyche and soma balancing and sustaining each other within the unity of the human person. It is important to keep this level of Adler's thought in mind if we are to appreciate the full depth of his approach to human beings.

3. THE STYLE OF LIFE AND THE MEANING OF NEUROSIS

Because he believed that the feeling of inferiority and its compensation involves a process inherent in human nature, Adler looked for its expression in the earliest situations of

[14] *Ibid.,* pp. 72-73.

life. The primary human relationship, he said, is that of a child with its parents; and in the human species, as a result of the slowness with which the oganism matures, paticularly in advanced civilizations, the parent-child relationship has an extended duration. The basic inferiority that the child feels in his relations with his parents because of his dependence on them is thus worked deeply into the personality, both because it is the first inferiority situation and because civilization causes it to last a considerable time. The relationship with other children in the family also plays an important role in the early appearance of inferiority feelings. An only child possesses the undivided attention of his parents, and when a new child is born he feels his position in the family to be threatened. The sense of insecurity that thus arises within the family unit from the relationship of the parents to the children and of the children to each other is now recognized to be of major significance in the development of the personality; but Adler was a pioneer in the field, and he was led to it by his fundamental conception of the role of inferiority in the development of the human organism as a whole.

In working out the various combinations of circumstance in which the child feels his first fears and seeks to overcome them, Adler developed his view of the "family constellation." The size and structure of the family unit and the relationships within it provide the atmosphere for the child's crucial years of growth. Everything depends, he said, upon the position of the child in the "family constellation," the way in which the child interprets his position, and the way he reacts to it. The family unit must be understood as the particular environment of which the child is most intimately aware, but the child himself is the active individual in the situation. Necessarily, it is the special requirements of the child's organism that determine the way he plays the role that falls to his lot in the family. There is thus, in Adler's view, a fundamental factor in the growth of the personality that must be considered prior to the family situation. This is the physical constitution of the child. Adler here referred to the extensive studies he had carried out during the earlier period in his career regarding organ inferiorities. The child is born with, or soon acquires through illness or accident, weaknesses in one or another part of his body. These may be either visible weaknesses of the external parts, the limbs, the skin; or they may be internal weaknesses affecting the functioning of the body. In any case, their effect will be felt, for the child's organism will respond by seeking to overcome these constitutional inferiorities on the psychic level. The child's personality begins to shape itself from within by a process of psychic compensation for physical weaknesses, and the family constellation provides the field in which this balancing process takes place. As the organism seeks to achieve an equilibrium of its psychic and physical natures, the child is simultaneously finding its place in the family constellation and coming to terms as best it can with the inferiorities of its position. In the interplay of these two basic situations of the child's earliest years, the underlying pattern of the child's personality is formed. On the basis of his work in his children's clinics in Vienna, Adler concluded that by the time the fifth year has been reached, the child has formed character traits and an approach to his environment, a "style of life," that is more or less permanently fixed.

"Each individual," Adler wrote, "adopts for himself at the beginning of his life, a law of movement," that is uniquely his. It is his own characteristic "style of life" formed during childhood and retained as the core of his personality through later years. "The law of movement is for each individual different in tempo, rhythm, and direction," [15] necessarily so, since it is a combination of inner balances worked out by the individual organism to meet its peculiar needs and situation. In every case it involves inferiorities and the effort to compensate for them in such a way that life will be livable mentally and physically for the individual organism as a whole.

"Every psychical expressive form," Adler said, "presents itself as a movement that leads from a minus to a plus situation." [16] And this inner urge to establish a favorable condition for the organism, ever "spurred on by a feeling of inferiority" involves an inner patterning of the individual's manner of experiencing life. The psychological and physical sides of the personality are equally expressed in this. The individual develops a particular way of carrying himself, a characteristic psychic "gait" that reflects his personality in its movements. The "style of life" reveals itself in all the activities and attitudes of the human being, not only psychologically but somatically as well. The body speaks both by its illnesses and by the behavior of its organs in health. Adler referred to this as "organ dialect," and he claimed that because the body and psyche are encompassed by a larger organismic unity, the man who understands the body's language can understand the depths of the psyche as well.

As Adler conceived of it, the "style of life" of each individual is unique; it is for each his special way of facing life. In its uniqueness, however, it is also inherently social because of the fact that the human being is able to express his personality only in relation to the community. In this connec-

[15] *Ibid.*, p. 37.   [16] *Ibid.*, p. 37.

tion, Adler postulated a fundamental trait in man that he called "social feeling." The original expression he used was *Gemeinschaftsgefuhl,* a loose though suggestive expression that is particularly difficult to render into English. In its overtones, it conveys an inner sense of intimate connection with the community, and it has been translated variously as "social interest" or "social sense" as well as "social feeling," depending on the immediate context. The basis of the conception was essentially Adler's view of human evolution, and especially his belief that man was able to survive as a species only because he compensated for his physical weakness by learning to live in societies. Because of this last point, the relation to the group has a primary importance in the development of the individual personality. It is reflected in the first clear formations of the style of life, for the attitude of the individual toward other persons inherently involves his attitude toward himself. Adler thus concluded that the way in which social feeling is expressed in the style of life —the degree to which it is expressed or is inhibited—is a key to the genesis of neurosis; and he made this the hub of his analytical work.

Under what circumstances does the child first form his pattern of approaches to life? How does he develop the "law of movement" that becomes the characteristic mark of that individuality with which he participates in the community of mankind? In one form or another, whether because of the weakness of an organ or because of his position in the "family constellation," or because of both, the child begins life with a sense of inferiority that his organism works to overcome. At the same time, he is necessarily drawn towards the group to share in relationships with others. There is thus a continuing interplay of inferiority feelings and social feelings,

and it is out of the synthesis of these two divergent tendencies that the personal style of life emerges. The process by
which this takes place is not conscious by any means; the
individual is hardly aware of it, and he could, in any case, no
more direct it consciously than he could guide the flow of his
blood. "There can be no question here," Adler points out,
"of anything like a repressed unconscious, it is rather a question of something not understood, of something withheld
from the understanding." [17]

The formation of the individual's style of life takes place
by a natural organismic process. It does not involve unconscious fantasy fulfillment of repressed wishes, but the teleological expression of tendencies latent in human nature. It
was for Adler an affirmative unfoldment of the human organism, and this, we should note, was the key to the conception of the "unconscious" that he was placing in opposition to Freud's.

Because he followed the assumption that the life processes,
both of the body and of the mind, always have a purpose
hidden somewhere behind them, Adler approached the
problems of the mental life in terms of what it was working
toward. In dealing with a neurosis, he would ask the question: what is it seeking to accomplish? He believed that, as a
general rule, the psyche of each individual governs itself in
such a way that it eventually crystallizes out of the various
tendencies in its nature a total pattern of existence that
makes its life both livable and meaningful, at least from
within its own point of view.

The individual may not be aware of the "meaning of life"
that he experiences; he may misconstrue its content and its
significance; and he may even fail to recognize that such a

[17] *Ibid.*, p. 16.

meaning exists at all in his life. Adler insists, however, that whether the individual is aware of it or not, there is necessarily a "meaning" operative in him psychologically, and it is expressed in such unconscious aspects of the personality as the individual's psychic "gait," the rhythm and pattern of his "law of movement," his "style of life," and so on. Because the individual is usually not aware of it, Adler claimed that the sensitive psychologist is very often in a better position to know the actual meaning of the person's life than the person is himself. He was, of course, referring here to the "meaning of life" in the specific and restricted sense of its functioning as a psychological experience. The metaphysical question of the ultimate meaning of human existence he understood to be something quite separate, to be dealt with on another level.

Seen from a psychological point of view in the light of evolution, the individual's inner experience of the "meaning of life" is an indispensable factor in the survival of the organism. It is, therefore, a natural psychological process for the personality to work toward establishing a meaningful style of life by integrating its dual urges to overcome its inferiorities and to express its social feelings. Such an integration comes into being gradually and unobtrusively as the individual grows to maturity. At various points in its development, however, it may reach a stalemate where things go wrong and the "meaning of life" is no longer clear.

When such an impasse occurs, it is most important in Adler's view to maintain a large and affirmative perspective and to conceive the problems of the organism in terms of the purposes toward which its development as a whole is tending. The questions Adler then asks are: What is this organism striving to accomplish? What is it requiring its psyche to do? What inferiority is it trying to overcome? How is it going about the problem of compensating for its weakness? And how is it related to the community in its inferiority and in its attempt at compensation?

The point behind these questions was not to "diagnose" the neurosis but to discover the meaning and purpose behind it. Adler's aim was to assist the organism in restoring its natural self-healing powers; and for this, he needed to identify the subjective meaning of life that had broken down for the individual and determine the reasons that it had become unable to operate any longer.

Assuming the neurosis to be a symptom of impasse in the growth of the personality, Adler's point was that this impasse need be no more than a passing difficulty. It arose in the first place, he said, because the individual was stymied in his growth; and if the natural processes of psychic growth could be restored the difficulties would resolve themselves naturally, much as a healthy body heals its wounds. His underlying conception was that the human psyche is drawn irresistibly toward a personal goal that it envisage as "perfection" though it can neither describe it in advance nor explain its reasons for seeking it. "Man knows more than he understands," Adler wrote.[18] He is led onward by a principle within himself that guides him where he cannot see. He falters when he loses touch with this principle, and he is healed when he returns to it.

[18] *Ibid.*, p. 258.

4. PAMPERED CHILDREN, OEDIPUS, AND A THEORY OF DREAMS

In his analytical reconstruction of the way the personality develops, Adler, like Freud, stressed the importance of the early years of life. Necessarily, the relationships within the "family constellation" have a formative effect upon the child, but Adler recognized that the cultural ground surrounding the family, the values of life that it absorbs from the community, may be even more important. In particular, the modern type of society stresses the competition of individuals on all levels of life. By the example of the elders, it teaches its children to seek "success" through achieving economic advancement or a higher social position; and this tends to bring about a special kind of personal psychology in the modern world.

Parents complain, Adler pointed out, that their children will not carry out their wishes; but they do not realize that their children are merely expressing the same attitude of competitive aggressiveness and self-centeredness that they themselves have unconsciously instilled in them. The education that serves as a preparation for modern life is concerned mostly with "spurring on the ambition of the child, and awakening ideas of grandeur in his mind." It is not mainly the fault of the schools or of the parents individually, but it is a necessary consequence of the social atmosphere that the child absorbs in his daily life. It occurs, Adler said, "because our whole culture is permeated with similar grandiose illusions. In the family, as in our civilization, the greatest emphasis is placed upon that individual who is greater, and better, and more glorious, than all the others in his environment." [19]

As a result of this social situation, a particular pattern of development has become characteristic for the modern personality. Adler calls it the psychology of the "pampered child." The child whose every whim is granted to him matures with an ego-centered style of life. He becomes accustomed to having his desires satisfied by others, and quite understandably he begins to think of his personal pleasures as ends in themselves. He is the object of attention, and so he regards other individuals as nothing more than the means of satisfying his desires.

Pampering reduces the social feelings to a minimum, Adler says, for "the spoilt child wants to have everything." [20] And this is precisely the attitude that causes so much difficulty in the modern world. The individual seeks his pleasures in himself, particularly in the comforts and satisfactions of his body. With his interests concentrated upon his own existence and not related to the community, his self-centered world becomes insecure and he can perform only "with difficulty the normal functions that evolution has established." The frequency of the neurotic condition in modern times is thus, in Adler's view, directly attributable to the competitive individualism that dominates western culture, for it results in a type of personality whose social feelings are severely underdeveloped and whose drives toward self-indulgence display the main characteristics of the pampered child.

We are bound to notice that the type of personality Adler is describing here is one that follows the "pleasure principle" in its style of life; and it was upon this principle that Freud's

[19] Alfred Adler, *Understanding Human Nature, op. cit.,* p. 64.
[20] Alfred Adler, *Social Interest, op. cit.,* p. 213.

fundamental conceptions were based. Freud conceived of the human being as seeking pleasures of a kind that could be experienced directly, and more or less tangibly, within the biologic organism. The drives and satisfactions he described were therefore libidinal, essentially sexual, rather than social in nature. Adler was not at all shy about drawing the inference, then, that Freudian psychoanalysis was essentially a description of the competitive, ego-centric pampered personality, since that was the type of person Freud encountered most in his practice. If that is the case, Freud's error would consist essentially in the fact that he attempted to build a general theory of human nature on the basis of a particular type of neurotic personality. The cultural climate around him prejudiced Freud's work, Adler says, for "Psycho analysis was far too encumbered by the world of spoilt children." "The result was that it always saw in this type the permanent pattern of the psychical structure, and the deeper layers of the mental life as a part of human evolution remained hidden from it." [21]

Two main areas in which this aspect of the Freudian theories becomes clear are the wish-fulfillment theory of dreams and the Oedipus complex. The important position that the Oedipus theory holds in psychoanalytic thought is a sign of the degree to which it expresses the essential spirit of Freud's point of view. The little boy who dominates his mother's attention becomes accustomed to having all his wants and desires satisfied by her. The problem, according to Adler, is that when he grows older he has to face situations in which other persons are involved, and then he finds that it is not as easy for him to have his way. Society rebuffs him when he seeks to gratify his ego-centric desires, and it is

[21] *Ibid.*, p. 36.

then that the boy—even if he has already grown to "man-hood"—recalls in the depth of his unconscious psyche that satisfaction was not denied him by his mother in days gone by.

He remembers—or fantasies—that she was sufficient for his needs, and he dreams, according to his "style of life," that if he could still possess his mother all would be well. This, in Adler's construction, is the basis of the Oedipal situation of mother and son. It derives from the mentality of the spoiled child who is so accustomed to the attention of others that, psychologically, he has no alternative when reality frustrates his wishes but to satisfy his desires in fantasy. Otherwise the "style" of his psychic functioning would collapse, and his ego with it.

The fantasies that arise in such circumstances are often severely aggressive and antisocial. The pampered type of person, Adler says, frequently "gets into such a frenzied state that he even harbors murderous designs against other persons who oppose his wishes." [22] When it is the repossession of the mother that the pampered child seeks, the father is the individual who inconveniently stands in the way. The fantasies are thus bound to involve the elimination of the father from competition, and given this purpose, father-murder in the Oedipus pattern is only the extreme—and generally merely symbolic—solution. It was this theme that Freud found recurrently in his own dreams and in the dreams of his patients. In Freud's analysis it became the core of the Oedipus complex; but in Adler's interpretation, such symbolism in dreams is only a product of the pampered personality in modern times who cannot bear to leave his wishes unfulfilled.

[22] *Ibid.*, p. 214.

Sexual desires that the individual has been unable to satisfy with other women, or that he has been afraid to attempt to satisfy without the protecting care and presence of his mother, may also be projected upon the mother with corresponding hostility toward the father. But this also must be understood in the context of what the personality is unconsciously trying to accomplish. The organism is seeking to keep itself in the state of childish self-gratification that his mother's pampering made possible. "Freud's so-called Oedipus complex," Adler says, "which seems to him to be the natural foundation of psychical development, is nothing else than *one of the many forms that appear in the life of the pampered child,* who is the helpless sport of his excited fantasies." [23]

Adler's approach to the interpretation of dreams makes the significance of this point even clearer. He begins with the general conception that the dream life and the waking life belong to a single psychic continuity, for they are contained by "the unity of the personality." Whatever its particular subject or content, therefore, the dream necessarily expresses the same style of life that the individual displays in his ordinary waking activities. The dream, however, like a fantasy, is different from conscious life by virtue of its freedom. It is not confined like waking experience to a world of inconsiderate facts where other persons also have wishes and pit their wills against our own. The dream is not hampered by the hard facts of reality for it is free in its world of fantasy to create a reality of its own. This new and autonomous universe in which the events of the dream transpire bears the stamp of the dreamer's style of life. The psyche, after all, can proceed only according to its own pattern, and

[23] *Ibid.,* p. 51.

the world of fantasy that the dreamer creates is necessarily cast in the dreamer's own psychic image.

The dreamer is, in a sense, creating a set of circumstances in which it will be possible to fulfill the wishes that were thwarted in life. But Adler insists that something larger than wish fulfillment is involved. In the dream the psyche as a whole is moving in the direction set by the style of life. The individual is, in other words, continuing to work toward the goals he had already been consciously seeking. Because of the confusion that clouds consciousness in the neurotic state, however, the personality often does not know what its goals really are. The individual's development is, therefore, stymied on the conscious level; but it is free to proceed once the restrictions and tensions of consciousness are relaxed by sleep.

Dreaming carries forward the psychic work that has been stalled by the conscious mind, and it moves in various, essentially unintelligible ways, toward the stabilization of the organism as a whole. It does this, Adler says, in accordance with "the supreme law of both life-forms, sleep and wakefulness alike," namely, "the ego's sense of worth shall not be allowed to be diminished. Or, to adopt the terminology of individual psychology: the struggle for superiority in accordance with the ultimate goal rids the individual of the pressure of his feeling of inferiority." [24]

The dream is thus working toward an inner balance, seeking to strengthen an ego made insecure by its feeling of inferiority in the competition of life. "We know," Adler says, "the direction the path takes." The unconscious purpose of the dream "is to find a solution suited to the style of life." The dreamer, therefore, expresses his style of life in his

[24] *Ibid.*, pp. 255-256.

dream, and with the greater freedom for fantasy that dreaming permits him, achieves a life solution of a kind that his personality requires but cannot achieve in the world. The solution for its life problem that the organism finds in the dream is able to satisfy the needs of its style of life at the cost of its social feelings. The dream permits this because it does not need to take the desires of other human beings into account. That is why, Adler points out, "the dream as the purposeful creation of the style of life seeks to keep at a distance from social feeling and represents that distance." [25]

Finding his solution within the safety of the dream, the dreamer is freed also from the limitations of common sense. In fact, Adler says, that is one of the main purposes of dreaming, "to lead the dreamer away from common sense." It involves a "self-deception," but one that is psychologically necessary. The individual is faced with "a problem for whose solution his social feeling is inadequate," but he saves his ego by willingly deceiving himself in his dreams. There he is able to follow "his style of life so that he may solve his problem in accordance with it; and—since he sets himself free from the reality that demands social interest—images stream in upon him that remind him of his style of life." [26]

In Adler's view, dreaming is a psychic mechanism by which the individual escapes from a reality that he cannot face. The neurotic finds in fantasy a solution that seems more suitable to him because it accords with the subjective needs of his personal style of life. The constructive value that Adler finds in dreams is that, despite their lack of social feeling and their flight from common sense, they do carry the psychic life forward and provide an area of freedom for psychic activity that consciousness inhibits. When the dream

[25] *Ibid.*, p. 257.   [26] *Ibid.*, p. 259.

is over, there are overtones, "feelings, emotions, and a frame of mind," that remain behind; and these may be of help to the conscious development of the personality if the capacity for social feeling is increased. As a whole, however, Adler's interpretation of dreams is limited; it is reductive in spirit and essentially analytical. Most important, as we will see in later discussions, because he avoided the dynamic conception of the unconscious that was developed in the work of Freud and Jung, Adler did not perceive the depth dimension of dreams. He could see that the uninhibited flow of dream material speeds the process of psychic compensation in the organism and thus helps stabilize the personality; but he could find in dream symbolism little more than a retelling of old personal problems with new metaphors. At one point he compared dreams to the words of a man who tries "to defend his mistakes with far-fetched arguments," [27] for, fundamentally, dreams did not make sense to Adler. But that was precisely what gave him his clue for the particular type of dream interpretation that he developed. Dreams are very often unintelligible, he said, because their very nature requires them to make no sense. Their purpose is specifically to permit a release from common sense, so that the individual who finds the world's requirements too hard for him can reconstruct reality in keeping with his private style of life.

This conception of dreams has a general resemblance to the Freudian theory of the unconscious wish, but it tries to set wish fulfillment in a larger context. In general, in Adler's view, the dream is much less concerned with gratifying a particular repressed wish than it is in securing a channel for the free expression of the style of life as a whole. If the

[27] *Ibid.*, pp. 261-262.

style of life of an individual is of the egocentric type that Adler attributed to the "pampered child," the dreams will show a tendency toward the fantasy fulfillment of frustrated wishes; but that will be the case only to the extent that the individual's style of life requires it. The symbolic situations presented and enacted in dreams are to be understood in the terms provided by the unconscious patterns of the dreamer; the pampered child, for example, will have wish-fulfillment dreams of an erotic nature. But where the style of life follows another principle, the pattern of dreaming will be quite different and will not correspond at all to the psychoanalytical theory of sexual wish fulfillment.

In this perspective, the Oedipus theme that Freud regarded as an inherent part of the human psyche can be clearly seen to be a specialized type of dream content characteristic only of a particular mentality. It is the dream of those who have been so completely protected and gratified by their mothers that they cannot bear to share her with another, even their father, while they fear to risk seeking new gratifications in the outside world. It is this combination of fear and possessive desire for the mother and the comfort she represents that is exceedingly common in modern times; and that is the reason, according to Adler, that the theory of the Oedipus complex has seemed to so many persons to be a true description of the facts. The popular acceptance of the psychoanalytical theory of sexuality, he wrote, "was due to the predisposition of the immense number of pampered persons who willingly accepted the views of psycho-analysis as rules universally applicable. For by endorsing the theory they were thereby confirmed in their own style of life." [28]

[28] *Ibid.*, p. 36.

5. THE COMPLEXITIES OF BEING SIMPLE

Adler intended this comment to undercut the Freudian position, but its consequences are not as serious as it seemed at first. All psychological theorizing is inevitably, as C. G. Jung phrased it, a "personal confession." That is true of the creative individual who has the original insights and formulates a new system of thought; and it is true of those who support the doctrine and become its advocates before the world. The man who originates a point of view necessarily expresses something of himself in his conceptions; but those who accept his theories do so because, seeing something of themselve also reflected there, they are able to recognize the germ of truth that it contains.

To say this, however, is merely to state one of the fundamental facts upon which all the history of thought depends. To say that Freud's conceptions of the functioning of the human psyche were accepted by individuals who felt their personal psychology to be described in them does not undermine Freud's position; for the same point can be made with regard to every school of psychological thought. We are faced here with a psychological fact that is so inescapable that it really should be self-evident; but to state it calls attention to the partiality and inevitable incompleteness inherent in all analytical psychological theories. The fact that Freudian psychoanalysis reflects a particular attitude and style of life does not mean that it is untrue, but rather that it is true only when it is used to interpret the specific mentality that called it forth and that it is able to describe. In the nature of the case, psychoanalysis remains relevant and essentially accurate as a description of a large segment of the modern mind; but if it is not placed in a larger perspective it can give an altogether misleading impression. This perhaps is the heart of Adler's criticism, as it was later of Rank's. Adler felt it necessary to stress that psychoanalysis is not valid as a general or universal psychology and that it should, therefore, not be applied to questions where moral values and the meaning of life are involved. These limitations of psychoanalysis are, however, more widely recognized today, and it is no longer as necessary to stress them as it was in Adler's time.

It is interesting to note the correspondence that Adler consciously drew between the development of his own style of life and his psychological theories. In a letter quoted by his biographers,[29] Adler tells that his "earliest recollection is of sitting on a bench, bandaged up on account of rickets, with my healthy elder brother sitting opposite me. He could run, jump, and move about quite effortlessly, while for me movement of any sort was a strain and an effort." Adler was about two years old at the time. While he had this illness, all the members of the family were especially solicitous of him, but when a younger brother was born he naturally received a great deal less attention. And Adler says, "I have a vague idea that I took this apparent loss of attention on the part of my mother very much to heart."

Oddly enough, Adler does not have a clear recollection of the birth of this younger brother, but he recalls that when he was about four years of age his younger brother died. At that time it seemed to him that his mother smiled sooner than she should have after the death, and he attributes that

[29] References here are from Phyllis Bottome, *Alfred Adler: A Biography*, *op. cit.*, pp. 9-13. This letter is also cited in Hertha Orgler, *Alfred Adler: The Man and His Work* (London: C. W. Daniel Co., 1939), pp. 19 ff.

to a resentment he carried against her for many years, until later in life he concluded that he had misjudged her. It may not be far off the mark to surmise, in the light of Adler's theories—and also Freud's—that the smile that he saw coming too soon to his mother's face was but a projection of his own repressed desire, for which he blamed his mother as he meant to blame himself; since that younger brother had been his main competition for his mother's attention.

Because of his early illness, Adler had a slow start in developing his physical capacities and his elder brother was always ahead of him. To overcome this, Adler says, "I did my utmost to excell at running, jumping, and rushing around—activities of which my elder brother was constantly making me aware." The development of his style of life was, at least from this self-description, a step-by-step illustration of his main theories. In his earliest years his attack of rickets gave him a serious organ inferiority, but he realized too that because of it he was the center of attention in his family. He experienced feelings of jealousy towards a younger brother and was constantly driven in his youth by a desire to surpass his elder brother who had been the first basis of comparison from which his feelings of inferiority were derived. Thus we find in Adler's life the two main types of inferiority feelings that he later described: those derived from organ weakness, and those resulting from relationships within the family constellation.

Adler maintained that a patient's earliest recollection was always of the greatest significance for the style of life, and in his own case, that earliest memory is of an illness that kept him on the sidelines while his elder brother was at play. It is small wonder, then, that Adler points to "the accord existing between the facts of my childhood and the views I expressed in my studies of Organ Inferiority." We can surely agree with him when he says that, "The similarity between my experiences and the basic views of Individual Psychology is not without interest"; but we cannot help wondering whether there is not more to the story than meets the eye. We shall find some additional clues a little further on in our study.

One of the most common objections to Adler's work is the charge that he oversimplified his material in order to make it fit the pattern of psychological formula. Freud, for example, in his "New Introductory Lectures," told an anecdote to ridicule what he called the "repetition-compulsion" that led Adler to interpret psychological conditions of every kind in terms of the inferiority complex.

"In the neighborhood of the little Moravian town where I was born," Freud said, "and which I left as a child of three years old, there is a modest health resort, beautifully placed in a setting of green. During my school years I often spent my holidays there. Some twenty years later the illness of a near relative of mine afforded me an opportunity of seeing the place again. In a conversation with the doctor in charge of the place, who had attended my relative, I enquired about his dealings with the—I believe—Slovakian peasants, who were his only *clientele* during the winter. He told me that his medical treatment was carried on in the following way. In his consulting hours the patients came into his room and formed up in a line. One after another they came forward and told him their complaints. One of them might have pains in the back, or a stomach-ache, or a feeling of tiredness in the legs, etc. The doctor then examined him, and, when he had formed his conclusions told him his diagnosis, which was in every case the same. He translated the word to me, and what it amounted to was: 'bewitched.' I was astonished, and asked whether the patients made no objection to his saying the same thing to all of his patients. 'Oh no!' he answered, 'they are very much pleased; it is exactly what they expect. Each one as he goes back to his place in the line says to the others by his looks and gestures: "There's a fellow who knows what's what." At that time I little thought in which circumstances I should meet with an analogous situation.

"For whether a person is a homosexual, or a necrophilist, or an anxiety-ridden hysteric, or a shut-in obsessional, or a raving madman—in every case the Individual Psychologist of the Adlerian persuasion will assign the motive force of his condition to the fact that he wants to assert himself, to over-compensate for his inferiority, to be on top, and to move over from the feminine to the masculine line."

And Freud continues, in a vein that is rather comparable to Adler's remark that the popularity of psychoanalysis is a derivative of the large number of pampered children in the modern world. "But, to the mass of mankind, a theory like this must be exceedingly welcome, which takes no complications into account, which introduces no new and difficult concepts, which knows nothing of the unconscious, which removes at a single blow the problem of sexuality, that weighs so heavily on everybody, and which confines itself to revealing the devices by means of which people try to make life comfortable." [30]

This story of Freud's calls to mind an incident related to me by a Jungian psychiatrist in Europe apropos of a comparable tendency toward simplification found among the "Freudian persuasion." The doctor had been called to de-

[30] Sigmund Freud, *New Introductory Lectures on Psycho-Analysis*, trans. W. J. H. Sprott (New York: Norton, 1933), pp. 192-195.

liver a lecture before a group of psychotherapists in support of the Jungian interpretation of dreams. When his lecture was completed, a Freudian analyst came up to him, shook his hand warmly, and said, "That was very good, Doctor. You said much with which I can agree. But *this*," and here he held up a long, thin, bony finger, wiggling it significantly, his eyes agleam and fervent with symbolic meanings, "*this* is the key to the whole thing."

It seems, indeed, to be an unavoidable fact that when the analytical method is applied to psychological study a one-sided oversimplification inevitably results. The charge can be made against each of the various schools of thought that they stress particular aspects of the psyche at the expense of others. It is true even of those psychologists who stress "wholeness" like Adler and Jung that they emphasize the particular interpretative principles that seem most appropriate to them in the light of their own temperaments, and necessarily they leave other principles to one side. Perhaps that is why we find that adherents of a particular "school" of psychology are sincerely convinced that they have placed a true construction on the facts,—as they have usually, from within the self-consistent framework of their assumptions—whereas to those who look at their work from outside their premises and point of view, their interpretations seem to be artificial, out of balance, and often beside the point. Freud's impatient critiques of Adler and Jung are examples of this, for Freud was much too completely encased in his own orientation to be able to see sympathetically what the other men were trying to achieve from their individual points of view. And it is quite the same when Adler looks at Freud, or at Jung, and vice versa.

The charge of "oversimplification" that Freud made

against Adler, claiming that Adler ignored the problems of the unconscious and sexuality, signifies mainly that Adler approached these questions with concepts foreign to psychoanalysis so that Freud did not recognize them in the terms of his accustomed framework. Because the goals of Adler's work were different from Freud's, the structure of his thought necessarily followed a different pattern, and issues like sexuality and the unconscious therefore arose in another kind of perspective and in contexts different from Freud's. There is in Adler's work, nonetheless, an unmistakable tendency toward simplifying the form in which his concepts are presented. Intellectually, Adler's books are much less impressive than the major works of the other three authors we are discussing here. They move softly and try to be as uncomplicated as possible. Adler's writings have neither the massive sweep of Jung's nor the historical range of Rank's; and they do not display an incisiveness at all comparable to the powerful dissective mind of Freud.

On the other hand, Adler's simplicity can be highly misleading, and to be appreciated it must be understood in terms of what he was trying to do. His aim was to carry out a work of healing that would reach beyond the small proportion of individuals who are able to come for private psychological treatment, for he was convinced that the ultimate field where depth psychology must make its contribution is in the community as a whole. To this end, Adler practiced a severe economy in formulating his concepts, believing that the lighter he traveled, the more ground he would be able to cover, and the better he would be able to accomplish his goal of social healing. His simplicity was, therefore, deliberate, and expressed something very fundamental in Adler both as a man and as a psychologist. It is revealed by Phyllis Bottome in her biography when she relates the standard reply that Adler gave when he was confronted by the charge that he had oversimplified his material. "I have taken forty years to make my psychology simple," his answer would be. "I might make it still more simple. I might say, 'All neurosis is vanity'—but this also might not be understood." [31]

6. VANITY, WHOLENESS, AND THE EXPERIENCE OF SOCIAL FEELING

We should ask, then: If Adler had actually crystallized his point of view into the simplest and most compact form possible, if he had actually condensed his lifework into the statement, "All neurosis is vanity," what would have been the essential message he intended to convey? And why did he feel that the full meaning of what he had to say was bound to be misunderstood?

To answer these questions we should think in terms of the development of Adler's thought as a whole, and consider where it was leading him. With countless variations, the leitmotiv of his work was his conception that inferiorities act as a sort of motive force for all of life, both in the evolution of species and in human society. Weakness was, to Adler, the starting point for all achievement. He knew this as a fact of his personal experience, and it may well be that the main drive behind Adler's researches was his need to find the secret of overcoming weakness, first for himself and then to teach to others. He began with inferiority as his problem, and the key that opened his understanding was a general con-

[31] Bottome, *op. cit.*, pp. xii-xiii.

ception of evolution based on "wholes" in a manner akin to the views of Jan Christian Smuts,[32] and specifically based on the hypothesis that there is a balancing principle—which Adler called "compensation"—inherent in all organisms. In human beings, feelings of inferiority are based on an implicit self-comparison of the individual with other members of the community. The sense of inferiority implies egotism, a wounded egotism, and the process of compensation acts to strengthen the ego, usually overcompensating the feeling of inferiority with one of superiority, pushing the psyche to an opposite extreme and creating a new kind of problem.

The shuttling of the human psyche between feelings of inferiority and superiority was at variance with what seemed to Adler to be a basic fact of evolution, the fact that the human species was able to make good its survival by forming groups in its struggle with nature. The human individual requires a community to sustain his life, and yet the dynamic psychic factor of inferiority and its compensation involves an incipient egotism. Feeling its weakness when compared to others, the ego seeks to strengthen itself, to overcome its weakness, and thereby to rise above its fellow men. This is the basic vanity inherent in human life, the invidious comparisons both of inferiority and superiority which makes the individual a shuttlecock of egotistic desires. As long as the person is caught in the ever-shifting movement from low to high that the process of compensation involves, he must remain on the edge of neurosis.

In Adler's terms, inferiority/superiority feelings are a sure sign that the social feelings are weak, for they indicate that the individual is still trapped in his self-centeredness. A man can advance beyond neurosis only when he transcends both

[32] See Smuts, Holism and Evolution (New York: Macmillan, 1926).

his sense of inferiority and his desire for superiority and learns to think of himself as a part in a larger encompassing whole, as an individual who participates in life and shares immortality as a member of the community of mankind. "The general welfare and the higher development of humanity," Adler wrote, "are based on the eternally imperishable contributions of our forefathers. Their spirit lives for ever. It is immortal as others are in their children." [33] All the past lives in us and is for us to carry forward. Whoever experiences the reality of this as a fact and undertakes to play his role in the continuity of life will find that his social feelings are at once greatly strengthened. And it is only by this pervasive and creative social feeling that the vanity that is the sign of neurosis can be lastingly overcome.

It is plain that for Adler "social feeling" signified something much more meaningful than mere sociability, as the term itself might imply. It was for him a profound experience of togetherness, an intimate connection of man with man extending across the largest reaches of history. In the analytical part of his work, Adler described the "meaning of life" as an aspect of the individual's "style of life"; this was a "meaning" of life subjective to each personality, but necessary for each as a functional, psychological fact. Now, however, Adler was speaking not of *psychological meanings* of life but of *the meaning* of life. There is a meaning that reveals itself in man's life, he felt, and particularly in the great historical expressions of social feeling. There is a "goal of perfection" that lies before humanity, that has revealed itself in evolution and in history. "When we enter life we only find what our ancestors have completed as their contribution to evolution and the higher development of all mankind. This

⁕ Adler, *Social Interest, op. cit.,* p. 278.

one fact alone should show us how life continues to progress, how we get nearer to a state in which larger contributions and greater co-operation are possible, and in which every single person in fuller measure than before represents a part of the whole." [34] Man is called upon then to move forward and contribute to "an ideal society amongst mankind," which would be, if it ever were achieved, "the ultimate fulfillment of evolution," for in it the social feelings would reach their highest form.[35]

We have ample evidence to remind us of what the result will be if the modern man fails to redevelop his social feelings. "What has happened to those people who have contributed nothing to the general welfare?" Adler asks. "The answer is: They have disappeared completely. Nothing remains of them; they are quenched body and soul. The earth has swallowed them. It has happened with them as it did with animal species that have become extinct because they were unable to get into harmony with cosmic facts. Surely there is a secret ordinance here." [36]

The capacity to "get into harmony with cosmic facts" was the ultimate goal of Adler's psychological work. His analytical theories appear as a preparation for this culminating insight and purpose. A first step was the analysis of the style of life in an effort to bolster man's tendency to compensate for his inferiorities by enlarging his social feelings. This was a necessary beginning in order that the ego-centered vanity of the modern psyche might be cleared away. Before the individual can hope to know the transcending meaning of life, he must be able to recognize with honesty the subjective meanings he has been ascribing to his personal existence.

Adler's analytical work played a preliminary role in the development of his ultimate conception of life. Beyond his analytical psychology there came to him a larger vision of man's place in evolution and of the transcending goal of history. It involved a deep sense of connection to life and a belief in the eventual achievement of a universal community of mankind through the fuller development of man's "social feeling." To work toward this was *the* ultimate meaning that Adler perceived in life. He recognized the fact that it was not at all objective, that it was only his own personal belief, and to that extent subjective. But he was convinced that the feeling of close relationship to the continuing life of mankind has an objective basis, and that it can become a reality for all human beings in the terms of each person's style of life.

The important fact of which Adler himself was profoundly aware but that he found so difficult to communicate to others was that a reawakened "social feeling" could not be brought into existence by a conscious decision in rational terms. It was not something that could be accomplished on an intellectual level. It had to be experienced in order to be known. And that was why Adler felt certain that no matter how fully or how deftly he would simplify his ideas—even with the statement, "All neurosis is vanity"—his fundamental message would inevitably be misunderstood. The best that he could hope to do was to build in people the psychological capacity for a direct personal experience of the inner continuity of life so that they could feel in harmony with the cosmos and share his ideal of human wholeness in a future community embracing mankind.

Adler thus directed his practical work in his later years as far as he could toward opening a psychological road by which others might achieve a sense of cosmic relationship through deepened social feeling. Simplifying his statement of his work and his intentions—as was his habit—he took the time-tested but much neglected dictum, "Love thy neighbor," as his motto, with the aim of making it a psychic actuality in modern times. As Adler stated the ultimate purpose of his psychology, it was to enable the modern person "not only to understand other persons, but to grasp the importance of social feeling and to make it living for himself." [37]

And we can believe that this aim was sincerely true with Adler, for it arose out of his own inner necessity and a searching of his soul. To experience "social feeling" in its profound cosmic aspect of human wholeness as something that would be "living for himself" was Adler's deepest spiritual need.

There was combined in Adler a great dread and a great hope. The dread was based on a sound historical insight and was borne out by events. The hope derived from his optimistic temperament, and from his affirmative dedication to life. in the years just before the first World War, Adler had heavy forebodings that a catastrophe was about to come to Europe. "I am always afraid," he is reported to have said in 1913 when the war clouds were hardly visible to others, "that—whenever my back is turned—someone will take my Vienna away from me." [38]

The war itself, however, was not the worst that was to come, and Adler was never rid of his dark premonitions until they were finally fulfilled in the nineteen-thirties. When he returned from his tour of army duties in 1916, it seemed to him that civilization was about to destroy itself because of its lack of social feeling. In the years just after the war and in the 1920's when Vienna suffered severely from inflation and from shortages of every kind, his sense of an im-

[37] *Ibid.*, pp. 306-307.   [38] Bottome, *op. cit.*, p. 106.

pending crisis in Europe became increasingly urgent and intense. It became to him a question of survival in evolutionary terms. If European culture was not to destroy itself, its ego-centered struggles for power would have to be overcome by deepened social feelings. But that involved something larger and much more difficult than the professional work of bringing analytic psychotherapy to a small number of neurotics. Such a goal would require a total re-education of the European psyche, an unhoped for if not altogether impossible achievement; but his concern with the problem led Adler nonetheless to change the tone of his psychology and move away from his earlier medical emphasis.

There are many indications that with the medical orientation with which his psychological work had begun, particularly his approach to the relation between organic weakness and the psyche, the Adlerian school was receiving a very favorable acceptance in medical circles. Adler's theories were certainly easier to handle and less distasteful than Freud's and much clearer than Jung's. Not only in Vienna, but in much of Europe and America as well, Adler's "Individual Psychology" was well on the way to becoming the psychological point of view with the widest medical support. By indirection in his "History of the Psycho-analytical Movement," Freud himself has acknowledged this, pointing, not without some displeasure, to the favorable treatment Adler's works received in the medical press. Phyllis Bottome records the statement of an early follower of Adler who complained that Adler "had only to make his psychology into a school of medicine for us to spread Individual Psychology throughout the world." [39] We cannot, of course, say how it might have come out if Adler had taken the medical path, but the fact

[39] P. Bottome, *op. cit.*, p. 116.

is that he chose to go in a widely different direction; and there is a great significance in his decision.

As a result of his intense experience of the cosmic aspects of what he called "social feeling," Adler perceived that the task before psychology was not primarily medical. The breakdowns of personality and the mental illnesses requiring medical treatment were only the *occasion*, the proximate circumstance, that stimulated the development of depth psychology. The real purpose that psychology had to serve was beyond the reach of the medical arts, at least in their professional aspect. Psychology, as Adler understood it, had been called into being to heal the modern personality of the destructive effects of its severe individualism; and the task before it was to replace the moral values that had broken down with psychologically effective spiritual qualities that would make social life possible once again.

Despite his strong position in medical circles, and despite the fact that his profession was as a medical doctor, Adler felt he had no choice but to turn in a nonmedical direction. That was the only possible way he could see of solving the ultimate problem facing Europe's culture after the first World War. Increasingly he directed his attention toward finding an audience for his social point of view outside medical circles. His lectures and books were constructed in as simple a form as could carry the concepts of which he spoke. He was concerned much less with specific psychological doctrines than with an underlying orientation to life. In this spirit, also, he concentrated much during these years on pedagogic work, and he was even fortunate enough, under the aegis of a favorable political regime, to have access to the Vienna school system for a time. This was an especially valuable opportunity for him since he believed that in order for a work of social re-education to be effective in the long run, it must be practiced above all with children. Adler was always especially successful in his work with children, possibly because of his type of personality and because his theories could be applied most directly in childhood situations. He was becoming deeply involved in pedagogic work as a means of instilling "social feeling" in future generations when the *Furor Teutonicus* broke over Europe.

Soon Adler's worst premonitions were realized. History did not grant him time to teach the "social feeling" for the lack of which European culture was to die. He had to come as an *émigré* to America, where, in a strange though friendly atmosphere, he took up work in a medical college. He made a brave effort to carry on, but his world had been burned behind him. He had seen an urgent need, but now it was too late. Unfortunately, he had been right. Adler lived a few years in New York, but shortly after the Nazis brought tragedy to his eldest daughter in Europe, he died in 1937. He had made his major contribution, but he left the meaning of his work still unfulfilled.

In following the development of Adler's thought, we have been able to see that his artfully simple writings contain a deliberate and profound thrust toward the outer boundaries of psychological work. He began, like Freud, with an analytical psychology of a medical type, only to realize that such a psychology would not be adequate to meet the needs of the time. It would be able to ease the stress of mental illness, but it would not be able to meet the fundamental human problems that brought modern depth psychology into existence. Unless it widened its spiritual horizons, psychology would lose its reason for being, and it would die.

Realizing that, Adler also saw that for psychology to restore meaning to the life of the modern person, an act of religious dimensions would be necessary. He himself experienced what he called "social feeling" in a religious way; it was to him a unifying cosmic factor, linking the evolution of species with the continuity of mankind and giving him a sense of inner connectedness with life. It was certainly because of the spiritual intensity of this experience that Adler was able to bring a magnetic personal quality to his work of psychological healing. He saw the new direction that psychology must take, and he understood that the questions to be raised and the answers to be found would reach to the very depths of the human soul. But Adler himself felt that the task of transforming the egocentric neurotic personality and of restoring "social feeling" to the emotionally isolated human beings of modern times would be best accomplished with simple formulas that could be presented and assimilated on a popular level. As a result, there is a marked unevenness in his published work. In one place he is profound; in another place he glosses the surface. Perhaps what is most characteristic of him in this regard is his tendency to create concepts of great fertility and suggestiveness—like his view of "wholeness" and "social feeling"—and then to apply them only in a limited way without following through their implications and relationships. We will be able to look into this more closely, later in our discussion, when it comes time to consider the constructive value of Adler's point of view in relation to the work of Jung and Rank.

As a doctor, Adler had the great insight to see that depth psychology would miss its vocation and die an abortive death if it did not treat man as a spiritual being and learn to heal him from a nonmedical point of view. In a dedicated and courageous way, Adler risked his established medical reputation (certainly he weakened it in professional circles) by calling attention to the new directions necessary in depth psychology. Not all his conceptions had the depth that the subject may ultimately require, and there is much that his point of view baldly omits. Nonetheless, the fact remains that it was Adler who took the first steps in the direction of a development in depth psychology that holds the hope of a rebirth in the spiritual qualities of man.

IV

Personalities and pioneers

I. JUNG ON THE ROAD AWAY FROM FREUD

The rift between Adler and Freud took place in Vienna in 1911, and Jung was not directly involved in it. At that time in Zurich, Jung was still publicly identified with Freud; but privately his doubts had been maturing on the same points that were the basis of Adler's criticism. At least as early as 1907 Jung had begun to find that Freud's theory of infantile sexuality was a stumbling block for him, as it was for Adler. By 1909 he realized that it involved much more than sexuality; the entire theory of libido, or psychic energy, and the principles of dream and myth interpretation were at stake as well. At that time Jung had no idea where his doubts would eventually lead him, but by 1911, when he was still president of the "International Psycho-analytic Association," he was well on the way toward completing his book on *Transformations and Symbols of Libido*.[1] This book was the first public occasion on which Jung disclosed the extent of his differences with Freud. It was published in 1912, and in 1913 at the Association meeting Jung and Freud met each other for the last time.

This separation, as the second volume of Ernest Jones's biography indicates, was a bitter disappointment for Freud. He was, of course, unhappy about the dissension that had come to the fore with Adler's group, and he was anxious to avoid a repetition of such unpleasantness. He feared that it would injure the name of the psychoanalytic movement, but it seems, in addition, that Jung occupied a special place in Freud's thoughts and feelings. When Jung had first become interested in psychoanalysis he had been working as an assistant to Eugen Bleuler in the famous Burgholzli Clinic in Zurich, and it was through Jung's influence that Burgholzli became the first medical institution outside Vienna to give Freud's theories serious consideration. Freud accepted his Swiss support with great appreciation, for it brought him prestige and personal encouragement at a time when he was sorely in need of both. When he met Jung, Freud was, as he wrote in his *History of the Psycho-analytical Movement*, much impressed by Jung's "conspicuous talents," and from that time onward it appears that he projected upon Jung many of his own hopes and fantasies.

Freud was perhaps too sensitively aware of the fact that the main support he was receiving in those pioneering days came from a socially marginal group of Jewish Viennese medical doctors. He felt that this was bound to have adverse effects at the universities of Europe, since the discrimination prac-

[1] Translated under the title of *The Psychology of the Unconscious*.

ticed against the Jews would be directed against psychoanalysis as well. He was not wrong in this, of course, for psychoanalysis soon was labeled a "Jewish science" and came in for attack on racial rather than scientific grounds during the dark days of European anti-Semitism. The objective practical considerations were, however, not the only factors involved in Freud's thoughts on this subject. It was also an emotional problem for him and his reaction to it casts a revealing light on his "style of life" as a whole.

One of the major psychological difficulties experienced by the modern "scientific" Jew of Freud's type is the problem of facing persecution on behalf of a religion to which he no longer feels bound by belief. Freud had absorbed uncritically the nineteenth-century naturalism that was part of his medical studies and throughout his life, as his later writings on religion abundantly showed, he was never able to appreciate the spiritual aspects either of Judaism or of the Old Testament. Nonetheless, because he was personally an exceedingly courageous individual, Freud would not stoop to the opportunist step of disowning his Jewishness in the hope of avoiding its difficulties and smoothing his path of life.[2]

He accepted the burdens for himself and would not shirk them, but—and this is the characteristic and significant trait of the man—he wished so strongly to protect his intellectual discoveries that he was ready to sacrifice his own position and fame if that would help. In this sense, psychoanalysis was to Freud the most cherished work of his soul, a child of the spirit most intimately conceived and most passionately tended, like the "opus" of Jung or the "art work" of Rank of which we shall speak shortly. He wished to shield the work

[2] See the address that Freud delivered to the B'nai B'rith of Vienna on May 6, 1926. It is printed in the March, 1946, issue of *Commentary*.

that was his intellectual child from every possible difficulty in the hope that it might enter the scientific world on its own merits and be spared anti-Semitic jibes.

Once he was convinced of Jung's great competence, Freud seems to have pictured him in his imagination as a Swiss knight who would ride forth in shining intellectual armor and carry the cause of psychoanalysis before an unfriendly world, a world that would not listen to a Viennese Jew. It is interesting to note how quick, how willing, indeed how anxious, Freud was to place himself in the background. In 1910 he spoke of Jung as "the man of the future," [3] and he immediately set forth to bring that future into the present by nominating Jung for the editorship of the Yearbook and the presidency of the International Psycho-analytic Association. So intent was Freud on having a socially presentable figure like Jung at the head of his "cause" that he did not even pause to notice that Jung was not really interested in the administrative and public relations role that was being laid out for him. Jung was not temperamentally attuned to that type of work, and he was not disposed to give his best energies to it. He was, as his later work abundantly showed, primarily a thinker and a researcher. So great, however, and so unconscious, was Freud's projection on Jung that he did not pay attention to what was said by the others of the Vienna circle who insisted that Jung had purposes of his own, and that he had already stated significant objections to the basic Freudian hypothesis of sexuality. These reservations were bound to lead Jung in non-Freudian directions, as they eventually did; but, though Freud heard the words, he did not perceive the signs that were obvious to the others. He was caught in his

[3] Ernest Jones, *The Life and Work of Sigmund Freud*, Vol. II (New York: Basic Books, 1955), p. 140.

fantasy of having someone carry his message to the world, a gallant hero speaking in the name of science beyond the reach of anti-Semitic prejudice.

There was a certain plausibility in Freud's desire to have a non-Jew and a non-Viennese at the head of the psychoanalytical movement; but the intensity with which he tried to turn full power over to Jung, to give Jung the authority to censor articles and determine policies, did not seem to be called for by the facts of the situation. Only the protests of the Viennese doctors held him back, and Freud attributed these to the dishonest motives of jealousy. The extravagant way that Freud pinned his hopes on Jung as though he were deliberately raising another person and dismissing himself from the field clearly has personal overtones. It was an action, after all, that was quite out of place, since Freud himself and no one else was the only possible leader for the movement that carried his name; and subsequent events conclusively proved this to be the case.

It seems definite that in his relationship with Jung, Freud was once again caught in a transference situation of the kind that had involved him with Wilhelm Fliess; in fact, as Jones points out, when the relationship with Jung began to wane, Freud himself compared it to a corresponding point in his friendship with Fliess because of the fears and unhappiness he felt.[4] There was in Freud a marked tendency to seek out men with strong personality traits, and then, with deliberate unconsciousness, to make himself subordinate to them. He did this repeatedly with one man after another over a long period of his life, regardless of whether the individual who drew his projection was strong in reality or not, as Wilhelm Fliess apparently was not. Freud seems to have had a great

[1] *Ibid.*, p. 142.

need for someone in whom he could confide, someone to whom he could tell everything he did; and for someone upon whom he could lean for support, at least in his imagination.

Freud himself recognized this tendency in himself, and he attributed it to the compulsion that made it his fate to repeat a childhood relationship with an elder brother, in his case actually an elder nephew.[5] It may very well have involved something even more fundamental whose implications will be understood only when the interpretation of the life of Freud has been continued in years to come on the foundations that Jones has laid. It resulted, however, in Freud's periodic overeagerness to efface himself both in his personal affairs and in his work in the psychoanalytic movement. It vitiated his relationship with C. G. Jung, possibly with Jung's unconscious collaboration,[6] and was one of the main roots of that recurrent sense of martyrdom that was Freud's weakness as well as the source of his persistence and strength.

The presence of these emotional factors meant that the relationship between Freud and Jung was inherently unstable. From Jung's point of view, of course, insofar as we are in a position to fill in the facts, his association with Freud had represented an unexampled opportunity for a young psychiatrist still in his thirties. It was certainly a turning point in Jung's life because of both the intellectual stimulation and the recognition that it brought him. Nonetheless, Jung's involvement in the psychoanalytical movement seems to have deepened certain personal difficulties that Jung experienced from 1911 onward, and with especial intensity between 1913 and 1915. As the founder of the Freud Club in Zurich and

[5] See *Beyond the Pleasure Principle*.
[6] See Chapter IV, Section 3, concerning certain extroverted tendencies in Jung's personality at the time of his relationship with Freud.

president of the International Psycho-analytical Association, he was completely identified with the Freudian point of view before the public; and yet his doubts were becoming stronger. Jones reports that when Karl Abraham told Freud that Jung's continued adherence was in doubt, Freud replied that as a practical fact Jung "can hardly go back now; he cannot undo his past even if he wanted to, and the Jahrbuch he edits is an unbreakable tie." [7]

Freud felt that Jung was irrevocably committed to the psychoanalytical line of thought, if only because he had severed his connections with the more orthodox lines of psychiatric practice. My own conversations with Jung in his later years indicate that he shared Freud's opinion in this regard. He had cut himself off from the excellent prospects he had enjoyed under Bleuler in order to follow this new line of study. And now, after publicly identifying himself with it, he was becoming increasingly convinced that he could not continue to subscribe to Freud's theories. Where then would he turn? How would he be able to re-establish his career? These were serious and practical problems that beset him, and it was around this time that Jung was disturbed by dreams whose ominous overtones were most upsetting.

There are indications that Jung was inwardly greatly troubled at this juncture of his life. Particularly in 1913 when the publication of his *Psychology of the Unconscious* had completely cut him off from the Freudians, he had dreams of which he has spoken at great length in later years that unsettled his psychic equilibrium and made him feel most uneasy on that score. His book on psychological types that was to establish his reputation was not yet on the horizon, and he had at that time no way of knowing where his fortunes would

[7] Quoted by Jones, *op. cit.*, Vol. II, p. 138.

turn next. The possibilities did not seem bright to him, for he had burned both his bridges, orthodox psychiatry and psychoanalysis, behind him. The uncertainties looming in his career as well as other factors played an important role in the doubts that Jung felt about himself at that time. It did indeed seem, as he often thought and remarked to some of the Freudian circle, that he was a perpetual heretic, a perpetual "younger son." In such a situation it was small wonder that his "unconscious" was becoming active in the most disturbing ways, producing strange symbolisms that he was not able to interpret with the concepts then at his command.

Concerned as he was then with the stability of his personal situation—both psychological and professional—Jung did not suspect that the intense activity of his psyche was then in process of making him a pioneer in his own right. He had no way of knowing that he was being brought into touch with levels of the psyche below the depths that Freud had reached. Gradually, however, during the years of the first World War, Jung found his bearings and became confident of his psychological position once again; and it was then that he became capable of working out an intellectual interpretation of the confusing and disturbing symbolism that his dreams had shown him.

Reading Ernest Jones' account of the relationship between Jung and Freud as he describes Jung's recurrent protestations of loyalty interspersed with significant lapses and doubts, we can understand that his behavior certainly seemed to bear the stamp of instability when seen from the Freudian point of view. Nonetheless, it must be kept in mind that while that period was of crucial importance to Freud in his efforts to establish psychoanalysis on an international foundation, it was also a critical time in Jung's personal development. His conflicting statements and actions with respect to Freud, which must certainly have encouraged Freud's projections on him only to destroy them in the end, must be understood in terms of the predominant pressures of his creative work and the pangs with which his new insights were coming to birth. For various reasons we cannot here refer to personal material that would relate Jung's psychic life to the development of his theories more specifically. Our aim here in any case is only to point out the underlying trends of his personal development as they are significant for depth psychology as a whole. At some point, however, the time will come for the life and work of Jung to be recorded, in full detail, and if the task is fulfilled with an honesty comparable to Ernest Jones' treatment of Freud, it will be of tremendous importance for the history of depth psychology.

In the Spring of 1907, Jung wrote a letter to Freud that foreshadowed in a most significant way the development of his thought in later years. It even suggested a term, "psychoid," that Jung was to hold in the background and not present again until 1946 when he used it in restructuring his conception of the unconscious.[8] Unfortunately, we do not have the original letter that Jung wrote; but Jones has printed a meaningful excerpt from Freud's reply, and from that we can infer clearly enough what Jung had written.[9]

Jung had apparently indicated to Freud that the difficulties he was encountering in Switzerland were closely related to the sexual tone of Freud's terminology. He wanted to find a substitute for the suggestive phrase, "libido," with which Freud had designated the energy of the psyche; and he wanted also to change the term "unconscious" to "psychoid."

[8] See Chapter VI, Section 1.
[9] Jones, op. cit., Vol. II, p. 426.

Freud, however, was dubious about the value that such changes would have in terms of psychoanalysis as he conceived. it. "Even were we to call the unconscious 'psychoid,'" he wrote to Jung in reply, "it would still remain the unconscious; even if we were not to call the driving force in our broadened conception of sexuality 'libido' it would still remain the libido and every time we follow it up we should get back to the very thing from which the new nomenclature was supposed to divert us." And then Freud added in his characteristic way, "We cannot avoid the resistances, so why not rather challenge them at once? In my opinion attack is the best defense. Perhaps you underestimate the intensity of these resistances, when you hope to counter them with small concessions. What is demanded of us is after all that we deny the sexual instinct. So let us proclaim it."

After this spirited rebuke, Jung seems to have withdrawn his objections, pressing them into the background of his mind and not speaking of them to Freud again. The difficulties he was experiencing in applying the principle of sexuality had, however, not been overcome by Freud's letter. The problems remained, and Jung's doubts lingered in his mind and continued to grow. Jones has recorded several instances between 1907 and 1912 when Jung indicated to other members of the Freudian circle that he no longer found it necessary to follow sexual analysis as stringently as Freud prescribed. He seems never to have accepted Freud's conception of sexuality and the unconscious, despite the fact that he was president of the psycho-analytic association, editor of the yearbook, and Freud's main spokesman before the world.

Freud stressed the practical difficulties bound to be encountered in practicing psychoanalysis in Switzerland, but it does not seem likely that this was a major factor in shaping

Jung's point of view. Certainly, anyone who has had a friendly acquaintance with the Swiss must admit that Freud was right in his judgment of their rigid attitudes toward sex and their inevitable "resistance" to his theories. By the same token, however, anyone who knows Jung as an individual must realize also that such "practical" considerations could be of hardly any significance to him. It would be axiomatic for him to assume that if the one-sided emphasis on sexuality was factually correct, the prejudice against it would eventually be overcome. Creative men like Freud and Jung are able to do their lifework only in the implicit faith that truth is bound to win out in the end, at least in the realm of science. The main difficulty for Jung was not on the sociological level, as Freud thought; it was simply a matter of judgment. It seemed to Jung that Freud's dogmatic emphasis on sexuality tended to narrow the perspective of all his interpretations.

The emphasis on sexuality seemed untenable to Jung because it weakened the entire structure of psychological theory. For one thing, it involved an unbalanced view of the personality, and Jung leaned strongly towards Adler's conception that the human being must be considered as a unity, as an organism whose fundamental processes tend always to re-establish its wholeness. A second difficulty, following from this first point, was that as long as sexuality was conceived as the dominant energy of the psyche, all the phenomena of the personality would have to be interpreted in terms of a sexual root. This meant that everything of a psychological nature was ultimately to be reduced to a basic sexual content. And it meant, further, that both theoretically and in practice, the attention was turned away from the problem facing the individual in "the present moment" in order to press backward into the past via analysis in an effort to relate the patterns of adult life to sexual events in infancy. Jung was thus questioning two of the basic assumptions upon which psychoanalysis rested: firstly, that whenever a psychic condition had been thoroughly and successfully analyzed, it would be found to be derived from an event in earliest childhood; and secondly, that the conscious recognition of this analytical reduction would, in itself, have a healing effect.

Quite in addition to the narrowness of the stress on sexuality, the question of whether analytical reduction could be a healing principle raised a serious difficulty for Jung. As he realized its implications, it became one of the main impulses behind his effort to develop another therapeutic method. It might well be that the roots of the neurosis were in the past, but it was equally true that the neurosis of many of his patients could be resolved only by directing their energies toward the future. For many of them it was as though a meaning, or a purpose of some kind, was present in their lives without their being conscious of what it was; and it was a disturbing factor precisely because they were not aware of it and were not permitting it to fulfill itself. In this light, the neurosis seemed to Jung to be best understood in terms of what it was striving toward, rather than in terms of the abnormal symptoms that it manifested. Healing might be found by turning toward the future as that future was contained in the latent purposes of the psyche, rather than by returning to the past.

"Causality is only one principle," Jung wrote in 1916, "and psychology essentially cannot be exhausted by causal methods only, because the mind lives by aims as well." [10] In his use of the word "causal" in this context Jung was re-

---

[10] C. G. Jung, *Collected Papers on Analytical Psychology*, ed. C. E. Long (London: Balliere, Tindall and Cox, 1920), preface to first edition.

ferring to Freud's analytical method of reducing events to their predecessors in the past, and he was contrasting to this his own approach, which he called "synthetic and prospective." He had already arrived at Adler's opinion that a great dis-service is done the individual when his neurosis is labeled as an illness. Each psyche, both Jung and Adler agreed, must be understood in terms of the innate goals of its individual nature, interpreting neurosis as an intermediate period of upset without which a new creative condition could not be achieved.

After the publication of his *Psychology of the Unconscious*, and particularly during the years just after the first World War, Jung made an increasing effort to find a means of drawing forth the "prospective" meaning of neurosis. His goal at that time was to develop a psychological theory and a method capable of orienting the individual toward the future in terms of the inherent purpose emerging from the psyche. In the nature of the case, however, he felt that it would not be possible for him to understand the direction of growth in the future if he were not first able to interpret, at least in a general way, the psychic background of the individual's past. He decided that he would have to merge the two points of view. The human personality, Jung concluded, has to be approached simultaneously from opposite directions: teleologically in terms of the future, and analytically in terms of the past.

Jung undertook to build his new point of view with this in mind. The most fundamental change that he made in Freud's tools of analysis concerned the nature of libido. In the "broadened" conception to which he referred in his reply to Jung in 1907, libido meant to Freud that psychic energy in general has a specifically sexual root. Jung's alteration of this view consisted essentially in leaving off the last part of that statement. He conceived of psychic energy as a generalized force and he did not attempt to limit it in terms of any particular categories. It was enough for him to speak of libido pragmatically as the dynamic force of the psyche, for, particularly when he was writing his *Psychology of the Unconscious,* Jung felt that this would enable him to adapt the advantages of Freud's libido theory without the hindrances involved in reducing the psyche to sexuality. Jung was especially interested in "the Freudian comparison of the libido with a stream, which is divisible, which can be dammed up, which overflows into branches, and so on." [11] Applying this, he conceived of energy movements as a general characteristic of the psyche, describing them as either "progressive" or "regressive," and he interpreted the symbolic expressions of these movements in dreams, myths, and the products of fantasy. It was on this basis that Jung constructed the outlines of his theory of hero mythology, conceiving the life of the hero as a symbolic expression of the movements of libido in the psyche. The hero, like the energy of the psyche, is drawn forward toward a goal that is distant and difficult to achieve. He must overcome many obstacles. He may even be swallowed up in the course of his search, be submerged in the whale or captured in a cave (the mother, the unconscious), and he then returns only after a prolonged and forced withdrawal from life to continue his struggles toward his goal in the world.

[11] C. G. Jung, *Psychology of the Unconscious,* trans. B. M. Hinkle (New York: Dodd, Mead & Co., 1916, 1949), p. 139.

2. FREUD AND ADLER AS "PSYCHOLOGICAL TYPES"

In speaking of the "forward" and the "backward" movement of libido, Jung had not gone far from Freud's foundations. He had, however, rejected the theory of sexuality with all that it implied in terms of analysis, and he was thus left without any basic principle to guide him in his therapeutic work. There was thus a gap in Jung's psychological equipment, and he undertook to fill it by extending the conception of libido movement in a new way. In addition to its progressive and regressive movements, Jung pointed out that energy also moves outward and inward: outward toward the object (extroversion), and inward toward the subject (introversion). These movements, he said, can be found to apply to each of the four classical psychological functions: thinking, feeling, intuition, and sensation, and they do so in a compensatory way. They balance each other. If thinking is extroverted, feeling is introverted; if intuition is introverted, sensation is extroverted, and vice versa. According to which functions are dominant in the personality, Jung defined the various psychological types, the "extroverted thinking type," the "introverted intuition type," and so on, with an intriguing number of combinations and permutations possible.

The theory of "types" represents Jung's effort to find a working substitute for the psychoanalytic theory of character formation that he could not accept since he was working with a different conception of the libido. He needed to develop a framework in which to place and describe the varieties of human beings, and he needed a basis of comparison to give himself perspective in his therapeutic work. Jung has spoken of the formulation of the four psychological "functions" in his type theory as a kind of psychological compass, and that is indicative of the role it has played in his thought. He developed the conception of types as a means of finding his bearings and guiding himself anew after he had parted company with Freud and seemed to be lost without direction. The theory of psychological types is undeniably analytical in its structure, and in this sense it is subject to the same criticisms that Jung directed against the reductive approach of Freud. It has another aspect, however, for it is designed to be used in a teleological way. In fact, in the perspective of the mature development of Jung's thought, the significance of the type theory seems to be that it was the intellectual schema by means of which Jung began the process of freeing himself from analytical and reductive habits of thinking in his psychological work. Jung's theory of psychological types is open at both ends. It is a system of classifications, but oddly enough, its basis is the principle that all classifications eventually go into their opposite. And though it is an analytical method, it maintains that all reductive procedures tend to inhibit psychological healing, since the future must be left open for growth. Quite naturally not a little misunderstanding and confusion have resulted from this formulation since it is so flexible that it is ambiguous. It has, nonetheless, made valuable contributions to the development of depth psychology, even though it hardly seems likely that Jung's type classifications can be utilized in the form in which he developed them outside the boundaries of his special system. In our present context, however, the theory of psychological types is particularly significant because it opens a revealing aspect of Jung's relation to Adler and Freud, and also of Jung's relation to himself.[12]

[12] For fuller discussion of Jung's type theory, see my *Jung's Psychology and its Social Meaning*, Chapter IV, "Introvert, Extravert, and Psychological Types," and for a closer study of Jung's theories in general see Part I, pp. 53-156.

A. *Freud: The Sexuality of an Introvert*

In his essay on "The Normal and Pathological Mind" published in German in 1926 and in English two years later as the first of the *Two Essays on Analytical Psychology*,[13] Jung made the interesting experiment of studying the condition of a neurotic first from the point of view of Freud and then from the point of view of Adler. In the Freudian perspective, the sexual factor loomed large. The suffering of the individual seemed to be derived from the fact that the image of his father had been fixated in his unconscious. The sexual overtones of the neurosis seemed clearly visible according to Freud's principles, but, when the facts were interpreted in the light of Adler's theories, the situation seemed to Jung to be equally well explained. The neurosis was interpreted then not in terms of sexuality but of inferiority feelings and the fact that the drive to compensate for them had resulted in an unworkable "style of life." In Adler's context, the patient's condition was shown to involve an unconscious attempt to hold the center of the stage and to assert a control over others that he would not have been able to secure without displaying the symptoms of the illness. After developing these interpretations, Jung pointed out that they appear as flat contradictions of each other, but that, nonetheless, neither one is really "wrong." In fact, he said, each of them is a correct description of the facts from a given point of view; and, he added, both of them may therefore properly be used as part of the analytical work in psychotherapy.

[13] C. G. Jung, *Two Essays on Analytical Psychology*, trans. H. G. and C. F. Baynes (New York: Dodd, Mead & Co., 1928). See also the revised version published in *The Collected Works of C. G. Jung*, Vol. VII, Bollingen Series (New York: Pantheon Books, 1955).

If we accept Jung's diplomatic position and agree with him that the same psychological facts can be plausibly explained from two opposing points of view, the question then arises of why it should be so. Jung gives the answer in terms of his theory of types, for, he says, Freud sees the patient through the eyes of an extrovert while Adler does so as an introvert. The conflicting interpretations that result are logically consistent and reasonable within their own terms, but neither can be translated into the terms of the other. When Adler studies the psychology of an individual, he thinks of the sensitivities of the person, his feelings of inferiority, and his efforts to protect himself and establish himself in the face of the problems of life. When Freud approaches the same situation, however, the subjective attitudes of the patient seem to be of much smaller consequence. Freud is interested in the objective and external aspects of the relationship between the father and the son, the instinctive sexual drives, and particularly the tangible factors in the situation. In other words, according to Jung, Adler's reconstruction of a psychological problem is in terms of the subjective feelings, the "inner" factors that led to the neurosis, while Freud's reconstruction stresses factors that are more tangible and impersonal. And this describes also the main characteristics that Jung noted in distinguishing the "introvert" or inner-oriented person from the "extrovert" or outer-oriented one. His conclusion, therefore, was that the interpretations of Freud and Adler were different because they themselves were different types of human beings. They would look at the same object and each see a different thing. The introvert and the extrovert cannot help talking past each other, for each is speaking a psychological language that describes the kind of world he sees. The appearance of conflicting psychological theories is thus unavoidable because of the varieties of human temperament; but, Jung says, speaking somewhat with the air of a beneficent mediator, since each can be only partially correct, they must eventually be integrated within the framework of a larger encompassing system such as the theory of types makes possible.

Despite the neatness of Jung's distinction, his classification of Freud and Adler has resulted in considerable confusion among those whose psychological type does not dispose them to think in Jung's terms. Lewis Way, for example, in his excellent book, *Adler's Place in Psychology*[14] comes to the conclusion—much to his own surprise!—that Jung's classification of Freud and Adler is exactly the opposite of what their types really seem to be. "It may seem preposterous," Way says rather self-consciously, "that in this diagnosis Jung has misapplied his own principles"; but that certainly seems to be the case. Freud, after all, was certainly not an out-going person. He was aloof, withdrawn, even ascetic, a man capable of long periods of self-restraint and solitude. Now that Freud's biographical material has been published, there can be no question at all about the fact that his personality was predominantly introverted, just as Adler's Viennese sociability indicates an extroverted temperament. Way is certainly correct in his observation that "It must seem . . . as if Freud were most at home in the world of his depth psychology and Adler happiest in the world of human contacts; as if the one had an uneasy relation to the object and the other an uneasy relation to the subject." [15] Our general knowledge of the lives of Freud and Adler indicates that it was Freud who was the introvert and Adler who was the extrovert.

[14] (London: Allen & Unwin, 1950), pp. 287-290.
[15] *Ibid.*, p. 289.

An interesting clue to the relationship between Freud's psychological type and his theories appears in the lectures that Freud called, *A General Introduction to Psycho-Analysis*.[16] Speaking of introversion there, Freud refers to the introverted person as one who is in a precarious psychological situation. *"Introversion,"* he says, "describes the deflection of the libido away from the possibilities of real satisfaction and its excessive accumulation upon phantasies previously tolerated as harmless. An introverted person is not yet neurotic, but he is in an unstable condition; the next disturbance of the shifting forces will cause symptoms to develop, unless he can yet find other outlets for his pent-up libido."

The use of the term "introversion," we should note, corresponds to the usage that Jung had developed earlier while he was still working within Freud's psychoanalytic context, and before he had re-defined it in constructing his theory of types. In this older meaning, introversion signifies libido movement that is going not inward but rather "downward." It means the "regression" of libido, the withdrawal of energy away from the world so that it can turn into the psyche. Apart from the specific usage of the term, however, there is an even more significant difference in the meaning that Freud and Jung attach to "introversion." To Jung, introversion is an entirely neutral term. He applies it merely to describe a particular kind of libido movement and he does not assume at the outset whether or not such a movement is beneficial for the individual. It is simply a fact. Freud's conception of introversion, on the other hand, involves an inherent evaluation of the way in which the person is directing his energy. He prejudges introverted activity, assuming what seems to him to be self-evident, that his judgment is in accord with

[16] (Garden City: Garden City Publishing Co., 1943), p. 326.

objective scientific observation. And it is the very sincerity of his innocent good faith with which Freud makes his prejudicial evaluation of a particular kind of energy movement that demonstrates the unconscious bias of his "type." It tends to substantiate Jung's basic point that Freud's way of approach, as every other psychologist's, is rooted in the attitude peculiar to his particular temperament and psychological type.

Perceiving this fact takes us back to the discrepancy that Way found in Jung's discussion of Adler and Freud. Freud's negative attitude toward introversion is clearly a sign of an extroverted type; and yet, as we know from his biography, Freud lived as an introvert. There is an apparent difference between the "type," that is, the direction of libido movement expressed in Freud's habits of life, and in the psychological theories which he articulated.

The statement that when a person turns his attention toward the inner life he is turning his energies "away from the possibilities of *real satisfaction*" (my italics) represents a markedly extroverted point of view. It is then significant to note that this belief that *real* satisfaction is *outside* the psyche is the view of a man who devoted his life to the study of psychological facts, that is, the facts of the *inner* life. It becomes particularly significant when we recall that Freud was an individual who permitted himself few indulgences in external pleasures but disciplined himself rigidly in order to carry out his researches. Freud lived an austere, an ascetic life despite the fact that he himself has vividly revealed, that his erotic sensitivities were awakened at an early age. We can only infer, then, that the desires that stirred in him but were not gratified in his youth were pressed down into his unconscious from whence they returned in the direction of consciousness via the symbolism of dreams. And, as we know, it was the analysis of Freud's own dreams that provided not only the basic contents but, more important, the guiding spirit of his theories.

The repression of desires for outward pleasures—which is the cornerstone of the psychoanalytic point of view—describes a main part of Freud's life very well. Drawn with great passion toward a young mother closer in age to him than to his father, Freud gratified his passion not erotically —which, as his theory analyzed in detail, was forbidden him —but in fulfilling his mother's expectations that he would live a life of notable achievement. He gave himself to a disciplined existence quite willingly because in his childhood his mother had convinced him that the omens surrounding his birth, as Jewish folklore interpreted them, presaged immortality for him. He willingly dedicated himself and sacrificed his erotic desires, but he also resented it, if only unconsciously; and we can see this reflected in the fact that Freud persistently thought of himself as a martyr, as a man bound to suffer persecution by those who could not help but misunderstand him. The destiny of greatness to which he felt himself to be born expressed itself in him sometimes as ambition, and sometimes as anxiety, the fear that he would not succeed. He accepted his destiny gladly, and also with misgivings. The necessities of study prevented his taking part in the pleasures of life in gay, extroverted Vienna; and seen in the retrospect of his middle age, Freud may well have felt that it was but one step from mental illness to have lived his youthful years as an introvert in old Vienna.

We can thus understand the personal significance of Freud's remark that "real satisfactions" are to be found not within the soul, but outside in the gratification of the instincts. The psychoanalytic theories that Freud developed gave life and form to those insistent urges of his psyche that had to remain unlived. While he stressed the extroverted life and extolled it as the way of psychic health for every man, this was precisely the kind of experience of which he felt himself deprived. In his love for his mother, Freud had sacrificed his sexuality to his studies; and he spent his lifetime regaining it vicariously in others by means of a theory and a therapy. It is indeed true, as Jones says, that "It cannot after all be chance that after many years of distraction in other fields the one in which the chaste and puritanical Freud ultimately made his discoveries was in that of the sexual life." [17] With his highly developed consciousness and his intuitive perceptions, he staked out his claim to the life of extroverted pleasure that was not his to live; and by means of his rigid use of analysis he established his power over it. At the same time, he covered the introverted life with contempt and hid it from himself. Freud's introversion, which was the dominant characteristic of his "style of life," thus remained unconscious with him. He lived it, but he could not face it. The material that he brought to consciousness in his intellectual work represented the other side of his psyche, that part of himself that would have been extroverted *if* he had lived it instead of repressing and then sublimating it. It was thus that Sigmund Freud, the introvert, gave the world a psychological theory that is extroverted in its major characteristics and in its underlying point of view.

[17] Jones, *The Life and Work of Sigmund Freud, op. cit.,* Vol. II., p. 433.

B. *Adler: The Inferiority of an Extrovert*

In the case of Alfred Adler, we have a similar disparity between the theory and the theorist. The conception of the inferiority complex and the interpretations related to it express an introverted outlook on life. The prevailing point of view is one of sympathy for the self-conscious individual, and a sensitivity for his feelings of weakness. It is an attitude that clearly reflects an introverted temperament; and yet, as Lewis Way has observed, Adler's behavior revealed him to be a wholeheartedly outgoing person, an extrovert by all the ordinary criteria. There seems to be, therefore, a strongly marked contrast between Adler's personality and the orientation of the individual psychology that he created. But there is something more to the story. There are indications that Adler was not always an extrovert; and his psychological theories quite definitely did not always express an extroverted point of view.

One of Adler's simplest and most useful techniques was his practice of asking his patients to tell him their earliest memories. He was interested not only in the things that were remembered, but in the pattern and the meaning with which they were recalled. The "style" of the memories was for Adler a significant clue to the style of life developed in the individual's adult years. And that is certainly a valid principle in interpreting Adler's own life.

We have already referred to the earliest memory that Adler recalled for his biographer.[18] In it, he pictured himself as a sickly onlooker forced to sit on a bench while his brother

[18] See Phyllis Bottome, *Alfred Adler: A Biography* (New York: Putnam, 1939), pp. 9-13.

played. Adler remembered his physical weakness and his exclusion from his brother's sports because of it. But these, we must notice, were only the objective constituents of the situation. Much more important for the meaning of his memory is the fact that he recalled these things in the reflection of his feelings. The memory that Adler retained was not simply of his exclusion from the games; much more significantly, it was a memory of the intense way he experienced that exclusion emotionally. What Adler remembered primarily was his feelings. And that is the key to his basic psychological type. Because he was predominantly introverted in his youth, it was not the outer facts of his relationships but his inner experience of them that made the greatest impact on him. It was his intimate and emotional evaluations of his childhood years that he brooded over so that they worked on him and shaped his thoughts. What became characteristic of Adler's personal "style of life," then, his mental "law of movement," was his sympathetic concern with the private feelings and fancies of human beings. To him, a person's subjectivities were objectively real; for feelings to Adler were things. He experienced subjective meanings as facts, and that is the heart of the introverted attitude he expressed in his psychological interpretations.

Adler's theories thus display a most remarkable resiliency. They begin with the strong introversion that we see in Adler's underlying conception of human life. A "feeling of his inferiority and insecurity," he says, speaking of "man" in general, "is constantly present in his consciousness";[19] but this is a most revealing personal expression, for it indicates the

[19] Alfred Adler, *Understanding Human Nature* (Garden City: Garden City Publishing Co., 1927), p. 29.

apprehensions and sense of personal limitation with which Adler himself embarked in life. Significantly, however, the fact of weakness, and especially the awareness of weakness, was to Adler the most affirmative and creative force in life. He regarded the sense of inferiority as the greatest stimulus to human effort since it results in the overcoming of weakness. To turn a "minus" into a "plus," to move from a negative to a positive, was the characteristic both of Adler's style of life and his psychological point of view. By means of it, the person who is withdrawn from the world because of his sense of inferiority is brought forward by that very fact out into the world. He turns his weakness into strength and his inhibiting self-consciousness is enlivened by social feeling. Introversion moves toward extroversion, for the principle of compensation has a tendency to turn things into their opposite in the psyche. If that is not the psychic pattern for every man, it was at least the course that life followed in the case of Alfred Adler.

Adler's biographical material contains several indications of this change in emphasis from a personality withdrawn by its introverted sense of inferiority to an individual moving toward the world confident enough of his own strength to live in terms of social feeling. The contrast that Ernest Jones records in his impressions of Adler is interesting in this regard. During the years that they were together in the early psychoanalytic circle, Adler impressed Jones as "a morose and cantankerous person, whose behavior oscillated between contentiousness and sulkiness." In those years when Adler was in his late thirties and was still struggling to get his concepts into a form that he could apply and expound, his personality showed the characteristics of the introverted person.

"He was evidently very ambitious," Jones adds, "and constantly quarrelling with others over points of priority in his ideas."

This trait of overly strong ambitiousness has been commented upon by several who knew Adler during those years, and it indicates that his feelings of inferiority were still very strong. Seeking to overcome them in the midst of intellectual competition and with the delicate sensitivities of an introvert, he was bound to find himself in many arguments. The pattern changed, however, as his efforts to compensate for his weaknesses led him further into extroverted activities. "When I met him many years later," Jones recalls, "I observed a certain benignity of which there had been little sign in his earlier years." [20] At the time, Jones attributed that change in Adler's attitude to the success he had achieved; but it seems to have had more fundamental psychological roots.

In understanding a person's character, whose testimony can be more revealing than that of the family cook? Phyllis Bottome quotes the personal report of "Sophie, the family cook and mainstay for over twenty years." "When I first came to the Adler family," Sophie is reported to have said, "the Herr Doktor was never without a book or a pen in his hand. When he came in from his rounds, he would sit up to all hours of the morning, writing and reading. It was not so later, for people came to the house all day long—and far into the night; but when he was a young man he did not talk very much." [21]

Perhaps this change in the degree of "talking" is the most revealing clue to the change in Adler's type. If he was with-

[20] Jones, *op. cit.*, Vol. II, p. 130.
[21] Bottome, *op. cit.*, p. 30.

drawn in his early years, he was precisely the opposite later on. The indications are that Adler used the cafés of Vienna as his lecture platform, and particularly after he returned from his war service in 1916 imbued with his new dedication to "social feeling," he concentrated on spreading his thoughts by word of mouth rather than by his pen. In contrast to the introversion and sensitivity of his earlier years, Adler's activities in the second half of his life indicate a full and ever-increasing expression of extroverted traits.

It is this movement, this transformation of the psychological type through the principle of compensation, that appears in Adler's theoretical views as in his life. His point of view expresses both introversion—the attitude of inferiority felt in his youth—and extroversion—the feeling of social connectedness that became a deepening experience and dedication for him in his later years. And the relation between the two, appropriately enough, is the same in Adler's theory as in his life. They appear in sequence, the sense of inferiority acting as the stimulus that leads to personal strength and social feeling, the introvert of youth emerging as the extrovert of mature years.

3. THE DEEPENING OF JUNG'S PERSONAL PERSPECTIVE

It is interesting to note that the change in Adler's outlook, which in his terms is a result of the process of "compensation," has its counterpart in Jung's life, and in Jung's theories. We have already referred to the emotional difficulties that Jung experienced during the years when his work was diverging from Freud's. He was then in his late thirties. His private psychiatric practice was established, and he was well known in several countries as the leading associate of Freud. The attainments he had achieved as a result of his participation in the psychoanalytic movement were, in fact, the practical considerations on which Freud counted to insure Jung's loyalty, and they now weighed heavily on his mind. Almost fifteen years earlier, when Jung had completed his medical studies, an opportunity had come that would have opened a promising career for him in internal medicine; but he had deliberately passed it by because of what he later called a "hunch" that he should enter the then unpromising field of psychiatry. After some years he had begun to find a place for himself in this new work as the assistant to Eugen Bleuler at Burgholzli, and then once again he precipitously threw his prospects away, this time by linking himself with the unpopular, socially suspect point of view of Freud. Even that had flourished, however, and there were signs after his trip to America that the psychoanalytical movement was headed for great international success with appropriate rewards in store for him as president of the association and editor of the yearbook. And yet, here he was again, having done the hard work, ready to leave just before the harvest. It seemed quite clear that his actions were following a definite pattern in which, as a psychiatrist, he could not fail to recognize symptoms with serious implications. It might indeed be that he had a hard fate ahead of him; and Jung, in his later years, has freely confessed that in that uncertain period of his life, particularly in 1913 when he was thirty-eight years old, he had strong doubts concerning his own stability. These doubts and fears passed in time, particularly when he developed psychological concepts that enabled him to understand to his own satisfaction the confusing events taking place in his psyche. But it must certainly have been with much foreboding that Jung carried out his self-analysis at that time, faced as he was with increasing isolation now that his relations both with Freud and with Swiss psychiatry were broken. It may even be that it was because of the intense feelings of inferiority brought on by these doubts about himself that Jung was stimulated to do the psychic self-penetration that culminated eventually in his profound discoveries.[22]

In addition to the uneasiness he felt over the pattern his life was taking, Jung was concerned about strange, disturbing dreams that were coming to him with increasing force. Especially from 1913 until about 1915, he found himself subjected to great, massive dreams of a mythologic scope, dreams that were deep and dark, perplexing, and generally ominous in their overtones. Jung could not understand these dreams. At least, their magnitude was such that they would not permit themselves to be reduced to the categories of interpretation he had learned from Freud. They were elusive, uncanny as the unconscious often seems to be, and all the more disturbing to him because he could not handle them with the rational tools of his profession. These were decisive moments for Jung personally and for the history of depth psychology in general. Sensitive as a psychiatrist is bound to be to such things, he was becoming all too acutely aware of a danger lurking in his own psyche. And in the midst of that precarious situation, he felt as though he were about to be overwhelmed by dreams that his psychoanalytical knowledge did not enable him to explain. His situation then was reminiscent of that of Freud who was driven to his discoveries by emotional pressures that had a substantial core of neurosis

[22] These remarks are based on my conversations with Professor Jung in 1953 and 1955, verified with certain written records, and correlated with the material published by Ernest Jones. See also an article written by Professor Mircea Eliade in the French newspaper, *Combat*, Paris, October 9, 1952.

(neurasthenia, Freud himself called it). Jung's dreams seem, however, to have come from a greater psychic depth than Freud's, if we can judge from the fact that their symbolism is more impersonal and mythologic, and that they show a greater power to possess the personality as a whole. These may well be signs that the tension leading to the dreams was greater in Jung than in Freud. In any case, they led him to an insight into the archetypal dimensions of the unconscious which Freud had suspected and suggested but had not actually seen.

The factors involved at this crucial point in Jung's development are varied and complex, and it would require a full-scale biography comparable to the work of Ernest Jones to do the subject justice. The psychological basis of Jung's relationship with Freud and its connection with the deepening of his insight into the unconscious is, however, of the greatest importance for the history of depth psychology, and for the aspect of its transformation with which we are here concerned. Like Freud, Jung has always followed the practice of retelling and reinterpreting his personal dreams in order to illustrate his theoretical points. Of these, there is a particular dream that he frequently discusses in quite another connection to illustrate his theory about the change that seems to take place in psychological type during the middle years of life, and it illuminates this critical period of Jung's life in an especially suggestive way. It is a dream that came to Jung probably early in 1914. It has been recorded in the privately printed version of the English seminar he gave in 1925 and is generally well known to students of Jung's work, particularly those who have had personal contact with him.

The gist of the dream in its relevant aspects is as follows:

Jung found himself in the mountains in the company of an odd little brown-skinned man. Both were armed, and as daylight came, Jung heard the sound of a horn that he instantly recognized. It was Siegfried, the hero of Teutonic myth, and he was coming down the mountain. As Siegfried came into view, Jung and his companion fired their rifles and Siegfried was hit in the chest. Jung turned away in horror and remorse. The little brown man went ahead to give Siegfried a fatal thrust with his dagger, but Jung could not bear to take part in this final act. He could not continue with the little brown man but ran away from him and went to hide where no one could find him. Two paths were before him, and Jung ignored the one that led down into the valley but chose the one that led farther up the mountain. The dream then ended in a torrent of rain that brought with it a great sense of relief, a sign that the atmosphere of the dream (which means also the atmosphere of the unconscious depths of the psyche) contained a great emotional tension, from which the dreamer had to be released.

Jung's interpretation of this dream relates it to the changes then taking place in his psychological type from a "thinking" to an "intuitive" type. In his view, as a man trained in science and medicine, his personality had been based on his "thinking function"; he was for the first part of his life a "thinking type" with an essentially introverted orientation. Since his thinking was the strongest factor in his personality, it was symbolized in the dream by the hero. Siegfried, according to Jung's interpretation, represented his thinking capacity that dominated the conscious portion of his psyche, and the message of the dream was that a fundamental change was about to take place. What had heretofore been dominant, the hero, would now be overthrown. Jung was no longer to be a "thinking type" for his "thinking function" had been killed. The actual murder was done by the little brown man whom Jung regards as a "personification of the unconscious." It was done, in other words, by the unconscious, and not by Jung as a conscious individual. The dream, therefore, meant to Jung that what had been unconscious and undeveloped in him, mainly his "intuition function," was now going to supersede his thinking side.

Such an interpretation can, of course, be valid only within the framework of Jung's theory of types, and must to that extent be considered an intellectual rationalization of the dream material. The very form of Jung's interpretation is, in fact, evidence in itself of the fact that the "thinking function," supposedly killed in the dream, remained exceedingly active, if not dominant, in his psyche. It does seem to be a fact, however, that a major change did take place in Jung's personality during those middle years of his life. He had been exceedingly intellectual in the decade following his academic studies, and it was with a predominantly analytical attitude that he had built his relationship with Freud; otherwise Freud would not have felt so close a kinship. Something seems to have happened within Jung, however, that disturbed his conscious orientation and made it necessary for him to come into a fuller relationship with his unconscious. The recurrence of deep, upsetting dreams from 1913 to 1915 was evidence that this need was very pressing. His personality had to change, or at least be modified, and that meant that his conscious emphasis on intellect would have to be altered. Actually the symbolism of killing in the dream seems rather extreme and inappropriate as a representation for the conception that Jung had in mind. The change that did take place in his psyche, at least with regard to his psychological type, was that he became less of a "thinking type" and more of an "intuitive"; and that he became less of an extrovert (less the man who organized the first psychoanalytical congress and founded the Freud Club in Zurich) and more of an introvert, concentrating increasingly on the intuitive study of myths. These were, however, changes only of degree and emphasis. They were not sharp, immediate, and complete, as the killing in the dream would suggest. The tenor of Jung's dream indicates that something of the greatest importance to him, something of heroic dimensions, was in danger of total destruction. It seems probable, therefore, that the dream was referring to something other than the slow and gradual changing of Jung's psychological type.

The date of the dream was 1914, not long after Jung had seen Freud for the last time at the meeting of the Psychoanalytic Association in Munich during September, 1913. He had not yet made peace with the fact that he had now finally cut himself off from Freud, and he did not know what the consequences might be. At this time, in the midst of his heavy dreaming, Jung's psyche was working to come to terms, even if only unconsciously, with this central event of his life. He needed to know what issues were really involved in his separation from Freud, and what its deeper meaning might be. And in that dream there was the answer.

The little brown man was not merely an abstract "personification of the unconscious." He was an actual human companion of Jung. And, when we think of it, there was in fact in Jung's living experience a rather odd, dark little man with whom he had only recently traveled as a companion. He had indeed gone hunting with Sigmund Freud, and the two of them together had covered dangerous ground, mountains and valleys, consciousness and the unconscious. Both of them had been well prepared and well armed. In the dream they had rifles, and intellectually they were both exceedingly good shots. When they fired, both of them hit the mark. Jung had thus come right to the point in suspecting that the analytical trend of his mind was involved in the dream in a negative way. He was as analytical as Freud, and equally as competent with analytical tools. He was as good a shot as Freud, and like him he had hit the mark when he fired. But what had they shot? Was it Jung's "thinking function?" It seems to have been something at once more specific and of a larger significance. It was Siegfried, the hero who is the embodiment of the Teutonic myths. It is of interest that at the first sound of Siegfried's horn Jung knew who was coming. He did not need to rely on his senses or on his intellect to know this, for his intuition, his "unconscious" told him clearly enough. Siegfried apparently represented an aspect of the Teutonic myths with which Jung was very intimately connected. It was something he would recognize immediately and directly from within his own being. Siegfried was that part of the Teutonic mythos still living in the historical levels of Jung's own psyche.

Now we can understand how, in the depths of his unconscious psyche, Jung was reconstructing his relationship with Freud. His dream was explaining what it meant, what the consequences would have been had he continued it, and why he had no choice but to run away from that funny little brown man who analyzed so sharply that he killed as with a knife. The dream described the facts realistically. Jung had already gone hunting in companionship with Freud, and together, armed with their intellects, they had shot at Siegfried and wounded him. The primordial myth that Jung experienced as "true" intuitively, not with his thinking side but from the depths of his historical unconscious, had been wounded in him as a result of his having joined forces with Freud. There was now very little life left in that myth, but it was not quite dead yet. That was why there was so great a psychic tension attached to the dream: there was still a choice to be made. Should he continue with his little brown companion or not? The dream describes the two possibilities. If he would continue with Freud, that odd little dark man would cut up the Teutonic hero with his analytic knife, and then the great old myth would be dead forever in Jung's psyche. It was this that Jung could not bear. Something unconscious in him held him back from completing the deed. To preserve the remnants of the Teutonic myth in himself, Jung ran away from Freud, in the dream as in life. He tried to hide from the whole bewildering situation. And then the dream makes a prediction, apparently in answer to an anxious question. Will Jung lose his position in the world? Will he have to take a downward path because he has left Freud? The dream says no. As a result of his decision to flee, the dream prophesies, Jung will come to a crossroads on the mountain, and there he will choose the path that will lead him upward. The prophecy was reassuring, and the dream therefore ended in a release from tension, a deluge of rain.

The prophecy of the dream was not wrong. Jung's path did begin to go upward some years after his separation from Freud. This dream, however, is not an example of precognition, but of something that is psychologically much more fundamental. It expresses a representative piece of the psychic organism, and it does so in terms of the symbolism of that segment of the psyche that is most severely affected. Thus the central image of the dream was Siegfried, a figure of special historical significance to the dreamer; and that is because the conflict in which Jung was involved concerned the deep historical (or "collective") levels of the unconscious. The dream, however, represents not merely the "collective unconscious" but the dynamic workings of the psyche as a whole as it moves toward the fulfillment of its inner nature. The dreamer is concerned with the immediate problem, the particular conflict in which he is entangled; but the psyche has a much larger perspective, and it reflects this perspective in the dream. As the psychic organism expresses itself in the dream, therefore, it clarifies the past, shows the workings of the psyche in the present, and indicates the general aspects of the future. It does this naturally because the wholeness of the psychic organism experiences time as a unity. That is why, also, the particular dream we have interpreted is like a window facing on the depths of Jung's psyche through which we can see the inner meaning of his life and work.

This dream is not directly related to the question of psychological types. What it does involve, however, is the conflict within Jung dividing his loyalty between the reductive psychological analysis he had learned from Freud and the historical myths to which he felt an unconscious attachment. From the subjective point of view of the dreamer, the dream is concerned primarily with allegiance, for it is charging Jung with having been untrue to an important part of himself when he shot Siegfried. In the dream Jung runs away and hides, but the implication is that he will eventually have to take a more affirmative attitude toward Siegfried and all that Siegfried represents to him. That means at the start, turning away from the dissective analyses of Freud, and then developing a positive relation to the historical aspects of his psyche in an intuitive way. The movement of the dream thus indicates a change in psychological orientation, for it was leading Jung away from his analytical consciouness toward a concern with unconscious factors that can be experienced only in a nonanalytical way. This is the aspect of the situation that Jung emphasized when he interpreted the dream in terms of a change taking place in his psychological type. That change in "type," however, was only a derivative of the problems that were then crystallizing within him. His psychological organism was working toward a definite goal as though it were guided by an inner purpose. Since this goal was still deep in the unconscious functioning of his psyche, Jung could not then be aware of it, but the dream gave it expression. It called attention to the fact that the historical side of the unconscious was now of primary importance in Jung's development. The big change, therefore, was from the analytical emphasis on personal psychological factors (such as the events of infancy, sexuality, and family relationships) to a concern with man's deeper relationship to the realities of myth and religion. And Jung's change of type from "thinking" to "intuition" was an aspect of that.

In a general way, the transformation of "type" in Jung involved a movement from extroversion to introversion. Jung does not consider himself ever to have been fundamentally an extrovert, but as a matter of relative emphasis it is a fact that he tended more toward extroversion during the first part of his life—up to the period in which he had the succession of deep dreams of which we have spoken—and more toward introversion during his later years. His clinical work and his activity in the organizational aspects of the psychoanalytical movement when he first joined with Freud are indications of his early extroverted tendency. The energy Jung spent in organizing the first psychoanalytical congress, the

Freud Club in Zurich, and his robust activities in many other groups on behalf of psychoanalysis may have been one of the factors that misled Freud into thinking that Jung would make a good administrative "official" for the psycho-analytical movement. Oddly enough, it was precisely during the years when Jung was undertaking to carry out a predom-inantly extroverted role in his association with Freud that his introveted side was becoming the dominant element in his personality. After 1915, Jung's main psychological tendencies were of an introverted cast, and this is most markedly seen in his major work of interpreting the symbolism and processes of the unconscious.

Quite obviously on the basis of his personal experience, Jung later made the generalization that the normal pattern of development is for the individual to follow a predomi-nantly extroverted orientation in the first half of his life, changing to an introverted point of view in the second half. The transformation takes place, he said, between the ages of thirty-five and forty-five (as it did in his own case) and it in-volves a reversal of the direction of libido flow, from out-ward to inward, also causing a different psychological "func-tion" to become the most active factor in the personality. The change in Jung's case was mainly from "thinking" to "intuition." His conception, stated simply, is that the prob-lem before the young person is to make use of the instinctual energy available to him in finding his place in the world. He has to find a channel for his sexuality; he must develop his conscious capacities; and he must work out a suitable means of adapting himself to the community. All this, Jung said, calls for a strong flow of extroverted libido, particularly in modern Western culture; but the situation goes into reverse when the individual passes the middle years of life. After that, it is as though the human being begins to prepare, in an unconscious and obscure way, for his eventual death. Then it is the discovery of the "meaning" of his life that becomes the primary psychological necessity.

"It is of the greatest importance for the young person," Jung said in a lecture delivered in 1929, ". . . to shape his conscious ego as effectively as possible, that is, to educate his will. . . . He must feel himself a man of will, and may safely depreciate everything else in him and deem it subject to his will, for without this illusion he could not succeed in adapting himself socially." "But," he continues, "it is otherwise with a person in the second half of life who no longer needs to educate his conscious will, but who, to understand the meaning of his individual life, needs to experience his own inner being." [23]

This pattern of change that Jung considers to be inherent in the psychological development of the human being describes the outlines of his own growth faithfully. He had spent the first part of his mature life in the extroverted activities of establishing a family and building a career; but when he had approached forty, his psyche had begun to turn in another direction. It had directed his libido inward to seek, by the introverted searching of his unconscious, some clues to the meaning of his life. At that time, Jung felt a pressing psychological need "to experience his own inner being," and it was this that impelled him to the study of mythology and the symbolism of the unconscious. The Siegfried dream of which we have spoken was, in his regard, characteristic of the underlying change in Jung's life. It revealed that his secret rebellion against Freud was connected with his un-

[*] C. G. Jung, *The Practise of Psychotherapy*, Bollingen Series XX (New York: Pantheon Books, 1954), p. 50.

conscious recognition of the fact that Freud's analytical way would destroy the old mythological "truths." The dream was saying that Jung needed somehow to keep Siegfried alive within himself; but it did not indicate what was to be done. It disclosed only that Jung would not complete the killing, and it left open the implication that he would need to come into closer contact with mythologic symbols in order to experience the "meaning" of life in "his own being." It becomes quite clear in this context that although Siegfried is a figure from the Teutonic mythology to which Jung is historically connected, the significance of the hero in the dream is not Teutonic exclusively. The larger needs of Jung's life at that point and particularly as revealed in his later development indicate that the central fact of the dream was the opening of his relation to the deep unconscious, and not his devotion to any particular myth.

The course of psychic life that was thus set in train for Jung around that period turned his energies ever deeper into uncharted areas of the unconscious. Because of what he had learned from Freud, he was able to keep his sense of direction and be aware at least of where he was going. He knew that he was being drawn deeper into the unconscious. And he also knew, because of what he had learned from Freud, that dreams and mythologic symbolism would provide the main materials of his work. Beyond this all-important starting point, however, his Freudian training was of little help to him, since it was precisely because Freud's procedures had offended some profound unconscious attachment in his soul that he had felt himself forced to leave Freud and seek a way of his own. Freud's conception of the depths in man was thus the foundation of Jung's new line of study. What Jung built upon it, however, was motivated by a different spirit, and increasingly tended to proceed in terms of its own premises and definitions.

One point of connection between Freud and Jung, however, is fundamental for the development of depth psychology, and that is the conception of the depth nature, the psychic magnitude, of the human being. Out of the uncertainties of this middle period of his life, Jung emerged with a view of the unconscious that derived from Freud's original insights, but which deepened the entire range of study to a considerable extent. In later years, Freud adapted some of Jung's points to press them into the general structure of psychoanalytical thought, but Jung continued to make basic reformulations of his theory of the unconscious and its operation as late as 1946. The cumulative effect of these developments in the work of Freud and Jung has been to alter the conceptual basis of depth psychology and to extend the transformation in its fundamental orientation. Since one of our aims in this book is to trace this transformation within depth psychology, it seems best that we pause at this point in our discussion of Jung in order to examine in fuller detail the conception of the depths of the psyche that came to the fore in the later writings of Freud and Jung. The gradual enlargement that was brought about in the theory of the unconscious opened progressively new vistas in the study of man, and these are of major significance for the new directions of depth psychology. When we have followed these lines of growth to see some of their implications, we will be able to return and consider the later developments in Jung's work in a fuller context.

V

The dialogue of Freud and Jung

on the magnitude of man

1. FROM OEDIPUS TO THE COLLECTIVE UNCONSCIOUS

It is a paradoxical fact that although the conclusions drawn from Freud's Oedipus theory are highly questionable, the conception of the psyche on which it is based retains its fundamental importance in depth psychology. From a dozen different directions the criticism has been made that Freud misread the ancient Greek myth, attributing to it meanings that belong to him and not to the myth itself. Though that may be so, the fact remains that even if Freud was altogether wrong in the way he developed his conception of the Oedipus situation, the principles behind his study were the starting point from which a much larger conception of the unconscious has emerged.

In following the line of analysis that led him to his theory of the Oedipus complex, Freud's aim was to trace the roots of those patterns of behavior that are inherent in the human species. He was trying to reach back into the structure of the psyche in its deepest historical aspects, proceeding on the general hypothesis that the psychic organism of the human species is everywhere the same in principle and that it can be studied with the same universality as the human body. Freud worked with the view that the psyche functions by means of processes that are inherent in human nature and are as inevitably, and as naturally, present in man as the circulation of his blood. He was thus seeking an explanatory principle that would be not the same as, but the equivalent in principle of a description of physiological processes.

The difficulty, as is always the case in psychological work, lay in the fact that the contents of the psyche are not nearly as tangible as those of the body. They are so elusive that they seem unreal to the matter-of-fact mind, and one of the major problems in the study of the psyche lies simply in determining what the actual subject matter is. Freud, however, was particulary gifted in being able to experience the intangibles of the psyche with the same vivid perception as physical objects. "They were," as Ernest Jones says, "as real and concrete to him as metals are to a metallurgist.[1] Once he realized, therefore, that dreams are not arbitrary but that they have a relationship to other contents of the psyche, he immediately began to think in terms of processes, just as he would do if he were engaged in physiological research. Once he had perceived, more as a result of intuition than of intellectual understanding, that dreams and myths have much in common, a large source of material

[1] Ernest Jones, *The Life and Work of Sigmund Freud* (New York: Basic Books, 1955), Vol. II, p. 432.

opened to him for empirical research. He was able, then, to undertake a comparative interpretation of symbolism; and this gave him a basis on which he could begin to identify the various processes of the psyche. Gradually he was able to fill in the details of the general and tentative conception of the "unconscious" with which his investigations had begun. One of the first and most fundamental conclusions he reached was a hypothesis that proved to be exceedingly useful in work in depth psychology, particularly in the researches of Jung and Rank. It was the insight that, just as dreams express the unconscious of individuals, myths express the unconscious of the human species as a whole: and, more important, that the symbolism of myths expresses the processes of the psyche in their quintessential form in contrast to the more personal contents of dreams deriving from merely individual experiences.

With these hypotheses, Freud was able to proceed in constructing an interpretation of the psyche in terms of universal processes. These, he felt, would appear naturally in all human beings, and would operate as inexorably as the processes of the body. He would find their essence in principle by deciphering the symbolism of myths. Then he would be able to apply the general principle to the particular case of the individual personality by relating dreams to myths, and he would thus demonstrate the forms in which the universal processes of the psyche occur in the varieties of human organisms. The processes that he would isolate and identify in this way might very well be misconceived; his descriptions of them might be one-sided, or even altogether wrong; but the basic understanding of the nature of the psyche and the perspective in which its processes were to be studied transcended all Freud's special theories. It was this that became the foundation for depth psychology, and particularly for the researches that Jung carried out in his efforts to find his way in the depths of the unconscious.

Jung followed Freud's lead and worked with a conception of the psyche as an independent, autonomously functioning part of the human organism. He experienced "psychic reality" in the same concrete terms as Freud, for that experience is certainly a prerequisite for any effective work in depth psychology. More specifically, Jung agreed with Freud as to the close relationship between myth and dream as linking the *tendencies* of the human species and the *actualities* of individual human beings. Likewise, Jung shared with Freud a general psychogenetic conception of man, holding that the basic experiences of primal times are transmitted across the generations, that is, as part of the natural inheritance of the psyche, so that they are present latently in the individual as general tendencies toward specific types of behavior. Both Freud and Jung held the view that what has been experienced primordially by the race is relived and re-experienced by the individual, in principle, in all subsequent times. In his later theories, Jung carried this hypothesis much further than Freud and articulated it more explicitly, but it was very definitely a conception that he derived from Freud. In a letter to Jung in the fall of 1911, Freud spoke of "phylogenetic memory" as something "which unfortunately will soon prove to be so." [2] The word "unfortunately" here probably reflects Freud's rationalistic attitude toward such conceptions; but he seems to have been convinced of it on a factual level. Describing Freud's way of thinking about these questions, Ernest Jones says, "There was, to begin with, the hereditary disposition, which in a few cases is all-important and in others

[2] *Ibid.*, p. 451.

hardly at all. It consists of the deposit of ancestral experiences. This was always Freud's view of heredity: 'If nothing is acquired nothing can be inherited.' What are nowadays called 'primal phantasies,' e.g., pictures of parental coitus, fear of castration, etc., were once long ago realities." [3]

Inherited memories like these, however, are to be interpreted as historical only in an abstract generic sense. They are part of the experience of man, regardless of the particular cultural line from which the individual is descended; at least, that was Freud's theory. He jumped from the basic experiences of a simple (primal) family nature to the human individual in all times and cultures; and Jung's critique was based on the realization that this left too great a gap. Between the human race and the individual there are the great cultural, historical groups. Each of these has its own special type of primordial experiences, and these are retained by the collective psyche of the people to be transmitted across the generations, transmitted orally by myths and legends, and also unconsciously via the depths of the psyche. The relation of myth and dream to the unconscious was thus carried a step further by Jung. He made Freud's psychogenetic conception more specifically historical by maintaining the integrity of the various mythologies, the Hindu, Chinese, Teutonic, Semitic, American Indian, and so on, and seeking to relate the dreams and personal psychology of modern individuals to the particular historical mythology from which their psychic life was most immediately derived.

This rather simple change resulted in many other alterations. Jung was still seeking the principles underlying the natural and universal processes of the psyche, but he was

[3] *Ibid.*, p. 222.

giving the historical and cultural factors greater consideration. The symbolism of myths could not legitimately be
interpreted in terms of a priori conceptions, but they were to
be regarded as meaningful in their own right. They were not
to be reduced to preconceived patterns representing sexual
and family conflicts. Gradually Jung came to the conclusion
that each myth was not only entitled to speak for itself
but that it could be understood only if its own inner logic, its
intimate assumptions about life were accepted in their own
terms and were not explained away. Jung thus took the cultural differences of myths as his starting point. He studied the
symbolism of religious beliefs, ceremonials, fairy tales, legends, and so on, in order to compare them with the corresponding symbols in other mythologies as a means of identifying the universal "motifs" with the mythologies that all
peoples have in common. His aim was still the same as
Freud's, to identify the processes of the psyche by correlating
the symbolism of individual dreams and historical myths, but
his method was different. He did not reduce the varieties of
myth to certain elementary sexual and family experiences;
but instead he tried to distinguish and describe those patterns of symbolism that reappear to the common themes and
motifs, the images and symbolic events recurring in the many
myths of mankind. He felt that, by finding the universal patterns of mythology, he would be led to the principles underlying the psychic life of man, and thence to the basic psychic
processes. This was Jung's aim and it determined the procedure that led him to his conception of the "archetypes."

With respect to the steps by which Jung's conception of
the archetypes was derived from Freud's point of view, it is
interesting to note that one of the earliest and most interesting of Otto Rank's books, *The Myth of the Birth of the*

Hero, first published in 1909, anticipates the germ of Jung's theory of the archetypes. In that book, taking a particular type of myth as his theme, Rank undertook to show that, because of the inherent nature of the psyche, there are patterns of symbolism that appear spontaneously in the most widely separated areas. He thus inferred, as Jung was to do more strikingly and upon a larger canvas in his *Psychology of the Unconscious* in 1912, that the basic symbolic themes are universal, and that they possess a common core that underlies the varieties of historical forms in which they appear.

When Rank wrote his book on the hero, he was very closely identified with Freud in Vienna, and he even had Freud's active assistance in drawing his material together. His book indicates, therefore, that the search for archetypes in depth psychology actually began in the midst of psychoanalysis and he had Freud's direct blessing. We can see from this that, although the discovery and designation of archetypes had been associated exclusively with Jung, it derives from a conception of the psyche that held an important position in Freud's early thought. That is why it seems highly probable that if Jung's theory of the archetypes had been his only, or even his major, difference with Freud, it would not have been sufficient to precipitate the separation between them; for even Jung's later developments of his archetype theory were either implicit in Freud's earlier views or were logically related to them. Freud might very well have assimilated the conception of archetypes into the main body of psychoanalytic doctrine as a further development of the line of thought that Rank's book on the hero had begun. It was much more Jung's rejection of the primacy of sexuality, a cardinal point of dogma to Freud, his critique of the reductive point of view in general, and certain temperamental differences that have appeared in our earlier discussions, that made the breach between them inevitable, and impossible to bridge.

There had been two very different aspects of the view of man that Freud had originally developed. On one side, the unconscious was described as the archaic base of the psyche containing primal urges that Freud reduced mainly to the son's Oedipal drive to murder his father and cohabit with his mother. On the other side, the unconscious was described as the container of frustrated desires, since it received the residues of those instinctual drives that civilization does not permit the individual to express. The archaic aspect of the unconscious was the truly dynamic base of Freud's theory, but in the practice of diagnosing neurotic patients, it was the other side that came to the fore. Freud's view was that those primal urges that cannot be expressed in consciousness are repressed. They are pressed back and down into the unconscious where they may or may not remain inactive. The net result is that the unconscious becomes the storing place for wishes that cannot be fulfilled.

This is the aspect of the unconscious that has always been stressed in Freud's works—necessarily so, since repression and unconscious wish fulfillment provide the practical base for his theories of dreams and anxiety and psychopathology in general—and the deeper, more dynamic aspect has tended to drop into the background. "We obtain our concept of the unconscious," Freud wrote, "from the theory of repression. The repressed serves us as a prototype of the unconscious." [4] But, he added a little later on, "Pathological research has

---

[4] Sigmund Freud, *The Ego and the Id*, trans. Joan Riviere. The International Psycho-Analytical Library, No. 12 (London: Hogarth Press, 1949), p. 12.

centered our interest too exclusively on the repressed." [5]

Psychoanalytic practice has thus, by its own admission, given good grounds to those critics who have charged that Freud's conception of the unconscious is negative, and that it deals with the backwash of psychic life rather than with the dynamics of personality. Adler, Jung, and Rank have all made this criticism of Freud, and, in their individual ways, have used it as a starting point and contrast for their own formulations. Of these three, however, Jung is the only one who continued to work directly with Freud's basic conception of the unconscious, undertaking to extend it in depth and to elaborate its contents.

From Jung's point of view, it was not merely a question of negativity in Freud's theory, but a question of understanding the functioning of the psyche in terms of its inner purposes as a constructive unity. Like Adler, Jung wished to be able to interpret the human being as an organism with special reference to the unconscious levels of the psyche. In the experiments with the "Association Tests" on which he had been working, Jung had followed the general hypothesis that there is something hidden, something underneath the veneer of the conscious personality. He found that the emotional affect attached to the contents that were repressed in the psyche tended to inhibit the associations or to affect them in other ways. It seemed that this fact carried at least a clue to the nature of mental disturbances, and Jung formulated it in his theory of the "complexes." He meant by a "complex" a combination of mental contents brought together as a functioning unity in the unconscious in such a form as to be capable of acting quite independently under the power of its own concentration of libido. As his work

⁵ *Ibid.*, p. 19.

with Freud proceeded, Jung developed the relationship between the complexes and the repressed contents of the unconscious that Freud had described. Jung's theory of the complexes was not Freudian in its origin, but it gained acceptance in a relatively short time and became a standard part of psychoanalytic doctrine and terminology.

It was the contents of the complexes that gave Jung something tangible to work with in defining the limitations of Freud's conception of the unconscious. He had found that the repressed material of the complexes as revealed in the Association Tests was always of a personal nature. It involved childhood wishes that could not be fulfilled, unrequited loves, desires, and experiences that were repressed as "sinful." The complexes were personal, and invariably of a negative character. The important insight then came from understanding the significance of dreams in revealing the nature of the complexes. Jung had recognized from the beginning that there was a special value in Freud's correlation of myths with individual dreams, but as he carried his own studies further he discovered a basis for this correspondence that Freud had not observed. Jung came across dreams of a type that he eventually called "big dreams": these not only contained symbols found in myths, but they seemed to carry a "message" not only for the individual but for his society as a whole. The prophetic dreams that appear in the Old Testament are examples of this type of dream whose scope transcends the individual personality both in contents and in significance. On the basis of the correspondence between such dreams and the cosmic conceptions found in mythologies both of primitive tribes and ancient cultures, Jung concluded that the more fundamental contents of the unconscious are not merely the result of unfulfilled personal desires, but have origins that are more than personal. His hypothesis was that the universal patterns of symbol formation (the archetypes) are expressed as objective entities in the unconscious, and that, as a result of their autonomous activity, psychic contents that are not personal at their core can appear in the dreams and complexes of individual personalities.

The theory of the unconscious that Jung then offered as his alternative to Freud divided the unconscious into parts. The more superficial part, the part closer to consciousness, contained wishes or memories that had been repressed. Its contents were psychic materials of a personal nature that the individual either could not raise to consciousness or had unconsciously suppressed. Jung called this the "Personal Unconscious." It covered that psychic "area" that Freud had designated as the "Preconscious," and also the main part of the Freudian unconscious, the "Unconscious Repressed." The more basic part of the psyche, the impersonal part deepest down and furthest from consciousness, Jung named the "collective unconscious," and this corresponded to the primal archaic core of the psyche referred to by Freud in his Oedipal theory; but there was a most important difference. Freud, for his part, tried to place the primal patterns of psychic life on a basis that was essentially biological, as the Oedipal yearning of the son for his mother; but Jung undertook to interpret unconscious symbolism in historical terms. He held that the archetypes are psychic patterns present in all mankind as a species, but that they are carried through time and reach the individual personality only via the symbolism of myths and the unconsciously held beliefs transmitted within national cultures. It was because Jung tended to deal with symbols directly in the forms in which they appeared in history, not reducing them in accordance with the psycho-analytical pattern, that Freud made his charge that Jung dealt only with the "manifest" (superficial) contents rather than the "latent" (hidden) ones. Jung's reply was that the sexual symbols found in myths are themselves symbolic representations of larger levels of human experience. To reduce them to sexuality, he said, reverses the actual life process that is inherently "prospective" rather than reductive. These seemingly sexual symbols are symbolic precisely because their function is to transcend the elementary facts of genitality and transform them in the richer contexts of life as a whole.

The new conception of psychic depth that Jung developed, the "Collective Unconscious," was an exceedingly fertile contribution to depth psychology; but it was an idea that was all too easily misunderstood. Particularly during the two decades preceding the second World War, when inflammatory racial ideologies were planting the seeds of the conflict to come, a term like "collective unconscious" was bound to be taken in the wrong spirit. The name that Jung gave to his most fundamental hypothesis practically asked for misunderstanding, and of course the misunderstandng came. In his later works, trying to overcome the misleading overtones of his original term, Jung sometimes used the phrase "objective psyche," but it has not come into general use. Its advantage is that it stresses the important fact that the effective power at work in the personality is independent of and prior to the conscious will of the individual; and this is a conception that is fundamental to Jung's way of thinking. The original term, the "collective unconscious," has, however, continued to dominate Jungian usage mainly because it expresses the essential distinction on which Jung's enlargement of the Freudian view of the unconscious was based.

Jung was stressing the difference between purely personal unconscious contents and those that have a root in the historical and group experience, particularly those that have a deeper root than individuality and consciousness. The main aim of Jung's new conception of the unconscious was to provide a larger frame of reference so that Freud's descriptions could be understood in a more adequate perspective. What Freud had previously described as the totality of the unconscious, Jung now divided into the Personal Unconscious and the Collective Unconscious. His view of the personality then involved a conception of strata. On the surface was consciousness; below that the Personal Unconscious; and further below that, the Collective Unconscious. The best analogy for this view is a cross-sectional drawing of a geologic formation. At the top is a thin layer of surface rock; this is consciousness. Just below that is another layer, thicker than the first, but still relatively thin; this is the Personal Unconscious. And below these two strata, as a deep formation of rock extending back to the Plutonic core of the earth itself, is the Collective Unconscious. This is really quite an apt analogy for the structure of the personality in terms of levels of depth. Jung has used it, and it has been taken up as characteristic of his thought and employed as a schematic means of giving people a general perspective for his point of view. It can be highly misleading, however, if one does not keep in mind that it really describes only a particular state in Jung's development of his conception of the unconscious. The representation in terms of layers was much too schematic, much too rigid, and when Jung realized its limitations he tried to expand it and make it more flexible. In his later writings we can see that one of the main aims of Jung's work was to build a dynamic conception of the psyche as a functioning unity; but it is true that the dichotomy and opposition between consciousness and the unconscious retains an important role in his thinking to this day.

2. THE SUPEREGO AND THE ID

Despite the lack of clarity in its formulation, Jung's theory of the "collective unconscious" enlarged the conception of the psyche in a most significant way. For various reasons, Freud was not inclined to admit that Jung had made an important contribution in this regard, but his writings indicate that he was taking Jung's points into account and placing them in the context of his own system. At the time when Jung brought forward his new ideas, Otto Rank was still a close disciple of Freud, a member of the intimate psychoanalytical circle in Vienna, and secretary of the international association. Rank's comments on the influence that Jung's theory of the unconscious had on Freud may therefore be taken as an eyewitness account more or less impartial as between Freud and Jung. Freud's Oedipus analysis had been based, as we have seen, on a hypothesis of dynamic depths in the unconscious. In practice, however, it was not this side of the unconscious, but rather the "unconscious repressed" that received by far the most attention. The conception of the unconscious that Freud used in his actual work was characterized mainly by its negative relationship to consciousness. Rank pointed this out in the years shortly before his death, interpreting it as a sign of the "purely rationalistic approach" and the "moralistic philosophy" that were at the root of Freud's point of view. It was, Rank said, "only after Jung had extended its content beyond the repressed material in the individual," that Freud attempted to deepen his perspective of the unconscious "with the broader but quite neutral term 'id.' "[6]

This clue that Rank has given us is of great value because it indicates where the fundamental connecting link between Freud and Jung is to be found. Oddly enough, in *The Ego and the Id,* the book that contains the major revisions that reflect Freud's effort to come to terms with Jung's "Collective Unconscious," Freud began with the flat statement, "I am as a rule always ready to acknowledge my debts to other workers, but on this occasion I feel myself under no such obligation." [7] We might easily be misled by this statement if we did not remember a principle that Freud himself taught us in his *Psycho-pathology of Everday Life.* He said no because he meant yes, and he inadvertently gave away the reason. The first impression we draw from that statement is that Freud is saying that the material he has used in *The Ego and the Id* is completely original and that unlike his other theories, it was not suggested to him by the works of any other authors. On closer inspection, however, it appears that all that Freud had said is that on this particular occasion he does not feel inclined to acknowledge the individual who stimulated him to develop his new conceptions. We can understand Freud's feelings on this point and even sympathize with them, considering that where Jung was concerned his pride must have had its reasons. The fact remains, however,

---

[6] Otto Rank, *Beyond Psychology,* published privately by friends and students of the author (Camden, N.J.: Haddon Craftsmen, 1941), p. 38.
[7] Freud, *The Ego and the Id, op. cit.,* p. 8.

that it was Jung's new theories to which Freud was addressing his argument. The omission of Jung's name is significant of the personal factors involved, and when we take that into account we realize that Freud's *The Ego and the Id* is best understood when it is read as part of a continuous (though undeclared) dialogue with Jung on the nature of the deep conscious. When that is understood, "this very obscure book," as Freud's translator refers to *The Ego and the Id*, becomes considerably less obscure.[8]

It was inherent in the way Freud thought about the unconscious that he related it directly to consciousness. That was the case for both the "Preconscious" and the "Unconscious Repressed." By the "Preconscious" Freud meant that part of the "unconscious which is only latent, and so can easily become unconscious." [9] By the "Unconscious Repressed," he meant the part that contained mental contents actively (Freud would say "dynamically") held back and kept out of consciousness. Both these aspects of the unconscious are clearly "negative" with respect to consciousness, as Rank pointed out, and Freud was inclined to admit that as far as it went this charge was true. He considered it to be a legitimate criticism because his own intention was also to develop an affirmative conception of the psyche that would reach deep into nature to trace the sources of consciousness. That inspiration had been present even in the early conceptions which had led to the Oedipus complex, but it had only been implicit there. Freud had followed a line of analysis then that was mainly biosexual. He had not followed up his original insight that there are universal forces of a

---

[8] Translator's Note, p. 6.
[9] Freud, *New Introductory Lectures on Psycho-analysis* (New York: Norton, 1933), p. 101.

historical nature in the depths of the psyche, even though he recognized the fact that discoveries in that field might alter the whole structure of psychoanalysis. While Freud concentrated on the practical side of the work dealing with the neuroses, Otto Rank had continued the deeper studies on a theoretical and cultural level. In 1909, Rank had developed some themes that had been implicit in Freud's earlier writings in his brilliant little volume, *The Myth of the Birth of the Hero;* and a few years later Jung had followed with a large, impressive work inquiring into the symbolism and processes of the unconscious at the mythologic level that Freud's Oedipus theory had touched. In writing *The Ego and the Id*, therefore, Freud was only returning to a line of thought that had begun in his own work; but, because he had neglected it, it had been necessary for him to be reminded of it and be recalled to it by others who had given it a new and larger significance. For the most part, the essay on *The Ego and the Id* is to be understood as Freud's tentative effort to reconstruct the basic doctrine of psychoanalysis in order to integrate into it those creative aspects of the unconscious that Jung's new formulations had brought to the fore, and thus open the field for further study.

The basic question that Freud was now considering anew involved the structure of the psyche as a whole, that is, the "area" within the human being where psychic processes take place. In this regard, Freud said, "the division of mental life into what is conscious and what is unconscious is the fundamental premise on which psycho-analysis is based." [10] It has of course been true that Freud's most basic contribution is the fact that he called attention to the importance of the un-

[10] Freud, *The Ego and the Id, op. cit.,* p. 9.

conscious and that he pioneered in studying it empirically. In describing the unconscious, Freud had distinguished various aspects of its operation and named them hypothetically according to their pragmatic value in treating pathological symptoms. Now, however, he was turning to the larger task of considering psychic life as a whole and describing its structure and divisions with reference to the fundamental distinction between consciousness and the unconscious.

To begin with, Freud said, "We have two kinds of unconscious—that which is latent but capable of becoming conscious, and that which is repressed and not capable of becoming conscious in the ordinary way." [11] These are, respectively, the "Preconscious" and the "Unconscious Repressed" of which we have already spoken. The difference is of particular significance because it leads us to one of the primary characteristics of unconscious mental contents. The fact that its material is latently conscious so that it can easily enter consciousness meant to Freud that the "Preconscious" is not fundamentally related to the depths of the psyche. Whatever truly pertains to the unconscious, his experience had taught him, can be brought to consciousness only with the greatest difficulty. Unconscious material is dark and obscure. It is not logically consistent in terms of time and place, and it does not respect the other rational limitations of the conscious mind. Unconscious material is strange to consciousness, but the material in the "Preconscious" is not strange because it is closely akin to contents that are already in consciousness. That is why it can be readily assimilated into the conscious level of the psyche. Thus, Freud pointed out, although he classified the "Preconscious" as part

[11] *Ibid.*, p. 12.

of the Unconscious, strictly speaking it does not belong there.[12] "While in the descriptive sense there are two kinds of unconscious, in the dynamic sense there is only one." [13] This one was the "Unconscious Repressed" whose material is so artfully veiled by the symbolization of the unconscious that its full meaning seldom reaches the conscious mind.

The conception of the unconscious in terms of deeply repressed material dominated Freud's work for more than twenty years. Nonetheless, he felt that it was now necessary for him to reconsider it. In the past, he said, he had treated the Ego as though it were altogether conscious; but in his practice he had accumulated evidence sufficient to convince him that the ego contains much that is unconscious. On many occasions, he explained, he had found himself with a patient whose ego was caught in the grip of a "resistance" but who had no idea of what was at work in him. "He does not know what it is nor how to describe it," Freud said. "Since, however, there can be no question but that this resistance emanates from his ego and belongs to it, we find ourselves in an unforeseen situation. We have come upon something in the ego itself which is also unconscious, which behaves exactly like the repressed, that is, which produces powerful effects without itself being conscious and which requires special work before it can be made conscious." [14] How are such experiences to be accounted for? A change in the conception of the ego seemed to be imperative.

Further than that, it seemed quite definite that the unconscious, material in the ego was not comprised of repressed contents, and neither was it preconscious. It did not include

[12] Freud, *New Introductory Lectures, op. cit.*, p. 101.
[13] Freud, *The Ego and the Id, op. cit.*, p. 13.
[14] *Ibid.*, pp. 16-17.

the kind of psychic contents that could easily become conscious, but it followed the style of expression characteristic of the unconscious. It did not fit into either of the two categories of the unconscious with which Freud was accustomed to work. Freud was, therefore, forced to "recognize that the unconscious does not coincide with what is repressed; it is still true that all that is repressed is Unconscious, but not that the whole Unconscious is repressed. A part of the ego too—and Heaven knows how important a part—may be Unconscious, undoubtedly is Unconscious." [15]

He found himself "confronted by the necessity of postulating a third Unconscious which is not repressed." [16] It was a disconcerting situation, for it implied that much more than some minor revisions of psychoanalytic theory would be necessary before the period of reappraisal would be finished. To reinterpret the ego in terms of the Unconscious, and then to alter the conception of the Unconscious in a basic way, might totally upset the neat little system that Freud had been building in his effort to make depth psychology a precise analytical science. If there is a type of unconscious that is not based on repressed material, Freud wrote ruefully, as though he were thinking aloud, "we must admit that the property of being unconscious begins to lose significance for us. It becomes a property which can have many implications, so that we are unable to make it, as we should have hoped to do, the basis of far-reaching and inevitable conclusions." [17] He had become so accustomed to emphasizing the importance of repressions that it would now be most difficult, even painful, for him to change his approach. Quite clearly Freud recognized this. He was certainly most reluctant to alter his conception of the unconscious in order to

[15] *Ibid.*, p. 17.   [16] *Ibid.*, p. 18.   [17] *Ibid.*, p. 18.

take C. G. Jung's view of the impersonal, nonrepressed forces in the depths of the psyche into account. And yet, since the facts indicated that it was a scientifically necessary step, he would not shrink from it; nor would he try to gloss it over, nor minimize its significance. That is characteristic of Freud's courage and intellectual honesty. In *The Ego and the Id* he faced as squarely as he could the task of critically revising conceptions that he had long accepted as part of the basic and permanent equipment of psychoanalysis.

The line of thought that Freud followed was clear and direct. The ego, he now recognized, was not mainly conscious as he had previously thought it to be; quite the contrary, it was markedly unconscious. Further, the unconscious aspects of the ego were sharply different from repressed contents. The ego had shown itself to be based neither on preconscious nor on repressed material, but on some "third" kind of unconscious. This led to a double point. In the first place it indicated that there is a most important part of the unconscious that is not repressed but which has not yet been described by psychoanalysis; and in the second place, it implied that when this third type of unconscious would be understood it would bring important clues to our knowledge of the ego. The search thus turned to the depths of the unconscious.

At this point, it is interesting to notice, Freud's style of argument also took a turn. He had been proceeding in a severely logical manner, drawing out the consequences of his observations, but his next step did not depend on logic and it was not based on any special empirical evidence. It was simply a definition. "We shall now look upon the mind of an individual," he said, "as an unknown and unconscious id, upon whose surface rests the ego." [18] In other words, feeling that an empirical account of the depths of the psyche was beyond his grasp at that time, Freud undertook a schematic description of the unconscious from an intellectual point of view. He simply postulated a division of the psyche into ego and id.

In working out this division, Freud seemed to be proceeding from opposite poles of the personality. The ego, he said, begins to form itself at the outer edges of the psyche where it meets its environment, while the id has its source in the inner depths; and somewhere in between, they meet and intermingle. The ego, Freud said, has as "its nucleus the Perceptual system";[19] it is based on the individual's conscious contacts with the world around him. The id, on the other hand, is derived from the vast forces of instinct. Its roots are in the deepest recesses of the unconscious, so deep that they are inherently inaccessible to the conscious mind. The id contains the tremendous untamed power of the psyche, and everything that is unconscious is ultimately encompassed by it. Thus, "the repressed merges into the id as well, and is simply a part of it." And "the ego is not sharply separated from the id; its lower portion merges into it." [20]

The picture of the psyche that emerges in this new view thus shows the id to be by far the predominant factor in the human being. It is the base of the personality and the ego rests upon it. To a limited degree, as the organ of consciousness maintaining the individual's relationship with the outside world, the ego is able to channelize and otherwise influence the activities of the id. At least, the ego tries "to substitute the reality-principle for the pleasure principle which

[18] *Ibid.*, p. 28.   [19] *Ibid.*, p. 28.   [20] *Ibid.*, p. 28.

reigns supreme in the "id." "The ego," Freud says, "represents what we call reason and sanity, in contrast to the id which contains the passions." The ego may make an impressive effort to hold the id in control, but in the end its influence is severely limited since it itself is dependent on the id. The illustration that Freud uses here is most significant. "In its relation to the id," he says, the ego "is like a man on horseback who has to hold in check the superior strength of the horse; with this difference, that the rider seeks to do so with his own strength, while the ego uses borrowed forces. The illustration may be carried further. Often a rider, if he is not to be parted from his horse, is obliged to guide it where it wants to go; so in the same way the ego constantly carries into action the wishes of the id as if they were its own." [21]

Having reached this point in deepening his conception of the unconscious, Freud found himself in something of a dilemma. He could go no further. He realized that in acknowledging the existence of a stratum in the unconscious more fundamental than the "repressed" he was upsetting the basis of all his previous work; and he was honest enough to confess it. "We at once realize," Freud wrote, "that almost all the delimitations we have been led into outlining by our study of pathology relate only to the superficial levels of the mental apparatus—the only ones known to us." [22] If any fundamental answers were to be found, they would have to

[21] *Ibid.*, p. 30. The significance of the rider on horseback illustration is emphasized by the fact that Freud repeated it in his *New Introductory Lectures on Psycho-Analysis*, to make the same point, that the ego is essentially dependent on the id, since "the rider is obliged to guide his horse in the direction in which it itself wants to go." *New Introductory Lectures, op. cit.*, p. 108.
[22] *Ibid.*, pp. 28-29.

come from a deepened understanding of the id. Freud recognized this to be so, but there was very little he could do about it. He was able to make some highly perceptive observations about the characteristics of the id in general, but he was not able to contribute anything more specific. Even a decade later, in his *New Introductory Lectures on Psycho-Analysis*, Freud freely confessed that he had been able to make no further progress. "You must not expect me," he said then, "to tell you much that is new about the id, except its name." [23] It was simply that he did not possess adequate tools of analysis for interpreting those unconscious areas encompassed by the id. The best that he could do was to concentrate on studying the ego more closely in the perspective of his new view of the unconscious.

In this effort, it seemed to Freud that the most important role of the ego is as an intermediary between the environment and the unconscious depths of the person. "Like the dweller in a borderland that it is," he wrote, "the ego tries to mediate between the world and the id, to make the id comply with the world's demands and, by means of muscular activity, to accommodate the world to the id's desires." [24] The ego plays the role of a guide for the id, but the question arises of what standards, what criteria of judgment, the ego itself uses in choosing the avenues of expression into which it guides the id. Toward what ideals does the ego channelize the energies of the id? And from what source does it derive these goals and purposes? Freud's answer was that there is a special segment of the ego that contains the "higher" values, the aspirations, and also the "conscience" of the personality.

[23] Freud, *New Introductory Lectures, op. cit.*, p. 103.
[24] Freud, *The Ego and the Id, op. cit.*, p. 83.

He called it the "Ego-Ideal," or, more popularly, the "Super-Ego"; and he described it as speaking to the ego with the voice both of inspiration and stern commandment.

In interpreting the superego, Freud took cognizance of a profound and most significant point. He noted that despite the fact that the ego seems to be acting with consciousness in relating the id to its environment, both the ego and the moral "precipitate in the ego," the superego, are fundamentally unconscious.[25] "Not only what is lowest," he pointed out, "but also what is highest in the ego can be unconscious";[26] and, further than that, it is precisely that part of the ego that contains the "higher" ideals—the moral values, religious beliefs, and the like—that "is less closely connected with consciousness than the rest." [27] This may seem paradoxical. We might have thought that the triad of id, ego, and superego would stand in a hierarchical order in the psyche, with the id as the instinctual base, the ego representing consciousness, and the superego corresponding to a sort of superconsciousness; but the facts show something totally different. The closest kinship seems to be between the id and the superego, the highest and lowest having the most in common by virtue of their relative lack of consciousness; and even that part of the ego that makes some tentative approaches to consciousness in terms of the "perceptual system" is never free from its dependence upon the unconscious substrate of the psyche in which both the id and the superego are contained.

"It is easy to show," Freud says, "that the ego-ideal answers in every way to what is expected of the higher nature of man." [28] This "higher nature," however, is nothing more than the conventional moralities that traditional religions en-

[25] *Ibid.*, p. 44.
[27] *Ibid.*, p. 35.
[26] *Ibid.*, p. 33.
[28] *Ibid.*, p. 49.

force. Their basis is by no means a "higher" consciousness, but is altogether unconscious. That conforms with Freud's earlier analysis of the Oedipus complex and its relation to religion. In the earliest conditions of primitive life, man had committed the "primal crime" that Freud described in his *Totem and Taboo.* The sons had killed their father and had then repented of their crime, Freud had said, and they had left mankind as their legacy for that act a burden of sin and a sense of guilt that are carried in the depths of the unconscious through all generations. It was not difficult at all to put that act in the context of his new formulation, at least in a schematic way. The basis for the "primal crime" was in the id, for it was darkly instinctive; and the code of moral behavior, the commandments and prohibitions that resulted from that act of father murder, were contained in the superego. Thus it is that the superego "is the heir of the Oedipus complex and . . . it is also the expression of the most powerful impulses and most important vicissitudes experienced by the libido in the id." [29]

With this, Freud found himself up against some of the knottiest and most fundamental problems that depth psychology has to face. How is it that the tendency toward particular kinds of moral and religious beliefs reappear throughout the history of mankind? The problem had suggested itself in Freud's first reconstruction of the Oedipus situation around the turn of the century when he was formulating his theory of the unconscious and dream interpretation. Freud's studies then had carried the implication that the fundamental patterns of human behavior are somehow ingrained in the structure of the psyche. Freud took it to be self-evident that conscious beliefs cannot be inherited—that

[29] *Ibid.,* pp. 47-48.

is, that the experiences of the ego cannot be transmitted from generation to generation—but he considered it equally self-evident that the tendency toward certain kinds of beliefs and conceptions is somehow inherent in human nature. It seemed to Freud, then, that some part of man's "mental apparatus" is responsible for the recurrence of similar patterns of thought in the primal and modern psyche. What he needed to know was: Which part of the psyche contains the basis for this continuity, and by what means it does so? Are the recurrent patterns of thought carried by the id? Or by the ego and the superego? To judge from the nature of these mental contents—that is, their closeness to religion and morality—it would seem that they are specially connected with the superego; but the superego, as a part of the ego, cannot transmit its experiences. On the other hand, Freud pointed out, "Owing to the way in which it is formed, the ego-ideal [superego] has a great many points of contact with the phylogenetic endowment of each individual—his archaic heritage." [30] There does then seem to be a direct link between the id and the superego that would make it possible for them to work together in some way in establishing the continuity of man's "higher" beliefs and experiences.

The question of how it takes place is, however, exceedingly difficult to answer. Freud was able to suggest only some tentative, though exceedingly provocative, hypotheses. The experiences of the individual, he said, do not have a lasting effect. They "seem at first to be lost to posterity; but when they have been repeated often enough and with sufficient intensity in the successive individuals of many generations, they transform themselves, so to say, into experiences of the id, the impress of which is preserved by inheritance."

[30] *Ibid.*, p. 48.

Individual experiences, in other words, have a cumulative effect in history and gradually penetrate to those depths of the psyche far below the ego level that actually can transmit patterns of behavior whether "acquired" or not. "Thus," Freud said, "in the id, which is capable of being inherited, are stored up vestiges of the existences led by countless former egos; and when the ego forms its superego out of the id, it may perhaps only be reviving images of egos that have passed away and be securing them a resurrection." [31]

This is as far as Freud could carry his speculations concerning these all-important depths of the psyche. He realized that he was on a most precarious path, but he had gone ahead with this line of research "in spite of a fear that it will lay bare the inadequacy of the whole structure we have so arduously built up." [32] On what was this fear based? Why did Freud consider this particular subject matter to be of such great consequence that he felt it necessary to overcome his personal misgivings and muster the courage to carry on the research? We will find the reason, I think, in Freud's recognition that what was ultimately involved in his investigations of the id and the superego was a conception of the unconscious fundamentally different from the one with which he had been working, fundamentally different, that is, from the conception on which psychoanalysis had been based.

We have already seen how reluctantly Freud accepted the conclusion to which his insight had led him that there must be a "third" kind of unconscious in addition to the "preconscious" and the "unconscious repressed." At that point, which was at the very outset of his new researches, there was the implication that this "third" unconscious would also be "third" in importance. But suppose, as Freud came increas-

[31] *Ibid.*, p. 52.   [32] *Ibid.*, p. 50.

ingly to suspect, that this "third" unconscious should turn out not to be of minor significance, but should show itself to be the most important unconscious of all, the very foundation of psychic life? If that were so, it would indeed be true that "the whole structure" of psychoanalysis that Freud had "so arduously built up" on the basis of the "unconscious repressed" would fall apart. There would then be no alternative but to acknowledge, in Freud's words, "that almost all the delimitations we have been led into outlining by our study of pathology relate only to *the superficial levels of the mental apparatus—the only ones known to us*.[33] He would then have to confess that the studies based on the "unconscious repressed," which have been the main output of psychoanalysis, were only scratching the surface of the human personnality, and that the really important forces of the psyche are something of a quite different order that need to be approached from another point of view. This was the danger that Freud truly saw. It can only be then because of the integrity of his dedication to knowledge that he himself plunged into the deepening search, despite the fact that he realized that new discoveries in this field were bound to undermine the discoveries of his earlier years.

In the statements of Freud that we have cited, and in the underlying spirit of his venture into the study of the id, we can see Freud's awareness of a transformation to come in depth psychology. The work he had done in the past had been based on a conception of the unconscious as repressed, as negative, and as centered on the personal wishes of the individual. He saw, however, that in the future emphasis would have to be placed on a conception of the unconscious that was not repressed but striving and creative; not negative

[33] *Ibid.*, pp. 28-29 (my italics).

but affirmative; not ego-centered but impersonal, with historical and spiritual vistas. In his later conceptions, Freud was groping his way toward the enigmatic ground of the psyche where the "highest" and the "lowest" come together, where the darkness of the id and the brightness of the superego blend into man's fate. In this hazardous search of his later years, Freud was able to go only as far as his tools of analysis would permit. The range was limited, but even in this he served as a pioneer. His anonymous dialogue with Jung in *The Ego and the Id* cleared the way for a further delopment by Jung that appeared in 1946.[34] Like Freud, Jung continued the dialogue namelessly, carrying further Freud's line of investigation, but not acknowledging Freud's contribution to this later stage of his work.

[34] See O. Froebe-Kapteyn, *Eranos Jahrbuch* (Zurich: Rhein Verlag, 1946). Jung's lecture there is printed as a long essay under the title, "Der Geist der Psychologie." It has been translated as "The Spirit of Psychology" in *Spirit and Nature: Papers from the Eranos Yearbooks*, ed. Joseph Campbell, Bollinger Series XXX, 1 (New York: Pantheon Books, 1954), pp. 371-444.

VI

C. G. Jung at the outposts of psychology

I. THE UNCONSCIOUS AS A PART OF NATURE: JUNG'S LATER VIEW

Jung chose his lecture at the Eranos Conference of 1946 as
the occasion for presenting a fundamental reconstruction of
his conception of the psyche. His hypothesis that archetypes
are the fundamental forces in the deep unconscious had
proved to be exceedingly fertile for the interpretation of symbolism both in dreams and myths, but its application had
remained abstract. The theory needed still to be tied down to
earth and to be related more closely to the functioning of the
psychic organism. Particularly, because of the indefiniteness
in the relation between consciousness and the unconscious,
Jung realized that it was important for him to place his conception of the archetypes in the perspective of a larger and

deeper view of the human being as a whole. And he undertook to do this by tracing the emergence of the psyche in the framework of natural evolution.

In the animal kingdom, Jung pointed out, each species has its own distinctive characteristics. The beaver acts as a beaver in all the things it does; the honeybee lives its life as a honeybee, and as no other creature. To say this is to state a most obvious truism, but it is a fact that is seldom taken into account in modern psychology. The inborn nature of each species contains the potentialities of the species, the possibilities and limits of what it is equipped by nature to do. A bird, after all, will build a nest according to its kind, and if not aquatic it will not try to swim the sea; and the human species likewise has its inherent propensities, which set the outer limit of what is possible for mankind to accomplish and provide the tendencies of what human beings will attempt to do. These "patterns of behavior," as Jung refers to them, are realities ingrained in the nature of the human species, and they comprise the primary facts of human nature with which depth psychology must begin.

Although this point seems self-evident, it is important to emphasize it in the simplest, starkest terms possible because it is an essential principle that underlies Jung's point of view. The aim of Jung's theory of the archetypes is to identify and describe those patterns of behavior that are generic to the human species in the same way that nest-building is generic to birds. In discussing Jung's work, one cannot repeat too often that the archetypes signify not "innate ideas" as he has often been misinterpreted to mean, but simply propensities that are part of human nature just as building dams is part of beaver nature. These archetypal propensities are present in the human seed merely as *possibilities of action*. They are latently present in the species, and whether or in what manner they will actually be expressed in any given individual depends on the situation of time and place, and on a host of special factors.

One of the unique characteristics of the human species is the infinite variety of ways in which it can express its basic patterns of behavior. The forms of these in society and history and in the psychology of individuals seem to be unending, and yet they are all based on certain basic tendencies that are inherent in the human species. It is this that Jung has in mind when he says, "No biologist would ever dream of assuming that each individual acquires his general mode of behavior afresh each time. It is much more probable that the young weaverbird builds his characteristic nest because he is a weaverbird and not a rabbit. Similarly, it is more probable that man is born with a specifically human mode of behavior and not with that of a hippopotamus or with none at all." [1]

According to Jung's interpretation, patterns of behavior are a significant datum for psychology because they provide the background against which—and from which—psychic contents arise; but they are not psychological in themselves. They involve activities that are performed automatically at dark and undifferentiated levels of being. They are expressions not of the individual ego or of consciousness but of a primal instinctuality—as the honeybee goes to its hive—and they have nothing in them that is at all commensurate with human modes of consciousness. On this account, zoollogists who have studied the social insects readily admit the great difficulty in understanding their patterns of behavior

[1] C. G. Jung, "The Spirit of Psychology," in *Spirit and Nature: Papers from the Eranos Yearbooks, op. cit.*, p. 436.

rationally. [2] We cannot "think" in their terms because their instinctual patterns are not expressed in our kind of thought. And the gap is no easier to bridge when we study the patterns of behavior of Homo sapiens, for on the primal, most fundamental level they are as far removed from consciousness in their operation, and as strange to consciousness, as those of any species in the animal kingdom.

If we proceed now, as Jung does, to seek to relate the primal processes of man as a species to the contents and functioning of the human psyche, we must begin by noting that these behavior patterns are inherently unconscious—in fact they are deeper and darker even that the unconscious—and in themselves they do not contain even the possibility of becoming conscious. Because of their very nature, their inner principle must remain hidden from man's consciousness, and that is why Jung points to the impossibility of describing them in terms of an intellectual formulation. There is, however, one observation upon which we can proceed, and that is the fact that the patterns of human behavior possess, in addition to their instinctuality, a psychic aspect. The process by which this psychic aspect emerges is unconscious, and the psychic components themselves remain unconscious. But, in the course of many transformations expressing the primary patterns of the human species, the specifically psychic nature of man develops: and it eventually culminates in consciousness. Jung refers to the totality of these patterns and processes as *psychoid*—meaning not actually psychological but psychlike—and he makes it his starting point in seeking to describe in theoretical terms the fundamental nature of the psyche.

[2] O. W. Richards, *The Social Insects* (New York: Philosophical Library, 1953).

We should keep in mind when discussing this phase of Jung's work that he uses the term "psychoid" in a very limited and tentative way. He is not by any means positing a definite psychic category of any kind. As he employs it, the term "psychoid" is *always an adjective, never a noun*. That is because it involves nothing more than a conceptual attempt to describe that most elusive part of the lifeprocess out of which psychic processes emerge. At certain points this conception touches common ground with some neurological hypotheses; but Jung proceeds with a much more general point of view, and his work neither conflicts with nor competes with studies of ideation and imagery in terms of the nervous system. With his psychoid conception Jung was groping his way toward that most intangible area of transition where biological phenomena are no longer only biological, but where, on the other hand, they are not yet psychological. It corresponds to the condition in nature where man lives by means of his instincts as a member of the animal kingdom while something more finely developed than instinctual behavior is beginning to disclose itself.

Strictly speaking, what Jung means by "psychoid" is neither instinctual nor psychological as such, but represents the primal level out of which both emerge. It should be thought of as a hypothetical substratum of the human organism at which psychological qualities are present but still unformed; they are potential but still undifferentiated in a way that is comparable to the capacity of speech still undisclosed in the human embryo. With growth, development and differentiation take place, and it is then that the activities of the organism begin to manifest the fundamental distinction between those actions that are blindly driven by instinctuality and those, on a higher level, that are guided formatively and selectively by mental images. This differentiation marks the emergence of the psyche as a distinct entity within the human being, and it indicates also that man has reached the point where he has become capable of civilization.

Like Alfred Adler, Jung considers the psyche to be the organ of human experience most closely connected with social life. Unlike Adler, however, Jung worked with a conception of the deep unconscious, and his interpretation of the unconscious symbolism of the psyche opened a new dimension for the study of culture. Without it, despite his profound concern with "social feeling," Adler was never able to undertake a large study of history. Both Adler and Jung placed the emergence of the psyche in the context of evolution, but the special contribution of Jung's later psychoid theory is that it provides a link between the animal events of nature and the intricate forms of civilized life. His key conception involves the functioning of the archetypes as emergents from nature that provide out of man's unconscious depths the varieties of conscious activity in history.

Each species, as Jung points out, has its own distinctive patterns of behavior. It expresses these instinctively without the guidance of consciousness, but oddly enough, despite the fact that the basic patterns of behavior are unconscious, they display a markedly intelligent purposiveness. The organism seems to "know" what it is doing and what its aim is, and it proceeds toward its purpose directed by a spontaneous insight that derives from a deeply unconscious source. This seemingly purposive insight, Jung says, indicates the "meaning" of each pattern of behavior, for, on the psychoid level of nature where consciousness and the unconscious have not yet been differentiated, the goal and the instinctual acts necessary to achieve it still are one.

Fundamentally, Jung says, every pattern of instinctual behavior involves a tendency that is more or less complete in itself, for the later stages of the line of activity as it approaches fulfillment are implicit in the first steps. The hatching of the egg belongs to the same pattern of behavior as the search for the straw with which the bird builds the nest. It is as though the organism is guided by an image of the entire process all through its activities, even though this image cannot possibly be made conscious. In the case of man, through the evidence provided by dreams and other expressions of the deep unconscious, we can see that patterns of behavior are actually expressed in images, and very often are forevisioned by images that indicate in advance the essence of a long course of activity that is to follow. In the case of animals, we are, of course, not in a position to say that anything like an image is present. But *in principle*, Jung says, the "meaning" of every pattern of behavior is contained in an image latent in the organism, a *proto-image;* and every instinct carries within its structure the imprint of the entire situation, organically and environmentally, the goal and the means to fulfill it. "Always it fulfills an image," Jung writes, "and the image has fixed qualities. The instinct of the leaf-cutting ant fulfills the image of ant, tree, leaf, cutting, transport, and the little ant garden of fungi. If any one of these conditions is lacking, the instinct does not function because it cannot exist without its total pattern, its image. Such an image is an a priori type. It is inborn in the ant prior to any activity, for there can be no activity at all unless an instinct of corresponding pattern initiates and makes it possible. This schema holds true of all instincts and is found in identical forms in all individuals of the same species." [3]

---

[3] Jung, "The Spirit of Psychology, *op. cit.*, p. 411.

The same principle applies equally to man. "As a biological being he has no choice but to act in a specifically human way and fulfill his pattern of behavior." The fact that each instinct expresses a guiding image is much more clearly seen in human beings than in animals. The psychic activities of man reveal these images in dreams, in fantasies, and in myths. Even in the events of history, we see individuals acting out patterns of behavior of whose meaning they are not in the least conscious. They are merely expressing an image latent in their natures that they are impelled to carry out in their overt activities. Jung cites an interesting example of this that he encountered on his trip to Africa. It is worth quoting in detail because it draws together the main issues involved in understanding the psychoid nature of the archetypes and the unconscious way that man expresses outwardly his inner experience of them.

"While sojourning in equatorial East Africa," Jung recalls, "I found that the natives used to step out of their huts at sunrise, hold their hands before their mouths, and spit or blow into them vigorously. Then they lifted their arms and held their hands with their palms toward the sun. I asked the meaning of what they did, but nobody could give me an explanation. They had always done it like that, they said, and had learnt it from their parents. Ask the medicine man, he would know what it meant. So I asked the medicine man. He knew as little as the others, but assured me that his grandfather had known. It was just what people did at every sunrise, and at the first phase of the new moon. For these people, as I was able to prove, the moment when the sun or the new moon appeared was 'mungu', which corresponds to the Melanesian word 'mana' or 'mulungu' translated by the missionaries as 'God.' Actually the word 'athista' in Elgonyi means sun as well as God, although they deny that the sun is God. Only the moment when it rises is *mungu* or *athista*. Spittle and breath mean soul-substance. Hence they offer their soul to God but do not know what they are doing and never have known. They do it, motivated by the same pre-conscious type which the ancient Egyptians, on their monuments, ascribe to the sun-worshipping, dog-headed baboon, albeit in full knowledge that the ritual gesture was in honor of God. The behavior of the Elgonyi certainly strikes us as exceedingly primitive, but we forget that the educated Westerner behaves no differently. What the meaning of the Christmas tree might be our forefathers knew even less than ourselves, and it is only quite recently that we have bothered to find out at all." [4]

When we consider the meaning of this behavior among the Elgonyi, the fact stands out that its roots are altogether unconscious. It can be said to be conscious only in the limited sense that the individual Elgonyi are aware of the specific actions that they take, that they deliberately raise their arms and do so at certain specified times. In the same way, a European who goes through various rites and rituals around the Christmas season is also conscious of his particular actions. What he is not conscious of, however, are the images deeply rooted in his nature that give these specific actions so much meaning to him and fill him with so much emotional affect at just that time of the year. The actions themselves are in consciousness, but the roots of the actions are unconscious. More important, the driving urge, the source of energy, is at a deep level, far removed from the conscious ego. The Elgonyi goes through his ritual as naturally as the sun rises. He does not think about it. He simply does it. It is part of the

[4] *Ibid.*, p. 420.

total structure of his life situation, and so it is something that he must do in order to express his nature. For the Elgonyi, it is part of the pattern of behavior that life requires just as the leaf-cutting ant cannot do otherwise than live out the pattern inherent in the nature of its species.

At its deepest level, then, the behavior of the Elgonyi is not psychological as such; neither can it be called instinctual. It takes place so close to nature that it is as though it were still part of the natural world. Instinct and archetype are still fused together there, and the individual acting spontaneously as a member of his species is really expressing himself merely as a phenomenon of nature. This is the core of Jung's point of view. At the level of nature, the pattern of behavior of each species expresses itself as an undifferentiated unity; brute necessity and purpose combined in one. The honeybee lives out its pattern of behavior because it must, because its nature will permit it to do nothing else. Its mode of existence is contained in the seed of its species and the meaning of the life of the individual bee, worker or queen, depends on that larger pattern. It is as though an image reflecting the course and purpose latent in the life of the species as a whole was present in the embryo of the individual at its inception; and this proto-image of the lifepattern of the species, deeper even than unconsciousness, imbedded as a *psychlike* factor in the psychological structure of the organism, is what Jung refers to as *psychoid*.

In animal species, the proto-image that directs instinctual activity is altogether unconscious. It involves simply a process of nature, and it can no more be described in terms of consciousness than can the growth of the animal's body. In the case of man, this is no less true. In man, as the psychoid aspects of his patterns of behavior are differentiated, the proto-images become sharper and more clearly defined, and eventually they even become articulate and visible. They are expressed individually in dreams and myths and in fantasies of all kinds, and that signifies that the psyche is coming into existence as a distinct entity in the human being. What has happened, according to Jung's conception, to permit the psyche to emerge as a factor operating in its own right, is that the psychoid proto-images of the organism have been separated from their physiological aspect. The proto-images formerly inseparable from the instincts on the psychoid level are now split off from them and appear independently as archetypes, the formative factors of the psyche. Separated from the instincts, the proto-images become archetypes; and as they are expressed in individual lives, they appear in the multitude of symbolic forms that constitute the phenomena of the psyche. It is thus that the psyche emerges in man by means of a process in which instinct becomes separated from archetype. The physiological and psychological aspects of man appear then as distinct areas, united on the common ground of the primal psychoid substrate of the human being.

In this context we can see that the great power of the archetypes comes directly from the role that they play in the scheme of nature. The patterns of behavior of each species contain their characteristic proto-images inherent in their nature, and these supply the meaningful direction of the organism's life. It is the proto-image that eventually becomes the archetype, for it provides the underlying psychic patterns and directs the individual's activities from a level far below consciousness. Just as the proto-images function to provide the essential purpose and drive behind animal patterns of behavior, so the archetypes fulfill the equivalent function in man. They are not the instincts themselves, but they guide the instincts. They give the instincts their direction. They give them form. They outline the stages and the phases through which the instincts must pass in human life. The archetypes are very close to the instincts, and neither is able to function without the other; but they are the opposite poles of the process by which the individuality of the person is eventually achieved.

The instincts are the driving urges and they represent the biological aspect of the organism; the archetypes represent the formative aspect of the instincts, their inherent pattern of development, their meaning. When Jung says, "the image represents the *meaning* of the instinct," the elusive point that he is trying to convey is that the archetype constitutes the essence, the purpose of the instincts in man; and it is this that is expressed in archetypal images. The archetypes are the psychic devices that nature has provided for taking human instincts in the direction in which they are *intended*— in which they are *equipped*, and, indeed, in which they *need*—to go. As part of this, we find that the archetypes shape the developments in human life, relating the phenomena of the psyche to the biology of the organism, to the stages in adult development, mating, social intercourse, preparation for death. The empirical data for this are most extensive, since all human life is included. We need think only of the various images in myths and legends of the mother caring for her child, or the story of Abraham and Isaac, to realize the great variety of archetypal forms that accompany the procreative instinct, for example. At some point it should be possible to attempt a full description of human life in terms of archetypal patterns of behavior, and that would be a definitive test of the value of Jung's point of view. Jung himself, however, has so far confined himself to the suggestive description of his general conceptions and he has left the application and testing of his hypotheses to a future generation.

From what has been said, we can see at least the general outlines of the stages of development that lead from the primal psychoid unity via the proto-images to the instincts and archetypes, and then ultimately to the historical varieties of imagery that comprise the contents of the individual psyche. In this large process, the archetypes play the central role, for they provide the psychological patterns by means of which the energies derived from the instincts can be expressed in meaningful activities. In a certain sense, the archetypes go ahead of the instincts as though their function were to make a road clear, to open a passage over which the raw energies of the instincts can flow. The archetypes cut through the wilderness of life, setting a specific direction and providing the itinerary over which the instincts can travel. These paths that the archetypes cut may be described also as channelizers in the sense that they direct the flow of energy out into specific areas of social life. In another connection I have described in detail how Jung interprets historical symbols as the mechanisms by which psychic energy is drawn into socially desired areas of life.[5] The active and creative power of archetypes can be seen vividly in the political ideologies of modern times where mass beliefs reshape the life of nations, both for good and for evil.

In our present context, however, it is sufficient for us to

[5] For the theoretical background, see Part II of my earlier book, *Jung's Psychology and Its Social Meaning*. For an application of Jung's conception of the archetypes see also my concluding essay on "The Power of Archetypes in Modern Civilization," in the volume commemorating Jung's eightieth birthday, *Studien zur Analytischen Psychologie C. G. Jungs* (Zurich: Rascher, 1955), Vol. II, pp. 379 ff.

consider the more general aspects of historical symbols. Since the archetypes themselves are merely "tendencies," they act only as guiding forces setting a general pattern. They have to be concretized with a specific form and content before their inner principle can become effective in life. They accomplish this by taking up and shaping according to their own nature the various materials and psychic contents present in the human environment. The actual constituents of such symbols may be historical (i. e., legendary) figures, natural events, cultural and personal material; but the archetype places its special stamp upon them and shapes them according to its own pattern. This special imprint bearing the characteristic mark of each archetype corresponds to the role that the proto-image had played in providing the meaning behind the psychoid patterns of behavior. The archetype structures the conscious material in such a way that it expresses symbolically the purpose, the direction, and the eventual meaning of the process that is taking place. As a proto-image, the archetype is present *in principle* at the very beginning of the process, and that is why it is a fact that dreams very frequently reveal an unconscious foreknowledge of the path of development that will unfold in the future in an individual personality. It is as though an acorn had a dream in which the leaves of a new oak tree were symbolized.

2. THE SELF AS SYMBOL AND REALITY

Of all his work, Jung's conception of the "Self" has certainly been the most misunderstood. Not even his much-abused theory of the "collective unconscious" has been so confusingly misconstrued both by loyal followers and unfriendly critics. And yet, the "Self" represents one of the profoundest, potentially most integrative, insights that modern psychology has so far achieved. It provides a large framework for study leading from man's primal emergence as a psychic being in evolution to the furthest reach of art and religious experience. It may be, however, because it undertakes so much that it encounters so many difficulties.

One of the sources of the confusion that has resulted from Jung's descriptions of the "Self" is the fact that the term has several different meanings in other systems of thought. It is, unfortunately, a term that has been used by others with connotations that not only differ from Jung's but that sometimes signify the very opposite of what he had in mind. To understand Jung's special meaning, therefore, we must eliminate from our minds the overtones that are attached to the term "Self" both as it appears in German Idealism and in Hindu and Theosophical types of philosophy. It is true, of course, that these large traditions of thought have contributed significantly to the development of Jung's ideas and have influenced him to the point where he chose the "Self" as the term to represent a fundamental aspect of his work. As he finally developed his conception, however, it does not depend at all on a metaphysical or philosophical substructure. Actually it derives from empirical material to a much greater extent than the abstract, semireligious nature of his formulation might suggest.

The psychoid substrate of human nature that we have been discussing is the factual basis for Jung's theory of the Self. In the world of nature, Jung says, each species follows patterns of behavior peculiar to itself. These patterns are implicit in the "seed" of the species, and this means that they are potential in each of its individuals. As the individual matures, the patterns of behavior inherent in the species express themselves in its life activities; and they do this, Jung pointed out, by a process of differentiation. A division takes place within the primary psychoid unity of the organism. The underlying pattern of behavior separates into two segments that complement each other from that point onward. One part contains the instincts, and it functions mainly on a biological level; the other part contains the images that give form to the instincts, and it tends to become psychological. These images are what Jung called the "archetypes," for they represent the underlying patterns and tendencies of action in each species. Always the instincts and archetypes go together, for they are, in Jung's conception, like opposite sides of a single coin. The instincts supply the energy for the unfoldment of the organism, while the archetypes channelize its growth and give it meaning. In principle, however, the source of the archetypes before they are differentiated is a single encompassing image that is the quintessence of the archetypes and contains as in a seed the latent purpose of the organism's life. Each species carries such a *proto-image* implicit in its nature, and in the human organism this image is the Self.

In these terms, the Self represents the first reality of human life, for it contains the primary constituents of what comprises specifically *human* nature. At the same time, the Self represents the culminating phase that brings the process of psychological integration to completion. This is really the same fact seen from another angle, for the fulfillment of the Self as a proto-image is necessarily the end result of the process as a whole. The Self is thus both beginning and end of man's life. It is the primal psychoid potentiality from which human development comes. It is the goal that draws this development forward and it is the ultimate achievement when the goal is reached.

Between the Self as the beginning and the Self as the end result of man's development there lies the psychological process that Jung calls "Individuation," the unfoldment and integration of human individuality. It is a process that is exceedingly difficult to define, not only because it contains certain inherent obscurities as a psychological conception, but because, if we could define "Individuation" with precision, we would be at the same time defining the ultimate meaning of human life. Because of its fundamental nature, Individuation eludes precise formulation, but that fact also gives us an important clue to what is involved in it. Individuation is the lifelong process in a human being by which what is potential in him is brought to realization and is integrated into the wholeness of a mature life.

Inherently, Individuation is not a conscious process. It represents to Jung *the* fundamental pattern of behavior in the human species, and as all patterns of behavior do, it expresses itself in the individual's life autonomously, as naturally and spontaneously as breathing, for it is equally basic to human nature. Its root is psychoid, and its functioning is, therefore, on a level that is even more fundamental than the unconscious. Individuation encompasses all the varied stages and phases of development by which the human organism emerges as a personality, at first unsteady and unsure of its individuality, and eventually stabilized with a fixed center. Individuation is thus a master psychological process present in all human beings by virtue of the fact that human nature tends toward wholeness. To Jung, however, Individuation is both a natural process in the psyche and a work to be done. It is ultimately a psychological task to be undertaken and carried through as a way of life in the conscious effort to bring the personality into harmony with the depths of the Self.

We can see now that Jung has two meanings in his use of the terms "Individuation" and the "Self," and to some degree the frequent misunderstanding of his conceptions can be traced to his failure to mark off these distinctions. On the one hand, *Individuation* is a natural process by which what is latent and potential in the human organism comes to expression on a psychological level. On the other hand, Individuation is a psychological discipline that seeks to work with the inherently integrative processes of the unconscious psyche in order to achieve a realization of the Self. Correspondingly, the Self is, on the one hand, the primal factor that is the basis of all psychological development; and, on the other hand, the Self is actually the final product of Individuation as the fulfillment of what is potential in man. The Self is thus both the raw material and the guiding purpose, the source and culmination of human life and of all psychological endeavor.

In all its phases, the *Self* is expressed symbolically, for it is only by means of the symbolism of the deep unconscious that man can experience the workings of the individuation process taking place within himself. This leads to an easily misleading aspect of the *Self*, for, as Jung conceives it, it is both reality and symbol. At the beginning, as it emerges from its psychoid root, the *Self* is the underlying reality of psychic life, the formative factor in man's development. All through the process of individuation, however, it serves as a symbolic goal drawing the work forward. The basis of this is also psychoid, for the *Self* is a *proto-image*. It is, in the example we have used, as though an acorn had a dream in which the future development of the tree was symbolized. The important point is that, as a *proto-image*, the Self represents a reality that is an actual possibility for the human organism, and it herefore is intimately involved in all the stages of man's psychological development. The archetype of the Self is expressed in the form of many historical symbols that represent various phases of the individuation process in the life history of nations. A particularly frequent symbol of the Self is the "Divine Child," which often appears also as a savior-messiah. In alchemical types of symbolism the Self as the ultimate achievement of psychological work is represented as "the pearl of great worth," the "philosopher's stone," or other symbols that convey the emergence of a small precious jewel as the result of the integration of the psyche. Apart from the traditional patterns of symbolism in history, such symbols often appear in dreams or in fantasies; and Jung claims that they very often have not only a redemptive meaning, but a psychological healing effect as well.

The religious traditions of western civilization have generally conceived the psychological process by which the realization of the Self is achieved and made actual—in other words, the crystallization of the individuation process—under the general heading of "redemption." Since a great variety of psychological processes are involved in this, it turns out that, when it is fully entered into, the work of "saving the soul" is highly intricate and requires much more than a simple, overt declaration of faith. The transformation of the dross material of the personality that is alluded to in the symbolism of the alchemists involves, as Jung interprets it, a long process that calls for many difficult steps; and these are found to be described within the frameworks of varying symbolisms both in Eastern and Western thought. For most of western civilization, however, the process of spiritual redemption centers on some form of the symbol of Christ, and this is true for heretical groups as well as for the various orthodoxies. Since the figure of Jesus has become basic to the psychology of Christendom, its symbolic representation has varied in a thousand different ways to express the many aspects of the basic messianic experience, the salvation of the personality.

When Jung refers to Christ as a "symbol of the Self," he means to indicate this fact: that for the western psyche some variation of the image of Jesus Christ is inevitably the center around which the symbolism of individuation is expressed. His meaning is not that Christ is to be understood as "only psychological"; nor does he imply that Jesus is any the less real as Christ. Jung's meaning rather is that the validity of the Christ symbol grows out of the primary reality of the Self and that, from a psychological point of view, the authenticity of the Christ symbol derives from the fact that it expresses the Self in a symbolic form. What the western man experiences as real when he participates in the symbol of Christ is only proximately Christ and ultimatley is the Self, which is a universal reality for man transcending the historical variations of the forms in which it appears. In Oriental and other non-Christian traditions, symbols other than Christ are experienced as representing the Self, and to Jung these are no less real than Christ. By Jung's criteria, it is the Self that is the reality since that is the ultimate psychoid fact encompassing and underlying all others.

For those persons who feel it necessary to hold specific symbols up to the test of "truth," Jung points out that a symbol is valid to the extent that it represents the fullness and depth of the Self. But now, as the traditional symbols lose their power in modern western civilization, it is difficult indeed to find a symbol that still succeeds in expressing the profundity and magnitude of the Self. Even the power of the Christ symbol is found to be waning, its meaning becoming obscure, and the devotion to it ambivalent. As the traditional symbols become ever less adequate, and therefore less valid and less "true," we are thrown back on the Self itself as the foundational fact of our being. We are no longer able to come to the experience of the Self via a symbol, but we are forced to open ourselves to it directly. Now the very fact of the conception of the Self as it is emerging in modern times becomes a symbol for us; that is, it becomes a channel of experience by which man can encounter his larger nature, and it is in this sense that Jung raises the possibility that the conception of the Self may turn out to be itself the symbol for the "new age" that western civilization is so earnestly awaiting.

Since the Self is not a personalized figure like Jesus or Buddha, it cannot be expected to serve as the type of symbol that inspires faith in the historical religions. Its value as a symbol for the new age lies mainly in the psychological perspective that it can give, and in the possibility that it can open an experience of the personality that will reach beyond the restrictedness both of special religious dogmas and the relativism of the rationalistic psychologies. Conceived as a symbol, the Self is an image of man himself, which is essentially what the various symbols of the personal saviors also are; but the Self as symbol represents man's nature in an abstract impersonal form. In his theoretical work, Jung conceives a symbol to be an image that represents an aspect of reality that no concept can encompass but that can be penetrated and comprehended only indirectly in a nonintellectual form. In this sense, then, the Self is a symbol that represents the nature of man at the point where man is more than a merely psychological being, at the point where man touches the cosmos, or begins to perceive, at least, that such a transpersonal contact is possible. There are many archetypal symbols that reflect this cosmic sense of the human being, but the Self is the quintessence, the archetype, of all of these. To speak of the Self as the symbol of the new age, therefore, has a generic meaning, for it signifies that the Self is an archetype transcending and encompassing all other symbols of a historical nature by which man in modern times can come to an experience of the cosmos.

From the early work of Sigmund Freud to the later writings of C. G. Jung we have observed a progressive enlargement in the conception of the unconscious depths of the psyche. The beginning was with Freud's "Unconscious Repressed," which opened a new field of study. Soon Jung added an historical dimension by charting the indefinite realm of the "Collective Unconscious" and setting the stage for a closer definition of the "archetypes." Stimulated by this, Freud then undertook to extend his original point of view by studying the primal darkness of the "id" and the "higher" beliefs that the "superego" draws from the psychic depths. The progress that he could make in this direction was severely limited since the irrationality of the "id" draws a curtain that keeps it beyond analytical interpretation; but Freud's efforts to search out the sources of the unconscious did indicate the kind of depths that needed to be reached. In his later years, Jung took up Freud's study of the "id" in a larger perspective by making a new attempt to trace the emergence of the Deep Unconscious out of the world of nature. Like Freud, Jung was able to find only the barest quantities of specific data to use as his basis in describing man's dim prepsychological origins; but he made it possible to experience human nature in a new light nonetheless.

Studying the patterns of behavior in animal species, Jung pointed out that a psychoid *proto-image*, darkly unconscious and yet purposeful, guides the development of every organism; and in the human species, this *proto-image* is the Self. The Self represents the basic realities of human nature, the potentialities and the limits of man's life; and since it is an image that eventually takes a psychological form, the Self is experienced as a symbol of the meaning and the goal of man's existence. In a variety of archetypal forms that cover the virtually unlimited symbolism of redemption, the Self draws man forward by relating his activities to larger contexts of life beyond his immediate knowledge. It leads man beyond himself, and it does this necessarily because the fundamental psychoid nature of the human species requires an attempt at spiritual transcendence. In order to fulfill his nature, man must reach beyond his own life to an experience of something in which he is encompassed but which we can never define. He may seek it in the heavens and find it there, but if he finds it, it is because a mystery of life has revealed itself to him out of the depths of the Self.

"The Self that encompasses me," Jung writes, "also encompasses many others. . . . It does not belong to me nor is it characteristically mine, but it is universal. Paradoxically, it is the quintessence of the individual, and at the same time a continuum for all [collectivum]." [6] Jung's personal ex-

*C. G. Jung, *Paracelsica* (Zurich: Rascher, 1942), p. 167 (my translation).

perience of the Self is, in other words, as a symbol that represents *the* reality of life. To Jung it is self-evident that man can come into contact with ultimate cosmic (that is, metaphysical) facts only by means of his psyche since he possesses no other apparatus for spiritual perception; but that makes the experience itself no less valid, and its contents no less real.

His effort to demonstrate the basis in actuality for man's transcendent experiences was one of the main reasons for which Jung developed his conception of the Self as a psychological category. Abstract though its formulation may be, and difficult though it is to verify in the experience of the average person, the Self has a major significance as Jung's effort to clarify an aspect of man's life that eludes the analytical techniques of psychology. As a psychological term, the Self represents the infinite depth and magnitude of human personality; and at its furthest reaches it touches the deepest ground of Being where man experiences the "boundlessness of the soul" as an evident fact. The Self is thus a psychological term that is more than psychological by its very nature, for its function is to direct the modern mind by means of consciousness to levels of experience that transcend the ordinary range of intellectual understanding.

It may seem odd, but it is precisely because Jung's conception of the Self reaches beyond psychology that it has so rich a contribution to make to modern studies in depth psychology. We will be able to see the reason for this more fully, however, when we have examined the hypotheses presented by Otto Rank in the writings of the last decade of his life.

VII

Otto Rank's two steps beyond psychology

I. A DISCIPLE'S DILEMMA

Describing the growth of the intimate group in Vienna in his *History of the Psycho-Analytical Movement*, Freud tells how Otto Rank first joined with them. "One day," he writes, "a young graduate of the technical school was admitted to our circle through a manuscript which showed very unusual understanding. We induced him to go through college and the university, and then devote himself to the non-medical application of psychoanalysis. Thus the little society acquired in him a zealous and reliable secretary, and I gained in Otto Rank a most faithful helper and collaborator." [1]

The manuscript of which Freud speaks was Rank's first

[1] Sigmund Freud, *History of the Psycho-analytical Movement*, Modern Library edition, p. 946.

work, *Der Künstler* (*The Artist*), which he wrote while a reluctant student of engineering. He had read three of Freud's early works, the book on dream interpretation, the three essays on sex, and the study of wit and the unconscious, and with those as his foundation, he had made a precocious attempt to interpret the psychology of the artist.[2] The creative personality was the subject on which Rank's attention centered from his first work to the last. Years later, in his *Art and Artist*, he enlarged some of the themes of his early book into a conception of creative experience as a whole, from the heroes of mythology to the modern age; and the question recurred in still another form in *Beyond Psychology*, the book he was writing when he died, and in which, as the unfinished, posthumously printed version reveals, the problem he had faced in his youth was still unsolved.

Rank's consistent interest in the artist, and particularly the spirit of sympathy with which he approached the difficulties of the artist's life, refusing to follow Freud in diagnosing the artist as neurotic, indicates a strong urge to creative activity in his own personality. There can be no doubt about the fact that Rank saw himself reflected in the kind of individual he called the "artist type"; and yet he did not participate in artistic work directly: he contented himself with writing books *about* the artist's life. Side by side with his impulse to creative art, he had a powerful intellect that was especially gifted analytically and trained in the scholarship of the *Geisteswissenschaften* (the humanities) in the Viennese manner; and the two contended within him throughout his life. The signs of the conflict are particularly evident in his

---

[2] Otto Rank, *Art and Artist*, trans. C. F. Atkinson (New York: Knopf, 1932), p. xx.

last writings, for these by their unevenness suggest that Rank's inner tension was deepening to a crisis just before he died. *Beyond Psychology* is a book that might well have been written by two separate personalities, so sharp is the change of tone and subject matter from chapter to chapter. At one extreme, it presents the severe intellectual analysis of symbolism by means of which Rank probed the depths of history; and at the other extreme it reveals the spirit of an artist straining to convey at least the outlines of his personal religious experience. These two sides of Rank's life were not integrated in that book, perhaps because he died too soon, and perhaps because the schism that they expressed had reached too deep within the man and was already too wide to be bridged. It was, however, because of the intensity of his problem that Rank was given a glimpse into the irrational hinterlands of the psyche, and it was from this that he made his major contribution to modern thought.

When Rank came to Freud in 1905 hardly twenty-one years old, the ready acceptance that was given him made it seem that psychoanalysis would provide a wonderful channel for both his artistic and his intellectual talents. In those early pioneering days, the psychoanalytical movement was greatly in need of creative personalities who would be able to match the pace of Freud's discoveries, and carry their own share of the work. Freud was particularly sensitive to such things and he was quick to recognize creative capacities in others. He encouraged Rank to work for his doctorate degree, even helping him to do so, and he brought him to the center of the movement by making him secretary of the group. Even at that early date, Freud realized that the field of history and culture would be the final testing ground for his new depth psychology.[3] Rank's cultural knowledge thus made him a particularly welcome addition to the circle that was then composed predominantly of medical men.

Although he was the youngest among them, it was not long before Rank was recognized as the most brilliant of the Viennese disciples. Ernest Jones, for example, recalls the awe he felt before Rank's encyclopedic knowledge, and the pride he felt when Rank approved of something he had written. Freud took a benevolent and even paternal attitude toward Rank's welfare and the knowledge of Freud's interest in him gave him considerable prestige throughout the psychoanalytic movement. After 1912 when Jung published his *Psychology of the Unconscious*, Rank's role became increasingly important. Jung's critique had made extensive use of ethnological materials, and by doing so had called attention to the limits of Freud's knowledge in philosophical and cultural fields. Of all those who remained in the psychoanalytical group after Adler and Jung had left, Rank was the only one who could match Jung's competence in the interpretation of cultural symbols, and his stature as well as his value therefore rose in Freud's eyes. He had already distinguished himself with his book on the birth of the hero in 1909, and he had demonstrated himself to be the one among them with the greatest historical breadth and the most disciplined understanding of cultural issues. Oddly enough, it was these very qualities in Rank that led him eventually to his most fundamental criticisms of the Freudian position. Because of the large historical perspective that he developed in the course of his psychoanalytical work, Rank realized that psychology is a transi-

---

[3] See Freud's letter to Jung cited in Ernest Jones, *The Life and Work of Sigmund Freud* (New York: Basic Books, 1955), Vol. II, pp. 448-449.

tional phenomenon in modern history; and when he had comprehended the implications of this insight, he began to look "beyond psychology," as we shall see.

Under Freud's guidance and support, Rank devoted himself to many phases of psychoanalytical work. He carried out theoretical research, wrote monographs, edited a psychoanalytical journal, did organizational work, and practiced lay analysis. For the better part of two decades he made important contributions to the field, and consistently received Freud's praise and appreciation. As the doctrines of psychoanalysis developed, however, and as they began to harden into a fixed system, less of the creativity of the early days was required. Psychoanalysis was settling down to the professional repetition of prescribed analytical techniques. Increasingly Rank found that it was his intellectual rather than his artistic energies that were being called into play, and a major part of his personality was thus left unfulfilled. If we can judge from unguarded remarks in his writings and from the events that took place at the time, Rank felt strong psychological pressures then impelling him to seek a new and more adequate channel for his creative capacities. Nonetheless, his strong personal attachment to Freud—an attachment verging on dependence—and his sense of gratitude for favors received in the past prevented his breaking his connection in a deliberate or abrupt way. When he published his book on *The Trauma of Birth* in 1924, he dedicated it to Freud and he offered it as a further development of some of Freud's hypotheses. His presentation was altogether within the spirit of his master's work, and Rank intended it, at least consciously, as an original contribution to psychoanalysis comparable to those of his other writings that Freud had praised in the past. There were certainly considerable grounds for

Rank to expect that his new work would be received in a friendly way, and it seems that Freud began by doing so, although it may have been with reservations.

Even several years later in 1932 when he wrote his *New Introductory Lectures*, Freud spoke favorably of Rank's book. "Otto Rank," Freud said, "to whom psycho-analysis owes many valuable contributions, has also the merit of having strongly emphasized the importance of the act of birth and of separation from the mother." [4] Freud then added that neither he nor the others in the group could agree with the inferences that Rank drew from his observations regarding the trauma of birth, but it seems definitely to have been the "others" rather than Freud himself who led the attack on Rank. Freud would certainly have preferred to avoid still another defection among his followers, especially one by so close and devoted a disciple as Rank; and Rank himself seems to have been most reluctant to break his relationship with Freud. The criticisms of the Vienna circle were, however, sharp and bitter, and Rank thought to escape the brunt of them by leaving Vienna for Paris for a short period until calm would be restored. But there was no return. Once in Paris, a new phase of life began for him. When he had written *The Trauma of Birth* in 1923, Rank's conscious intention was simply to add a new conception to psychoanalytical theory; but in perspective we can see that the net effect of the book, and perhaps its *unconscious* intention, was to precipitate his separation from Freud, thus freeing the artistic side of his personality for creative self-expression.

In his later study, *Art and Artist*, written in 1930, Rank made the acute observation that one of the aftermaths of

[4] Sigmund Freud, *New Introductory Lectures on Psycho-Analysis* (New York: Norton, 1933), p. 122.

a creative act is an attack of guilt feelings, remorse, and anxiety. It is the toll that is exacted, in one form or another, for the one-sided concentration of energies in creative work. In making this point, Rank may well have been describing his own experience, for we know that when *The Trauma of Birth* drew strong attacks from the Freudian circle Rank was on the verge of retracting his views. The thought of being cut off from Freud became exceedingly painful for him, for he feared the isolation and ostracism it might bring. His book had, however, brought a challenge to his artistic nature, and the challenge could not be ignored. Without wishing to, Rank had created a situation that forced him away from Freud. He had left himself with no alternative but to withdraw from the psychoanalytical movement and to begin to articulate the independent point of view that would express his individual creative nature.

The feelings of guilt and remorse that Rank experienced are not difficult to understand. Publishing *The Trauma of Birth* was a fundamental creative act for him, and its first result was to upset his accustomed position as the loyal disciple of a revered master. After twenty years of devotion, Rank wished to express his individuality; and he wished also to retain his friendship with Freud, not only for professional reasons, but because his feelings for Freud were personally strong and affectionate. Freud had acted as a father to him in many ways, had established and protected him in the field of psychoanalysis, had given him a career and sustained him in it. Rank had much for which to be grateful, and his attachment to Freud was deep indeed. But how could he develop the artist in himself and fulfill his own need for creativity while remaining a loyal disciple? Here we have the underlying dilemma that haunted the last years of Rank's life. His devotion to Freud as a human being conflicted with the necessary unfoldment of his own individuality, and his act of self-liberation in writing *The Trauma of Birth* was followed by a sense of remorse that took many forms over the years and from which Rank never fully recovered.

Rank's later writings, particularly his last one, *Beyond Psychology*, reveal a profound betterness of spirit, as though his controversy with the Freudian circle and their attacks upon him had permanently tarnished something deep within him. We see this in the gnawing negativity of his comments on Freud, and in his disturbed remarks on Judaism, for Rank was a victim of a kind of self-hatred, aggravated by Nazism, that he could never transcend. It seems that when the split came and his affirmative relationship with Freud was irrevocably turned into his opposite, the entire complex of factors encompassing Freud as a person and psychoanalysis as a doctrine became a psychological wound for Rank that would not heal. It was relatively simple for him to move away from Vienna and live at a distance from Freud, first in Paris and then in New York. But it was much easier to separate himself from Freud geographically than psychologically. The man and his teaching remained at the center of a continuous struggle in which Rank was forced to engage within himself. He needed somehow to come to terms with Freud and with all that Freud represented in his mind as the embodiment of his lifework up to 1924. Freud who had been his protector was now his psychic adversary.

As we follow the development of Rank's thought after he left the psychoanalytical movement, we perceive that it was only as his relationship to Freud deepened in its negativity that it began to have affirmative results. Between 1925 and 1929, Rank produced two works of three volumes each that are significant mainly because they embody the transition between his Freudian point of view and the valuable contributions of his later years. The first of these was his *Techniques of Psychoanalysis*, the second and third volumes of which have been translated under the title, *Will Therapy*. The other was his *Outlines of a Genetic Psychology on the Basis of the Psychoanalysis of the Ego-Structure*, the third part of which was translated as *Truth and Reality*. Both of these works began with a psychoanalytical frame of reference and gradually developed a theory of consciousness and the will that deliberately and specifically states the opposite of Freud. Rank gained some adherents on the basis of these works, but he himself could not be satisfied with a system of thought that he recognized to be fundamentally negative in its inspiration. He had to come to terms with Freud in a more searching and comprehensive way, and he thus undertook a large interpretation of history whose essential goal was to give him a perspective for understanding the significance of psychoanalysis, or more specifically, the life and work of Sigmund Freud. As a result of this theory of history, which is best expressed in his *Psychology and the Soul* and in his *Art and Artist*, Rank was able to see the inherent limitations of the analytical point of view of psychology as a whole; and in looking "beyond psychology" then, he reached a profound insight into the role and meaning of artistic and religious experience. At that point, Rank's negativity had gone full circle, culminating in an affirmative and original contribution to modern thought. He thus illustrated with his own life a distinction he had made between the "neurotic type" and the "creative type"; for while the "neurotic type" is caught in negativity and is unable to escape from it, the "creative type," whatever his other weaknesses and shortcomings, is stimulated by his negative experiences to struggle and break through them and emerge ultimately with a productive work, such as Rank himself accomplished.

2. THE WILL AS AN INTEGRATING PRINCIPLE: POINTS OF MEETING WITH ADLER AND JUNG

Like Adler and Jung before him, Rank directed his most basic attack against Freud's materialistic conception of the personality. In a sense, every fundamental critique of psychoanalysis must begin with this, since Freud's most obvious weakness lies in the determinism that underlies his work. His medical preconceptions made it almost impossible for him to deal with the purposiveness and creativity inherent in human nature, and in his later years Freud himself seems to have recognized his lack. He tried then to broaden his point of view, but there was very little he could do by that time since the difficulty was imbedded in the very tissue of his thinking. Rank realized how fundamental the problem was for Freud, and he therefore concentrated first on revealing the unconscious assumptions upon which Freud had built his system. At the beginning, Rank was effective in this mainly in a negative way. His criticisms of Freud hit the mark, but his first efforts to provide an affirmative substitute proved to be nothing more than a one-sided negation of psychoanalysis. They were transparent, and through them one could easily see that Rank had not yet recovered from his oppressive resentment of Freud. At that time—as we see in his *Will Therapy* and in his *Truth and Reality*—Rank was still in the throes of the painful period through which, apparently, he had to pass in order to free himself both from his personal attachment to Freud and from the Freudian habits ingrained in his thinking. Only when he had freed himself would he be capable of developing his ideas in an independent and individual way.

In his negativity, Rank began with an extreme and indiscriminate attack in which he brought the charge of determinism not only against Freud's medical conceptions, but against all theories of the unconscious in general. The conception of an unconscious substrate in man, Rank said, is inherently deterministic because it severely limits the conscious capacities of the will. Rank later refined this criticism and made it more balanced as he took note of the different kinds of conceptions of the unconscious with which depth pscyhology works. At this early point, however, he was interested mainly in stressing the degree of freedom that the individual possesses in contrast to the biological determinism implied in Freud's theory of instincts. In this regard, Rank took the view that Freud's original theory of the "unconscious wish" was superior to the later conception of the "id," for, Rank said, the wish is an aspect of the will and when he spoke of it Freud thus implied at least the capacity of the individual to choose. "Freud's original wish fulfillment theory," Rank wrote, "lay much nearer to this recognition (of the will) than his later doctrine of instincts, which actually only represented a biologizing of the unconscious wishes. We easily recognize in the Freudian wish the old will of the academic psychologists, although in the romantic guise of natural philosophy. . . . But the conscious wish fulfillment tendency of the ego, for the designation of which the suitable word 'will' exists, extends much further than he was willing to admit, while the instinctual impulse tendency in men is less extensive than he originally thought." [5]

At this point in his development, Rank's emphasis was altogether on consciousness. In his later writings he recognized once again the importance of Freud's theory of the "id," and especially the profound significance of Jung's interpretation of the historical levels of the unconscious; but at this intermediary period in Rank's life when his antagonism against Freud still dominated his psychological work, his negative feelings toward Freud were directed against the theory of the unconscious in general. "The 'psychology of the unconscious,'" Rank wrote polemically around that time, "unveils itself to us as one of the numerous attempts of mankind to deny the will in order to evade the conscious responsibility following of necessity therefrom." [6] In deliberate and exaggerated contrast to the theory of the unconscious upon which, as a psychoanalyst, Rank had previously based all his studies and his practice, he now wanted to consider the "conscious will as the central point of psychology, if not of world history." [7] He spoke now, rather enthusiastically, of "a constructive will psychology, in the center of which we again place the conscious ego, with its old rights and newly won prerogatives." "As soon," he promised, "as we restore to the will its psychological rights, the whole of psychology becomes of necessity a psychology of consciousness." [8]

With this point of view, Rank became the spokesman for many who had wished for a kind of psychoanalysis that would be simpler and easier to use than Freud's laborious

---

[5] Otto Rank, *Truth and Reality*, published as the second part of the volume, *Will Therapy and Truth and Reality*, trans. Jessie Taft (New York: Knopf, 1950), pp. 213-214.
[6] *Ibid.*, p. 234. [7] *Ibid.*, p. 232. [8] *Ibid.*, p. 233.

method. He found a particularly appreciative audience in fields like social work where time limitations make a brief form of therapy necessary, and Rank's emphasis on the use of the conscious will as a therapeutic agent gained considerable attention. It seems, however, that Rank himself was not nearly as enthusiastic about his new point of view as were some of his followers. He soon realized that if he would continue with his program of replacing the depth psychology of the unconscious with a psychological theory of the conscious will, he would merely be returning to the superficiality of pre-Freudian days. He could defend his therapy of consciousness only on the grounds of its pragmatic value, and in this regard Rank distinguished between the practical necessities of therapeutic work and the stricter criteria of psychological theory.

In the emergencies of life, Rank pointed out, therapy must be carried out under circumstances that place severe limitations on the degree of success that can be sought. In therapeutic work one must be satisfied with whatever can be accomplished; but in theoretical work truth is the aim, and there the standards of judgment must be much more exacting. Therapy and theory have to be kept separate, Rank said, and the work that is done in these areas must be judged by different standards. On the basis of this distinction, Rank held that the approach to therapy he had derived from his psychology of consciousness could be highly useful even though the theoretical principles upon which it was based were admittedly inadequate, and might even show themselves to be shallow if they were extended to a general interpretation of the human being. While he retained his "will therapy," Rank therefore pursued his theoretical work on an entirely different level. It is significant that as he continued his theoretical studies he changed his orientation and turned once again toward the depths of the psyche. In his later major writings, *Psychology and the Soul*, *Art and Artist*, and *Beyond Psychology*, Rank reached far beyond the psychology of consciousness with which he had briefly identified himself. His mature work is authentically a *depth* psychology that studies the unconscious in its historical dimensions, complementing and verifying from its special point of view the corresponding work of C. G. Jung.

Rank's insight into the nature of the will is the key to all his work, both therapeutic and theoretical. It is, therefore, in the deepening of his conception of the will that we see the foundation of his contribution to depth psychology.

In the early Freudian view under which Rank was trained, consciousness and the will were considered to be in a very close relation to each other. In general, the will was thought to represent the sum of energy available to consciousness; and since, as we have seen, Freud originally thought of the ego as being completely in consciousness, the will was considered to be the energy that the ego uses in its conscious activities. Placing himself in a position directly counter to Freud's, Rank undertook to reverse the formulation by interpreting consciousness as a derivative of the will. "Consciousness originally," he wrote, "is itself probably a will phenomenon; that is, consciousness was an instrument for the fulfillment of will before it advanced to the will controlling power of self-consciousness and finally of analytic hyperconsciousness, which on its side again interprets will and will phenomena continuously in order to make it useful for its momentary interest." [9]

From this statement, we can follow the genesis of Rank's

Ibid., p. 217.

theory of the will. The will, he said, is the instinctual force by which the human being emerges as an individual. At an early stage of development, the organism experiences certain desires and impulses that it seeks to satisfy on an animal level. At the point, however, where the organism realizes that these particular desires are its very own, a sense of individuality arises and the beginnings of consciousness appear. The organism then *wills* to seek the satisfaction of its needs, and in that act of will becomes for the first time psychologically an individual. "The realm of willing," therefore, Rank says, is "the actual ground of psychology." [10] The will and consciousness act to raise each other, for "Instinct lifted into the ego sphere by consciousness is the power of will." [11]

Underlying this interpretation, we can see the signs of Rank's early relationship to Alfred Adler. At the beginning of life, the will is only latent in the organism; it has to be aroused before it can express and develop itself. Just as Adler noted that the organism is impelled to assert itself by a "feeling of inferiority," Rank also pointed out that it is negative situations, situations of need and of opposition, that draw forth the will and stimulate its expression. Adler had spoken of a latent "will to power," which meant, essentially, an urge on the part of the individual to express himself in relation to his environment. It resulted in a process of "compensation" for "inferiorities" which, in Adler's simple but expressive phrase, worked to turn a "minus" situation into a "plus." Corresponding to this, Rank pointed out that it is only under the pressure of a man's conflicts with nature and with his fellow men that the will is stimulated to a high degree of development. That was why he believed that the situation in which a "tension of wills" was deliberately

[10] *Ibid.*, pp. 215-216.   [11] *Ibid.*, p. 232.

generated would have a dynamic and creative effect in psychotherapy.

Opposition draws forth the will and reveals it to be the quintessence of individuality. As the person acts he expresses his will, and it is then that he becomes aware of himself as an individual. Consciousness is stimulated and called forth by activities of the will. Gradually as it continues to assert itself, moving toward larger goals with increasing opposition and increasing tension, the will requires and generates ever greater capacities of consciousness. Impelled by the will, consciousness is thus raised to ever higher levels of development, and eventually the point is reached where consciousness can no longer be controlled and used as merely an instrument of the will, but becomes itself a master that uses the will for its own ends. The situation, in other words, moves into its opposite in Rank's analysis as it had in Adler's. The natural expression of the will requires consciousness to aid it, but as consciousness grows it itself shapes the will and determines it. The center of the personality then shifts from the primary base where the will is close to the instincts, and a condition that Rank calls "analytic hyperconsciousness" develops, in which the individual is drawn a precarious distance away from the natural capacities of his will.

It was this point that led Rank to see the weaknesses in the view of the psychoanalytic idea "that the bringing into consciousness of the unconscious must be the therapeutic agent." [12] The basis of this theory, Rank pointed out, is the belief that the personality will somehow be in a more secure position when consciousness is dominant. There is, he said,

[12] Otto Rank, *Beyond Psychology* (Camden, N.J.: Haddon Craftsmen, 1941), p. 277.

a "fear of the unconscious, that is, of the life force itself, from which we all seem to recoil." The modern person seeks refuge in consciousness, or, more precisely, in the conscious interpretation of the unconscious portions of his psyche; and analytical kinds of psychology cater to this desire. "What operates therapeutically," then—and here Rank introduces a most profound insight—"is the promise and hope of some kind of intellectual control over the irrational forces." Eventually the effort ends in failure because consciousness is only a derivative and a relatively weak factor in the psyche when compared with the irrational power of the will. In the long run, the apparent therapeutic effects of those methods that proceed in terms of "analytic hyper-consciousness" reveal themselves to be little more than rationalizing consolations. They seem to "work" only because they avoid the shaking contact with the depths of the psyche that is the source of their original fear, and would also be the source of a creative healing if the contact were permitted. In the nature of things, such analytic therapy can only be temporary, and at best, superficial. Its methods, Rank says, are "certainly not scientific, and least of all, constructive," because they make of consciousness a barrier to the free expression of the life-will of the individual." [13]

These statements, which have been quoted from *Beyond Psychology*, indicate a conception of the will that is altogether different from the view Rank had expressed in his *Will Therapy* and in his *Truth and Reality*. In the mature development of his thought after his early, unripe negation of Freud's work, Rank's point of view was the very opposite of a "psychology of consciousness." He would no longer say, "Psychology can of necessity be nothing other than a psy-

[13] *Ibid.*, pp. 277-278.

chology of consciousness; yes, even more, a psychology of consciousness in its various aspects and phases of development.[14] Quite the contrary, his main concern now was to show that the "over-estimation of the rational mind" gives certain kinds of psychology an illusion of success whereas they are actually retarding the full development of the personality.

As we look closely at Rank's later conception of the will, we realize that a full transformation had taken place in his thought. He had made a complete circle, returning to the depth psychology with which he had begun under Freud; but in the course of his journey, a new and all-important dimension had been added. He now conceived the depths of the psyche not medically and reductively, but creatively in terms of its emergent purposes. Rank still preferred not to use the term "unconscious," and he did so only inadvertently as in one of the passages quoted above where he spoke of the unconscious in terms that made it the equivalent of the irrational psychic depths expressed via the life will. Such references reveal the underlying tenor of Rank's thought. He had gone beyond both of his earlier theories that related the will to consciousness, the Freudian view of the will as an agent of consciousness, and his own view of the will as the power behind the "wish" and of consciousness. He conceived the will now as fundamentally unconscious, as deeply and darkly beyond rationality, and this was the conception with which he built his approach through depth psychology to history and to art.

Rank's criticism of the theory of the unconscious echoed Alfred Adler's view that dividing the psyche into conscious and unconscious segments is both arbitrary and artificial.

[14] Rank, *Truth and Reality, op. cit.,* p. 217.

The human being, after all, lives as a whole. Freud freely conceded this point, but he held that the overlapping of consciousness and the unconscious is inherent in the mobility of psychic contents and that the conception of an "unconscious" area in the psyche is an essential tool for psychologic analysis. Jung tended to agree with Freud in this regard, particularly during his earlier years when he developed his theory of the "collective unconscious." As his work progressed, however, Jung was increasingly convinced of the need for a unifying concept that would make it possible to study the unconscious in a depth perspective encompassing the psyche as a whole. His theory of the Self of which we have spoken was formulated in terms of this need, and Rank worked in the same direction. We find therefore that Rank's later, deepened conception of the will is comparable *in spirit and intention* to Jung's theory of the Self.

In this larger sense, Rank defined the will as "an autonomous organizing force in the individual which . . . constitutes the creative expression of the total personality and distinguishes one individual from another. This individual will, as the united and balancing force between impulses and inhibition, is the decisive psychological factor in human behavior." [15] Here we see the essence of Rank's advanced conception of the will as it corresponds to Jung's Self. The life will is the inner principle of the personality, the integrating principle. As such, it expresses all the unconscious potentialities of the person, his latent creativity and the irrational urges in the depths of his being. They differ mainly in their "style" of expression, but not in their essential content. In Jung's view, the Self unfolds by a "natural process," by the kind of silent workings with which a tree comes to bloom,

[15] Rank, *Beyond Psychology, op. cit.*, p. 50.

but Rank thinks of the will as a specific force. It is to him the essence of individuality, and also the power of individuality, for it is the organ of tension between human beings as individuals assert themselves counter to one another in the conflicts of life. The will is thus the inner principle of the psyche just as the Self is, but it is that principle expressed as energy. There is an inherent kinship between the Self of Jung and the life will of Rank for, with their slightly different points of emphasis, both were efforts to develop the basis for an integral and dynamic depth conception of man. They belong together, and should be understood as complementing each other. The Self as conceived by Jung is the psychological potentiality that emerges in each individual personality; and the life will as conceived by Rank is the vital force with which that potentiality is expressed and fulfilled in the world.

Other differences between the two conceptions are mainly questions of degree, or of implications that their authors did not make explicit. To Jung, for example, the Self has a cosmic aspect that was not as clearly articulated in Rank's theory of the will. But this very point, the possibility of transcendent experiences, was in the background of Rank's later years and was a major hope to which he aspired as he worked his way "beyond psychology." Another aspect of the Self that was not directly represented in Rank's writings was the theory of archetypes. But he balanced Jung's work here with a brilliantly perceptive interpretation of history constructed in terms of his deepened conception of the will. In this area, as we will see shortly, Rank's incisive approach to history tended both to support Jung's hypothesis of a "collective unconscious" and to cut through the indefiniteness of the archetype theory in a most provocative way. While Jung described the historical levels of the psyche, Rank took the additional step of setting the concepts of modern psychology in a historical perspective, and by doing this he opened the way for a fundamental transvaluation of the psychological point of view.

3. HISTORY AND THE QUEST OF IMMORTALITY

Only when he had reached his enlarged conception of the will was Rank in a position to undertake his mature life work. When he had returned from his too quickly conceived detour into a "psychology of consciousness," and was able to understand the will as the depth principle of the personality, an integrating "tendency inherent in the individual," [16] he had the key he had been seeking for the study of the human being. The first well-developed application of this insight was in his *Psychology and the Soul*, which he wrote in 1929 and 1930. All Rank's earlier works are tentative, probing steps leading to this. From the point of view of his permanent contribution to depth psychology and to the history of thought in general, *Psychology and the Soul* is unquestionably Rank's most important work. It contains the quintessence of a "system" that interprets both the individual and his culture within a single historical framework.

That Rank himself considered this book to be his foundation stone is amply revealed by the tone of his references to it in *Art and Artist, Modern Education*, and *Beyond Psychology*. It seems, in fact, that one of the most bitter disappointments of his last years was the wave of silence that covered

[16] Otto Rank, *Modern Education*, trans. M. E. Moxon (New York: Knopf, 1932), p. 206.

Psychology and the Soul. Like a pebble tossed into the ocean, it seemed to sink and disappear from view. It took twenty years to get it translated into English, for it did not appear until 1950, more than ten years after Rank's death. Writing in *Beyond Psychology*, in 1939, he could not hide his unhappy realization that his most basic book had missed its mark. Up until now, in fact, it has received the same silent reception in English as in German, very probably because of the terse obscurity of its style and the involved, cumbersome development of its argument. Its theme, however, is profound. In it, Rank presented the outlines of his conception of man's mental life and the foundation of his approach to all the forms of will expression in the individual personality and in civilization.

On the surface, the outline of the theory that Rank set forth is a schematic conception in which he divides history into four "eras." These are: Emamism, which is the primal era of the will; Animism, the "era of the soul"; the "sexual era"; and the "psychological era." As he describes them, assigning definite qualities and attitudes to each, Rank gives the impression that he is trying to mark history off into four separate stages of development; but that is not his aim at all. He was much too sophisticated a thinker to attempt a rigid theory of history, and what he actually did develop was a subtle, psychological reconstruction of the long-range inner trends of history. The method of presentation that Rank followed in that book was, however, most unfortunate, and it was bound to mislead his readers. Working with a massive accumulation of cultural data, he condensed his material into an outline form that highlighted its outer structure rather than its inner flow. He thus emphasized the external pattern of his thought and inadvertently deprived his theme of its essentially living quality. It was this fateful error of style rather than content that cost Rank his audience; but it does not detract from the significance of his underlying point of view. His interpretation of the forms of will expression in the perspective of history is a major addition to the development and transformation of depth psychology that we have been following in the works of Freud, Adler, and Jung.

As a theoretical system this aspect of Rank's work is very complicated, for it involves a severely intellectual integration of conceptions of sociology and depth psychology.[17] On a human level, however, his work is simple and direct, for it is based on an essential and fundamental psychological fact. The human being, Rank says, experiences his individuality in terms of his will; and this means that his personal existence is identical with his capacity to express his will in the world. Death, however, puts an end to the kind of will expression that man experiences in his mortal life. Individual existence seems to terminate; but if there is no will remaining to man, his connection to life is destroyed. Rank's point then is that the most basic fact underlying man's psychological and cultural history is the observation first made under the most primitive circumstances that death apparently brings the individual's existence to an end. One way or another, man must come to terms with this simple but unavoidable observation. Not out of idle curiosity but out of a profound psychological

[17] The closest correspondence to Rank in the field of European sociology is Karl Mannheim. See particularly his *Ideology and Utopia*. That does not mean, however, that Rank can be understood in terms of Mannheim. I think it is safe to say that Rank's depth-psychology perspective gave a dimension to his thought that has no equivalent among sociologists. The one exception to this is the striking similarity between Rank's historical point of view and the approach to history presented by Thorstein Veblen in his systematic book, *The Instinct of Workmanship*. This may be mere coincidence, however, since I find nothing in Rank's writings to indicate that he was acquainted with Veblen's work.

need, man interprets and reinterprets it throughout history, constructing and reconstructing his conception of the universe in order to establish a place for himself after his death. Man does this out of his deepest nature. He cannot live, or he can live only painfully confused and neurotically unsure of himself, if he does not possess a clear conviction of the continued existence of his will in some form. This, to Rank, is the psychological fact that underlies the development of the individual personality and the variety of man's works in religion, art, and civilization. The "urge to immortality" is man's inexorable drive to feel *connected to life* in terms of his individual will with a sense of inner assurance that that connection will not be broken or pass away.

Human history is rich with examples of the ways in which the "urge to immortality" has been fulfilled. One common form that has many varieties is the belief in the permanent existence of the "soul" after death, in a "heaven" or on an "astral" plane from which the departed soul may both interfere with and assist in mortal affairs; or it may be a belief in the transmigration of souls, or reincarnation. Another major approach to immortality is by means of sexuality, either directly through the procreation of children, or indirectly through the "ancestors" or blood ties such as clans, nations, or races. Shared beliefs, participation in groups whose members are "chosen" by some higher agency, or who possess an "eternal truth" or a secret ritual are other roads to immortality. And, particularly at the higher levels of civilization, a main expression of the urge to be immortal is the "art work," a tangible object or undertaking in any realm of life such as art or politics or science to which the individual dedicates his energies in implicit hope that the product of his creative will will outlive his mortal body.

The will strives for immortality in an infinite variety of ways. It may seem, when we speak of it thus, that "immortality" is much too exalted a word with which to describe the prosaic fact that man covers his fear of death with the most ingenious and grandiose fantasies. It must be clear however, that as Rank uses it, the term "immortality" is metaphysically neutral. He speaks of the belief in immortality as nothing more than a psychological fact; but he does not dismiss the possibility that there may be a cosmic fact of even greater significance behind the persistent recurrence of that faith. Rank's immediate goal, however, lay in another direction. His first aim was to place the different kinds of immortality belief in historical perspective in order to find their meaning for the individual personality in modern times.

The first belief in immortality was, in Rank's view, natural and naïve. Man was close to nature then, and his sense of the continuity of life was immediate and specific. The earliest human being could not conceive of something as abstract as everlasting life; but neither could he conceive of a condition after the end of his life. He lived, therefore, with a simple sense of the ongoingness of the present in the form in which he experienced it. His own person, and more important, the immediate group into which he was born, was the one reality of his existence; and since he could not conceive of any other basis or way of life, his main fear was that the group would change or would come to an end. The primal man identified his own existence with that of the group and, as in the *"participation mystique"* of which Levy-Bruhl speaks, the continued existence of the group was the equivalent of the individual's own self-perpetuation.

In this regard, Rank's historical analysis begins with a significant addition to the theory with which Alfred Adler had started. Rank accepts Adler's basic judgment that it was because of man's *social* nature that the human species was able to emerge in its present form from the competitive struggle of evolution; but he adds the observation that man's social nature inherently involved a sense of immortality that was originally experienced in and through the group. Thus, agreeing with Adler that a *social sense* is innate in the human species as one of the conditions of its selective evolution, Rank adds that a *sense of immortality* is also innate in the human being and is, in fact, inseparable from his social nature. The two are experienced together, for the *sense of immortality* is primarily a *social* fact whose main content is the culture of the group. In the early days of man's history, the individual considered as unreal and invalid every aspect of life other than the one in whose terms he experienced his identity with his group. There was in this era of Emamism, the primal era of the will, no spiritual reality, no soul and no heaven, for at that level of life man experienced his social existence as identical with his immortality. His personal will was totally invested in the group, and its continued life was not in danger as long as the group endures. Underlying the more obvious and superficial motives of warfare we see, therefore, man's endless struggle toward "self-perpetuation"; and this means, as Rank develops his conception, man's ubiquitous effort, inherent in his evolutionary nature, to secure his immortality by maintaining an identity between his individual will and the continuous historical life of his group.[18]

This earliest expression of the urge to immortality was able to avoid the problem of death as long as the individual was still submerged in the collective experience of life. As man became aware of his own individuality, however, the

[18] Rank, *Beyond Psychology, op. cit.,* pp. 40, 63, 130, 131.

stark fact of the physical death of the individual human being became increasingly difficult to ignore. A new conception of the world became necessary. Whatever the details of the particular culture, the new point of view had to satisfy man's innate psychological need for a belief in his own self-perpetuation, and it had also to reinforce his growing sense of individuality. The outcome of this was Animism, the second major era that Rank distinguished, the "era of the soul."

Man's dawning sense of death, Rank says, led him to make a distinction between the physical body and a spiritual "double" that is completely identified with the individual, but does not cease to exist when his physical body dies.[19] From the conception of the "double," of which primitive mythology provides abundant examples, there eventually emerged the belief in the "soul" as a definite spiritual entity. The "Animistic era," as Rank interprets it, presents a view of the underlying reality of life that is altogether different from the earlier era of the will. Man's "self-perpetuation" was no longer experienced on the naïve sensory level in terms of the collective experience. His enduring life was not physical at all, but was transferred to another dimension of the universe. The "spiritual era" discovered a new reality that had been hidden from the Emamistic era of the will, a "higher" reality that gave new meanings to all of man's experiences. It was now the "soul" and the "realm of the soul" that constituted the reality of life, and this provided the criterion by which the validity of all man's acts and thoughts could be judged. Immortality was no longer a col-

[19] Rank, *Psychology and the Soul* (Philadelphia: University of Pennsylvania Press, 1950), p. 34.

lective experience, but something that each individual had to achieve for himself on the plane of spiritual realities.

The nature of the change from Emamism to the "animistic era of the soul" is indicative of the basic though abstract point that Rank was trying to make in marking off the four eras of man's development. He wanted to demonstrate as graphically as he could that the fundamental conceptions that underlie man's beliefs about life have their sources beyond consciousness and beyond rationality. And even more important, he wanted to show that these deepest, unconscious, most intimately assumed beliefs about life are not fixed and final as the "realities" about which they speak, but that they vary with the transformations of history. The first point was common to depth psychology in general; it had been a theme of Freud and Adler and Jung in diverse forms. But the second point was particularly Rank's own, and constitutes one of his most significant contributions to depth psychology. On the basis of it, he showed that some of the components of man's life that modern psychology has assumed to be objective and permanent, such as the "instinct" of sexuality, are actually variable in history both in their form and in their effects. It demonstrated also that it is the very fact of their impermanence, their inner changes, and the conflicts involved in these changes that lead to some of man's major psychological difficulties. It is true of this subject, however, as of most of the others with which Rank dealt, that he developed brilliantly intuitive insights and hypotheses but did not live long enough to apply them in detail and harvest their fruit. The rather abstract conception of the four eras that we are here presenting in outline is such a theoretical system intuitively conceived but not carried to its ultimate implications. Rank's basic point is incontrovertible; the modern personality can be understood only in the large historical perspective of man's psychological development. And the outlines of the system that he presented provide some of the essential insights with which this can be done.

4. SEX, THE SOUL, AND THE END OF PSYCHOLOGY

One of the basic assumptions on which Freud had built his psychoanalytical theories was the belief that sexuality, since it is expressed in a biological act, is an instinctual and therefore a universal part of human nature. Rank's cultural researches, however, led him to another conclusion. "Primitive man's attitude during the presexual era," that is, the "era of the soul," "clearly indicates that sexuality meant something inner, and not something as realistic as a relation with the opposite sex." [20] Originally, Rank maintained, man did not think of sexual contact as significant in its own right. In most cases it did not seem important enough to primitive man even to be an object of guilt feelings. Sex was merely play then, and it was only at a later "stage of human evolution" that "there occurred what one may call the discovery of sexuality." [21]

The whole perspective of psychological thought changes when the consequences of this historical point are taken into account. Sexuality is not, as Freud assumed, mainly a biological fact of human existence independent of man's non-sexual beliefs. The times and circumstances under which the sexual act is carried out, and particularly *the meaning that*

[20] *Ibid.*, p. 37.   [21] *Ibid.*, p. 34.

is given to the act and to the resulting child depend upon other and no less irrational attitudes toward life. In the animistic era where the belief in spiritual realities provided the context of life, "sex and reproduction were," Rank points out, "sharply distinguished," and the basis for the distinction was to be found in the belief in the soul. In all the varieties of soul belief the physical body was considered to be ephemeral while the soul was an eternal reality which chose the body of a newborn human being only as its temporary home. The sexual act played no more than a secondary role in such a view of life. To people who thought in its terms, the mere fact that sexual intercourse had taken place did not mean that a child would be born. Birth would not be possible unless the divinities willed it, unless a soul was available and was seeking to enter the mortal realm, and a host of other contingencies that derive from the lore of spiritual immortality. "In general," Rank says, primitive man "believed that reproduction was mediated not by sexual intercourse, but by entrance of the soul of the dead into the body of women, who then effected rebirth and immortality of the soul. Therefore sexual tabus were not restrictions, but expressions of man's inherent belief in his individual immortality."[22]

In the "era of the soul," immortality was a spiritual fact; but in the "sexual era" that followed it, immortality could be achieved in a much more tangible way: simply by having children. Instead of approaching life in terms of a view of reality based upon belief in the soul, the sexual era conceived of its realities in terms of relationships deriving from the basic fact of procreation. Characteristic of the sexual era, for example, was its emphasis on family ties, inheritance, honor,

[22] *Ibid.*, pp. 34-35.

and obedience. Personal connections based on "blood ties" took precedence over all others, and even man's relationship to God depended on descent from a particular father. In the "animistic era," all these relationships had been experienced not biologically in terms of procreation but spiritually in terms of the belief in the soul.

The two eras differed with respect to their most fundamental preconceptions about life. Their styles of thinking were basically at variance, as were their conceptions of reality, but, since the change from one to the other took place gradually, most cultural situations involved a combination of the two. Historically, the point of view of the "sexual era" emerged from the "era of the soul," and the ideologies of procreation, as Rank referred to the beliefs of the sexual era, must therefore be understood against the background of the older spiritual teachings. Many myths and sagas seem, in fact, to be best understood when they are interpreted as expressions of the conflicts that were inherent in the transition from the animistic to the sexual era. There is indeed a profound insight in Rank's remark that, "Unless we can translate the language of the sexual era into that of the spiritual era, we cannot understand even the biological facts of sex." [23] It is an insight, we might note, that deepens the historical perspective of psychology to a considerable degree, but also reveals the scope of the problems that prevent a precise historical analysis on this depth psychology level. The four eras that Rank marked off do not permit themselves to be sharply differentiated. In actuality, they overlap and fuse with one another. Their contending principles and views of life are often expressed not only within a single myth and a single culture, but even within the same human being.

[23] *Ibid.*, p. 47.

One of the most sensitive psychological areas that Rank studied was the point where sexuality and spiritual belief come into conflict. On the surface it would seem that the attitudes of the animistic era, emphasizing experiences of the soul as they do, would inhibit the sexual impulses; but Rank points out that very often exactly the opposite is the case. "Under the primitive world view," he observed, "in which the spirits of the dead effected impregnation independently of the sexual act, intercourse was a natural act of pleasure to which man gave himself under certain circumstances and at certain times." [24] The very fact that the sexual act did not participate in the higher spiritual values of its view of life freed it, and permitted a greater leeway for sexual expression. Only in the age that made sexual activity the core of its approach to reality did sex become important enough to be associated with guilt. The "naïve playful activity" of the spiritual era "became tabu," and the sex act was hemmed in with restrictions and ritual observances both to control it and exalt it as the center of society's way of life. Sexuality "was restricted to impregnation for the sake of begetting children and achieving reproductive immortality," and indulgence in sexual activity for other purposes was looked upon as sin.[25]

"In the sexual era," Rank points out, "reproduction was required because it served procreative immortality, but the sexual act itself was avoided because it robbed man of his strength. In a word, reproduction that had been dangerous at first came into favor, and sexuality, which was originally a proof of strength, became tabu." [26] "The issue," Rank reiterates, "has always been one of immortality and of the salvation of man's soul from dissipation under the sexual era's

[24] *Ibid.*, p. 39.   [25] *Ibid.*, p. 39.   [26] *Ibid.*, p. 39.

ideology of fertilization." [27] Here we have a main theoretical key to the emotional complications that have seemed to be inherent in man's sexual activities since the earliest times. Although the animistic era permitted free play in sex within its own boundaries, when its spiritual ideals were carried over into the sexual era they had an inhibiting effect. In the context of the new procreative age, the old beliefs of the primacy of the soul could only confuse the individual and split his standards of action. We see this in the fact that to the extent that the "spiritual significance of sex" was still felt to be a reality in the sexual age, the individual remained under the influence of the old belief that he "might lose his immortality at the time his soul entered the child." [28] Because of it, a degree of "sexual resistance" was inherent in the sexual age from the time that it first emerged out of the spiritual era. The "sexual resistance" with its concomitant "anxieties" was the source of the "neurotic" forms of individual and social behavior that Freud described. But—and this is Rank's profound and fundamental point—the inner meaning and "cause" of this behavior was not sexual, as Freud thought, but spiritual; for its root lay in the old beliefs of the spiritual era upon which the ideologies of the sexual era had been superimposed.

The meeting of the points of view of the two eras and the resulting tension that remained in man ever afterward comprise the main source of those inner conflicts that a later age described as "psychological." A historical perspective is thus essential for understanding the problems with which depth psychology deals. By means of it we can understand *in principle* why the great affirmative force of the sexual energies became negative and was burdened with feelings

[27] *Ibid.*, p. 42.   [28] *Ibid.*, p. 38.

of guilt and sin. The road to immortality became uncertain, for man was caught in a confusion between sexuality and his belief in his soul. "As an expression of will," Rank says, "sexuality became evil, guilty, and a cause of death"; and these were precisely the characteristics that "had formerly been ascribed to the will" in the era of the soul. Sexuality became identified with the negative will, and it was from this point of view that not only Freud had proceeded but both his philosophic predecessors, Schopenhauer and Nietzsche, as well. "Since," Rank points out in a brilliantly perceptive passage, it seemed to the man of the sexual era who was still influenced by the old spiritual beliefs, that "will could bring about death," the will was labeled as bad in itself. "Yet it did not simply disappear; instead it became transformed into a negative power manifested as guilt feeling, and interpreted or explained causally under the concept of sin. *This was the beginning of psychology which only deals further with the broken, denied will and with guilt as a moral phenomenon, now shorn of its former connotations of power.*" [29]

As Rank interprets it, the emergence of psychology represents a new point of view, a new "era" in man's development. It is not, however, an era born of strength, but of weakness. Psychology, one can say, was born of death, the death of old beliefs that once gave meaning to man's life. The negativity of psychology is most clearly shown in the fact that it "explains" man's beliefs—man's ancient ideologies that recur still in the modern mind—but it has no beliefs of its own. Psychology is capable only of explaining, but not of believing. "For," Rank says, "the psychological ideology has never been alive. It came into the world, so

[29] *Ibid.*, pp. 164-165 (my italics).

to say, with an old mind." It "was produced from the neurotic type and corresponds to it." [30]

This last remark of Rank's is indicative of an ambivalence inherent in his life and visible throughout his later writings. It was because of his insight into the historical dynamics beneath the surface of the mind that Rank was able to have a vision that opened a vista for him beyond psychology; but he had been engaged in the psychoanalytical discipline for most of his mature life, and he could never altogether overcome its habit-forming effects. Thus we see him, in his old psychoanalytical way, labeling the Freudian point of view as "neurotic," even though the main burden and meaning of his lifework was to show how superficial that label is. "How presumptuous, and at the same time, naïve," he said elsewhere, "is the idea of simply removing human guilt by explaining it causally as 'neurotic'!" [31]

The problem of guilt cannot be "diagnosed" and conveniently rationalized out of existence. It arises from a conflict that is inherent in man's historical development, and it recurs whenever those fundamental historical issues are re-experienced in a modern personality; whenever, that is, an action undertaken in terms of attitudes of the sexual era is reconsidered from the point of view of the old spiritual beliefs. Sexuality seen in the light of the ideology of the soul seems to be sin, and this is where psychoanalysis, quite unwittingly, made its most significant contribution to therapy. It undertook to reinterpret the old moral beliefs of the spiritual era in a rational way. That is to say, psychoanalysis "analyzed" the old spiritual beliefs so that they would no longer be deterrents to the expression of sexuality. By "ex-

[30] Rank, *Modern Education, op. cit.*, p. 112.
[31] Rank, *Beyond Psychology, op. cit.*, p. 273.

plaining" them, the force of the old spiritual beliefs was largely neutralized, and the conflict between the sexual and the spiritual ideologies was, to that extent, removed.

We are now in a position to see the point of Rank's remark that psychoanalysis sought to remove guilt by simply calling it "neurotic." What Freud did, in effect, was to "analyze" the beliefs of the spiritual era as they occur in modern individuals and "reduce" them to sexual origins. Freud then added the "diagnosis," phrased in his "scientific" medical terminology that any person who evaluated his sexual and related experiences by the criteria of the old, to him outmoded, spiritual beliefs was, by that very fact, "neurotic." The experience of guilt with its profound historical roots in man's nature was thus expected to disappear when the psychoanalyst exclaimed his magic medical word.

Seen in this light, such healing effects as psychoanalysis may eventually achieve do not derive from a truly therapeutic method. They are the result rather of the reconstruction that psychoanalysis presents of the individual's experiences in the terms of its own ideology. "Psycho-analysis," Rank says, is "psychological knowledge only to a minor degree; it is principally an interpretation of old animistic spiritual values into the scientific language of the sexual ear." [32] And if it has a healing effect, that is, if it removes the emotionally disturbing consequences of guilt feelings, that is because "under this sexuo-psychological interpretation, spiritual values are just as comforting or 'therapeutic' for us as a naïve belief in immortality was for primitive man." [33]

In other words, the therapy of psychoanalysis is achieved

[32] Rank, *Psychology and the Soul, op. cit.*, pp. 87-88.
[33] *Ibid.*, p. 88.

by providing a psychological ideology with which to reinterpret those experiences that led to inner conflict when
they were considered in the terms of the two earlier ideologies of sex and the soul. "To put it bluntly," says Rank,
"in one sentence which shakes the foundation of the whole
Freudian system and of psychology in general, for that matter: Freud, without knowing it, interpreted the analytical
situation in terms of his world-view and did not, as he
thought, analyze the individual's unconscious objectively." [34]
And again, "Facts are no more explained by re-evaluating
them ideologically than ideologies are explained by labelling
them as psychological facts. The materials of psychology are
not facts, but ideologies, such as spiritual beliefs, which
again are not simply facts related to a definite reality, but
ideologies related to a definite mentality. Such concrete
manifestations of these ideologies as society or the family
must be understood for what they are and not as mere
psychological facts." [35]

To speak of psychoanalysis as a "psychological ideology"
implies nothing more than an acknowledgment of the fact
that Freud's work is the most articulate expression of the
point of view that underlies the modern "psychological era."
Because of the peculiar role that it has played in history, the
larger significance of psychoanalysis can be grasped only if
it is understood as an ideology, that is, as a subjectively useful
point of view, and not as the objective science it has thought
itself to be. The basis for the existence of psychoanalysis,
as well as those sister disciplines that are related to it, is
to be found precisely in the fact that they function as
ideologies. They have been helpful in practice just to the

[34] Rank, *Beyond Psychology*, op. cit., p. 278.
[35] Rank, *Psychology and the Soul*, op. cit., p. 89-90.

extent that they have been able to provide a believable frame of reference within which the individual could reconstruct his experiences in a way that would make his life seem reasonable and meaningful once again. The impact of the collapse of the older ideologies has unquestionably been softened by the fact that the various analytical types of psychology have functioned as ideologies. They have filled in the most painful gaps in the modern spirit, at least temporarily, and to that extent they have actually carried out their original intention of serving as a "therapy" for modern man. The nature of their "healing" has, however, been something other than their theories led them to expect. The main contribution of the psychological ideologies has been to alleviate the chaos of belief—or more accurately, of disbelief—in the modern personality. But the very fact that they have played such a role—and have done so inadvertently—raises some serious and significant questions regarding the nature and possible duration of the "psychological era."

The distinguishing characteristics of the "psychological era" are essentially negative, for psychology arises out of the collapse of the older ideologies. It proceeds on the basis of a pervasive skepticism that is, on the one hand, a studied and deliberate attitude toward the acquisition of knowledge; and on the other hand, simply a chronic incapacity to believe. Since man in the psychological era is not able to accept any of the old ideologies in their own terms, he interprets traditional beliefs "symbolically" or "psychologically," since that is the only way he can talk about them at all. He experiences himself, then, as an outsider with respect to the older, once strongly established ways of life, and he is led to a severe self-consciousness that culminates in doubts of the most fundamental kind. In the psychological era, Rank says, "the necessity of tormenting self-awareness became the virtue of therapeutic self-knowledge, whose results were esteemed as 'truth.' " [36] But the "truth" that comes from psychological self-analysis does not bring with it any new conviction as to the nature of the individual's life. The new psychological truth remains essentially an absence of belief, and its negativity extends even to man's fundamental ideology, the belief in the immortality of the soul, which is his oldest heritage.

This is the unique distinction of the psychological era according to Rank, for only in the psychological era has the belief in immortality been seriously endangered. Through all the vicissitudes of history, even the "knowledge of death," Rank says, "has been unable to shake the belief in individual immortality," except temporarily; [37] and then it has always been restored in the context of a new ideology, as we saw in the transition from the spiritual to the sexual era. Its form has changed from the primordial animistic view to the tribal conceptions of the sexual era, and these have been combined in the most varied permutations in subsequent cultures; but the basic theme of immortality has survived throughout. Only in the psychological era has the belief in immortality lost its inspirational force of a significant degree, and that, Rank says, is because "psychology . . . is a predominantly negative and disintegrative ideology . . . , an ideology of resentment in Nietzsche's sense. It destroys illusions and ideologies, which can no longer withstand its progressive self-consciousness. It becomes progressively unable to maintain even itself, and finally, as the last natural science, ideology, it destroys itself." [38]

[36] *Ibid.*, pp. 86-87.   [37] *Ibid.*, p. 96.   [38] *Ibid.*, pp. 192-193.

In the modern age, man needs an ideology capable of strengthening his will in a creative way. He needs a point of view through which he can experience his immortality in a believable and livable form, as an enduring and productive connection to life. More important than a therapy to quiet his illnesses and soothe his old wounds, the modern person requires an affirmative ideology of education capable of drawing forth the latent "genius" of the individual and inspiring a new "collective vitality" in a tired civilization. But psychology cannot possibly carry out such a role, "for," Rank said, "with the appearance of the different psychoanalytic schools, psychology seems exhausted." It seems "to have arrived at its end rather than at the beginning of a new development." [39]

By 1929, when he was writing his provocative essays on *Modern Education*, Rank was already convinced that psychology, as developed by Freud, had passed its most useful years. Certainly the various psychological methods for individual treatment would still be able to survive; they would continue to have their "therapeutic" success by carrying on their ideological work under cover of a medical terminology. But eventually they would all show themselves to be unequal to the great need of the time, the task of re-educating the will and refurbishing the energies of the modern personality in a creative way. In the task of educating a new generation, psychoanalysis can hope for little more than "the avoidance of neuroses," for its negative approach is alien, by its very nature, to the creative experiences of religion and art. [40] And since this is the case, Rank concluded, since psychology is as good as dead where a fundamental, spiritually re-creative

[39] Rank, *Modern Education, op. cit.,* p. 112.
[40] *Ibid.,* p. 111.

work is concerned, let us accept the fact, and take it as our starting point. Indeed, "what could be better," he said ironically, "than that we should have a *finished psychology* before it is applied to pedagogy!" [41]

The perspective of his cross-cultural study of the forms of will expression had led Rank to see the inherent instability of the psychological point of view. Modern man, he perceived, needs something more than psychology. He has to go beyond psychology to solve the problems that concern his deepest nature. Unfortunately, the pathways there are still uncharted; but the question of what lies beyond psychology dominated the last decade of Otto Rank's life.

5. THE ARTIST LOSING HIS STRUGGLE WITH LIFE:
   ANOTHER DIMENSION OF THE ARCHETYPES

When the phrase "Beyond Psychology" first occurred to him, Rank was engaged in writing three books that presented his mature psychological point of view. [42] These books completed the difficult process of self-liberation by which he had freed his mind from its dependence on Freud. During the first years of his "secession" from the psychoanalytic movement, Rank had concentrated on formulating his own orientation in a systematic form, particularly emphasizing the capacities of the conscious will in contrast to Freud's determinism of the unconscious. He stated the results of this phase of his work in his *Will Therapy* and in his *Truth and Reality* as what he called a "psychology of consciousness." On the

[41] *Ibid.*, p. 112.
[42] These three were. *Modern Education, Psychology and the Soul,* and *Art and Artist.*

basis of these two books, Rank gained a significant following in America, but the conceptions he developed there
played only a transitional role in the growth of his thought.
Rank recognized the superficiality of his emphasis on consciousness, for such a psychology could not satisfy his high
intellectual standards for very long, and he soon undertook
to construct a larger and more adequate frame of reference.
He turned his energies, then, toward liberating himself from
the anti-Freudian system that he himself had created; and it
was while he was thus occupied that he conceived the title
phrase, "Beyond Psychology," as an apt description of the
new directions of his thought.

The meaning of this phrase seemed clear to Rank when he
first thought of it, but in the course of the decade from 1929
to 1939, it revealed depths he had not originally perceived.
In the preface he wrote for *Beyond Psychology* only a few
months before he died, Rank candidly discussed the changes
that had taken place in his understanding of what was to be
found *beyond psychology*. There he disclosed that he had
thought at first that, since both psychoanalysis and his own
psychology of the conscious will had been concerned predominantly with the emotional problems of individuals, his
step beyond psychology would involve mainly a change in
emphasis. What he would accomplish, he thought, going
beyond psychology, would be to bring an end to psychology's
analytical preoccupation with personal and subjective factors
by developing a cultural and historical perspective. At that
time, going *beyond psychology* meant to Rank going *beyond
individuality* to the deeper social foundations of life that
provide the background of the individual personality. He
conceived of himself then as studying the cultural dimensions of psychological events; but later, when his work had

brought him to a deeper level of personal experience, he perceived an even more important area *beyond psychology* that opened a new vista for his lifework. During the years around 1929, however, Rank's aim was specifically to go beyond psychoanalysis and its derivatives so as to bypass the psychologies of neurotic individualism. He thought that he would be able to do that most successfully by means of a social psychology; but he recognized that he would need an interpretive principle deep enough and comprehensive enough to study the historical expressions of the human will.

At this point in his work, Rank was seeking to overcome the weaknesses of two different kinds of individualistic psychologies. The first, which he had learned from Freud, considered instinctual drives to be the foundation of personality development, and the other, "a psychology of consciousness" that he himself had formulated, treated the conscious will as the most important organ of human action. Going "beyond" the two contrasting principles of instinct and consciousness, Rank now offered his "Third Principle." "Our view of human behavior," he said, "as extending beyond individual psychology to a broader conception of personality indicates that civilized man does not act only upon the rational guidance of his intellectual ego nor is he driven blindly by the mere elemental forces of his instinctual self. *Mankind's civilization, and with it the various types of personality representing and expressing it, has emerged from the perpetual operation of a third principle which combines the rational and irrational elements in a world view based on the conception of the supernatural.*" [43]

The essence of this "third principle" was expressed in the outline of an historical system that Rank presented in his

[43] Rank, *Beyond Psychology, op. cit.,* p. 62 (my italics).

"Psychology of the Soul." There, as we have seen, he interpreted *the will to immortality* as man's innate sense of connection to life in all the aspects of his experience, personal, social, and cosmic. In that book, Rank had shown that while the striving for "self-perpetuation" is inherent in human nature, its expression is not biological but social. Man's native tendency to express his will becomes an urge to maintain his individual identity beyond the limitations of his body. Man strives with death, and though he cannot overcome it physically, he overcomes it "ideologically." The last word is the key to Rank's point of view. Man's *will to live forever*, he says, expresses itself and satisfies itself in terms of belief—manifestly so, since the very nature of immortality prevents man on earth from having definite knowledge in advance and limits him to an act of faith. Immortality inherently belongs to the future, but man works toward it in his present life in terms of various beliefs about it, most of which he draws from the attitudes and habits of thinking, the "dominant immortality ideology," prevailing in the period of histories in which he lives.

The variety of forms in which man strives for immortality are virtually infinite. Sometimes the individual identifies his personal existence with that of his group, his tribe, or his nation; and then, though he dies, he feels assured of immortality in the survival of his people. In other circumstances, the belief in the existence of an individual and indestructible soul is the basis of the faith in immortality. Often the striving for immortal life is expressed in a *work,* a master opus, into which the individual invests his full life energies. It may involve a deed of heroic proportions in battle, in politics, or in religion; or it may be a special production, a work of art or of science. Rank's point is that whatever the means by which immortality is sought, it is always in terms of *beliefs* that derive from the community and from the particular historical moment in which the individual lives. In those cases, however, where the urge to immortality expresses itself in unique works of individuality —heroic acts or artistic productions—the community provides the raw materials for the creative individual's work— but the creative act itself embodies the assertion of the individual's own will counter to the fixed patterns of the culture. It is precisely by creating something that alters the will of the community that the creative individual establishes the uniqueness of his will and thereby gains his immortality. But, this also is an "ideology," for the belief that immortality can be attained by individual artistic works is itself derived from the community and appears only in certain periods of man's history.

The will to immortality is thus the principle that Rank followed in his effort to interpret man from a point of view beyond the individualistic psychologies. This was the "third principle" to which he referred. Man's urge to strive for enduring life is inherent in his nature, but it is not instinctual in Freud's biological sense. Equally, although it is experienced in acts of consciousness, it is fundamentally unconscious. Its roots are irrational. It operates not individually, but socially, for it both draws upon and creatively reshapes the forms of cultural life. The urge to immortality is an experience of the individual seeking to perpetuate his individual will. It is also, however, inherently *beyond individuality*, for immortal life by its very nature extends beyond the individual earthly personality. It reaches out to larger realities; ultimately, for the artistic and religious person, it reaches toward transcendent facts; and for those who seek a more earth-bound immortality, it reaches toward historical and traditional facts, or, as Rank would say, toward "ideologies."

All those beliefs that are strong enough to inspire the personal will to immortality and to become identified with it are essentially *impersonal.* They are, that is to say, beliefs derived from the historical collectivity of mankind. They are powerful and capable of leading to creative work because they reach far into the primordial depths of human nature. All those beliefs that are spiritually authentic, Rank says— and here he echoes a profound insight of C. G. Jung's—have their source in a level of the human spirit that is more than individual.[44] That is why deeply valid spiritual experiences are never subjective, even though, because they express the irrational depths in man, they may be incommunicable. They represent social factors in the human psyche that have an objective reality as links between man and the cosmos via the experience of the will.

When the lives of creative individuals are seen in the retrospect of history, the social quality of their work is much more clearly visible than at the time the work is being done. The actual act of creativity involves an intense personal struggle for the artist because he must first "free himself from the prevailing art-ideology in order to forge his individual expression." [45] The artist experiences his personal vocation as an intense expression of his individual will, and he therefore feels himself to be in conflict not only with the general traditions of his culture but with the attitudes toward his art immediately preceding his own innovations. The artist must struggle against art, Rank says, in order to

[44] Rank, *Psychology and the Soul, op. cit.,* pp. 126-127.
[45] Rank, *Art and Artist, op. cit.,* p. 368.

crystallize the work that will express his individual will. When the work is over and can be seen in perspective, however, the observer perceives that its "uniqueness" was only the momentary experience of the individual artist. In direct relation to the depth and authenticity of his work, the artist's personal act of creation serves to give tangible and permanent form to a spiritual experience of an impersonable type whose sources and meaning far transcend his individuality.

The contents of the art works of great creative individuals, Rank says, are fundamentally impersonal, for they are derived from the historical store of beliefs and experiences that comprise the collective heritage of a people. As the creative person brings these to expression in word and deed, he articulates what others have felt vaguely, though no less strongly, and their potential spiritual experiences are actualized by means of his work.[46] It is because of this that the artist is often regarded as a hero, for he is a living prototype of man's creative will. He experiences creatively what is dormant or suppressed in others, and they are thereby enabled to experience their own latent creativity through him.

What Rank has in mind here is far from the old social theory that the artist is merely the man who crystallizes the "spirit of the times" in a work that is the most widely accepted because it is the most representative. Despite his insistence on the fact that no expression of the human will can be understood outside of its cultural context, Rank's most basic emphasis is not on society but on the individual. His point is simply that the raw materials for creative experience are provided by the culture, but that the creative

[46] *Ibid.*, p. 103.

act itself is the unique accomplishment of the artistic type of personality who uses and transforms the collective heritage in an especially meaningful way. Rank's appreciation of the will, in the deepened conception of it that we described earlier as the organ of creativity in man, leads him to an essentially activistic view of art. The artistic individual is not the representative man of his era. Just the opposite. He is the unique man, and his uniqueness consists in the fact that, in his individuality, he expresses a spiritual experience —that is, an experience of the inner realities of the "soul" —which "touches," awakens, and inspires the longings of the will of many other human beings.

At this point, Rank's conception of the creative person tends toward the theory of C. G. Jung concerning the "archetypes." The archetypes, according to Jung, are patterns of imagery and symbolism that are universally present in man, although in different cultural forms; and, in his view, the great creative artist is the one whose work succeeds precisely because it transcends personal subjectivities and reaches the "universals" in the depths of the human spirit. Where Jung relates these experiences to the "Self," Rank places them in terms of the will; and here again we see that at the advanced levels of their thought Rank and Jung were dealing with essentially equivalent concepts. The main differences between them in this area of their work is, in fact, largely a question of their individual "styles" in working out the relation between the universal factors in the psyche and those that are historically variable.

Jung's work began as an analysis of the cultural varieties of myths and symbols, but as he framed his theory of the archetypes he tended more and more to emphasize their underlying sameness rather than their historical differences.

He did this because of the unifying tendency of his mind, and because he was convinced that the task of identifying the various universal patterns of the psyche was the major contribution he was destined to make to psychology. Rank, on the other hand, recognized only one factor of a universal scope, man's *will to immortality;* and from that point on, his studies are historical because he was interested not in the will to immortality as such, but in its consequences from the diverse forms of man's cultural behavior. While Jung proceeded from historical symbols to their underlying universals, Rank worked in the opposite direction in his effort to follow the movements of the will in history. Their styles of study were different, but their subject matter was essentially the same. Their central concern was with the impersonal foundations of man's personality, and this was directly expressed in their conception of the creative individual. The artist's work, Rank and Jung agreed, is authentic to the extent that it is drawn from the objective, more-than-personal contents of the human spirit. When subjective material predominates in an artwork, it was to them a token that not art but a spontaneous attempt at self-therapy was involved. The artist whose work expresses mainly subjectivities of a personal psychological kind is carrying out his art in unconscious answer to a therapeutic need that must be satisfied before he will be capable of creative work that will have an objective spiritual validity. Jung diagnosed the appearance of such subjectivities in the terms of his analytical psychology of the "complexes," while Rank sought to interpret the artist dynamically as a distinct type whose "neurosis" indicates only that his will has not yet been sufficiently developed to make creative expression possible. In a larger frame of reference, however, when he took the first of his two major steps beyond individualistic psychology, Rank placed the modern artist in the historical perspective of his theory of the "eras," and this yields some exceedingly suggestive insights into the problems of the creative person in our time.

Rank's point in studying the artist in historical perspective was to show how the transition from the "era of the soul" to the "psychological era" has affected man's creative capacities. The main characteristic of the "animistic era" as Rank described it was that the thing that seemed "real" to people living within its terms were the intangible experiences based upon the belief in the soul. These "realities" existed on a spiritual plane, and were comparable for the most part to the kind of perception that takes place in dreams. In the "ear of the soul," dreams were regarded as real. What modern man would tend to think of as the more tangible realities of everyday life were interpreted in that view of things as derivatives of the prior realities of the "spiritual" realm of the dream. "Primitive man," Rank says, "took the dream to be absolutely true"; and this meant "not that he confused it with reality, but that he saw it as a higher reality. The dream neither predicted reality to come nor recalled that which had gone, but portrayed the true reality corresponding to the spiritual world view." [47] If "the dream contradicted reality, the contradiction was neutralized by adjusting reality to suit the dream. The basis for this correction did not lie in any wish merely to improve reality, because this was rarely desired and less often achieved. It lay rather in the compulsion to bring reality into agreement with spiritual belief in order

[47] Rank, *Psychology and the Soul, op. cit.*, p. 98.

to sustain that belief," [48] and more particularly "to verify this belief by *making* it real." [49]

For the hero of the animistic age, the belief in the transcendent validity of the dream was akin to a belief in God. The voice that spoke to the hero was the voice of immortality. He obeyed it in his waking life with the conviction that even if he perished in the work, the immortality of his soul was assured. It was this faith that sustained him in his hazardous adventures. The exploits of the hero may have been dangerous to his body, but they were not at all dangerous to his soul. On the contrary, they were undertaken specifically to secure the safety of his soul, to protect it from death. In the spiritual era of which Rank speaks, men believed that they were required to carry out the instructions that came to them in a dream, in a vision, or by a voice communicating from the "realm of the soul." They felt they had to translate that spiritual message into the tangible reality of their physical lives, thereby "*making* it real."

This task of converting a spiritual reality into an actuality of the world was the heroic enterprise of primordial times. Should a man succeed in it, he would indeed be worthy of "immortal life," and that was the reward that the hero sought: to "save his soul" from death. Because his very life was at stake, not only his mortal soul but more important in the terms of the spiritual era his immortal soul, he devoted all his energies to the work. His life became identical with his work, and it is in this fundamental respect that the hero of the spiritual era is the prototype of the creative individual in all future ages.

Descriptions of the exploits of such heroes are to be found in the myths and legends of all races. It is highly probable

[48] *Ibid.*, p. 99.   [49] *Ibid.*, p. 101.

that although most of these traditions purport to be literal recordings of historical events, they have in fact only a slim thread of actuality as their basis: but they are true nonetheless *in principle*, for they are faithful expressions of how man's creative will can be *lived* in the context of a spiritual universe. The fact is that men in later ages did not possess the same powers of personality that were attributed to the primordial hero. He had received a direct message of a spiritual reality to be expressed in the world, and he had placed his whole life unreservedly in its service; but men in later generations could only recall it, wish for it, and re-interpret its meaning to fit within the framework of their present lives. Occasionally a "strong-willed individual" would feel impelled to re-enact the life of his heroic proto-type; but his effort would inevitably end, Rank says, in "tragic failure." [50] The creative work of artists after the spiritual era was confined to singing songs *about* the heroic life, to recounting its glories, and translating the beliefs upon which it had been based to make them seem "reasonable" by the standards of a new age.

The fundamental change that had taken place to prevent creative individuals in later eras from living as heroes was simply that the realm of the soul was no longer experienced as the primary reality. To the primordial hero, his "higher" guidance was a self-evident fact to be obeyed in the light of immortality, but for men of a later age the encounter with spiritual reality was much less intense. It was cushioned by traditions, and weakened by new ideologies that hedged man's ancient belief in the soul. The power of the creative will was remembered; but the artist in that vast sweep of history that Rank calls the "sexual era" was not capable of

[50] *Ibid.*, p. 101; Rank, *Art and Artist, op. cit.*, p. 283.

emulating the hero in life. He could not reproduce the hero's experiences in himself and he therefore required another means of achieving his personal immortality. He needed a substitute for the creative lifework of the hero that he venerated out of respect for the group's historical memory but that he could not verify in his own experience since he did not share the earlier ideology of the soul. The artist had to discover a new road to immortality for himself. Instead of duplicating the hero's life in his own, which he could not do, he undertook to re-create the hero's life by retelling the old stories in versions of his own, thus identifying himself with the immortal soul achieved by the hero's exploits, and yet expressing his own individuality.

In the act of discovering his new vocation, the artist of the "sexual era" found a new function for dreams that fulfilled the needs of his new point of view. He no longer conceived of the dream (and the creative inspirational aspect of the "unconscious" in general) as the spiritual instrument it had been to the hero; instead, the dream became for him a tool for fantasying. By virtue of his belief in the earlier ideology of the soul, the hero had regarded his dreams and visions to be messages from a transcendent reality that he was bound to obey and "make real" in the world; but the artist did not feel as close to the spiritual substrate of life as the hero had been, and he therefore experienced the dream portion of his psyche simple as an organ of imagination. The dream became a medium of creative fantasy to him so that, by articulating unconscious wishes and wish fulfillments in artistic forms, the creative person could have a tangible "work" that would bring him a limited immortality of a personal kind and thus provide a satisfying substitute for living the life of the hero.

Since the hero is the prototype of the creative individual, the underlying patterns of behavior expressed in the hero's life apply *in principle* to the life of the artist as well. The creative personality seems to contain a "typical destiny" inherent in its nature, and thus involves it in similar kinds of situations through all the changing circumstances of history. [51] It seems as though, beneath the surface of the artist's existence, there is a substrate of "mythical stuff" that contains the inner necessities that ultimately come to the fore in his life. [52] He must, for example, have a channel in which he can express his will in a unified and dedicated way. "Compared with the average man," Rank remarks, "the artist has, so to say, a hundred-per-cent vocational psychology." [53] The hero was the man who made his life his work and achieved his immortality by devoting his life to the task of converting a spiritual vision into an actuality to "make" it true; but the artist is not capable of that, and so he comes as close as he can. He makes his work his life "by living himself out entirely in creative work." "This fact is so obvious," Rank adds, "that when we intuitively admire some great work of art, we say the whole artist is in it and expresses himself in it." [54] And for the artist, because of the mythical theme that is the inner reality of his being, this act of total dedication is an absolute necessity. He "needs his calling for his spiritual existence, just as the early cultures of mankind could not have existed and developed without art." [55]

One of the qualities that distinguishes the artist from the artisan is the fact that the artist's calling comes from within. He does not choose it because others approve or be-

[51] Rank, *Art and Artist, op. cit.*, p. 289.
[52] Rank, *Beyond Psychology, op. cit.*, p. 170.
[53] Rank, *Art and Artist, op. cit.*, p. 371.
[54] *Ibid.*, p. 373.   [55] *Ibid.*, p. 371.

cause it will bring a livelihood. Rather, "the creative type nominates itself," [56] and does so because of an autonomous inner direction comparable to the spiritual guidance followed by the primordial hero. To the extent that artists in later periods of history retain man's old animistic beliefs and still possess a sensitivity to the experiences of the soul, the "call" that convinces them of their work has a strong and independent, an objective spiritual quality. If the artist does not possess such a belief, however, he is bound to question his artistic vocation. If it did not come to him from the "realm of the soul" (as he believes it did not), what other source could it have? The artist then begins to examine his creative nature in a negative way. He compares himself to others in the community, and he perceives the difficulties he is encountering in his life because of his artistic vocation. Not feeling that his "call" has a spiritual meaning, he is easily led to doubt its authenticity. He "hedges" his art work to satisfy more practical considerations, and thus he denies himself the total dedication that is the prime requisite of the hero's creative life.

The step that follows the artist's doubt of himself and his work is self-consciousness, and then self-analysis. At that point, "his aim is not to express himself in his work but to get to know himself by it." [57] The artist who is not secure in his spiritual convictions "cannot express himself without confessing." Out of touch with the older creative ideologies, he seeks to use his art as a means of "knowing himself." "This individual realism," Rank points out, "which reveals itself as a search for truth in art and life, only intensifies the conflict in the person of the artist. The more successful his

[56] *Ibid.,* p. 371.   [57] *Ibid.,* p. 390.

discovery of truth about himself, the less can he create or even live." [58]

Thus it is that "While his prototype, the hero, through his self-generating activity, had given rise to a new belief in the immortality of creation, the artist type became more and more self-conscious of his individual difference, and consequently, losing his original creativity, became an artificial type himself, a mere artisan of technical skill." [59] No longer sure of either the basis or the nature of his existence, he anxiously studied himself, and he became as fascinated by the analysis of the "reasons" for his interest in art as he had previously been in art itself. The artist thus completed the journey that has been characteristic of modern man in many fields of life and went from spontaneous creativity to psychological self-analysis.

This is the dead end of the artist's life. When the creative type of person regards his personal problems as part of the struggle that is inherent in the heroic life of art, he can overcome them and soon cease to be an *artist manqué;* he will then no longer be an artist who is suffering simply from the fact that he has not yet been able to fulfill himself. But if the creative person loses his nerve and begins to analyze himself negatively as a neurotic, the inner source of creativity is closed off. The will to create in the light of immortality then becomes nothing more than a "narcissistic attraction to one's image," and psychoanalysis becomes not only the death of art but of the creative personality in general. [60]

---

[58] *Ibid.,* p. 390.
[59] Rank, *Beyond Psychology, op. cit.,* p. 101.
[60] *Ibid.,* p. 101.

6. CREATIVE PERSONALITY BEYOND PSYCHOLOGY

When the artist type first came to psychoanalysis and tried it, he was in search of "a new artistic ideology." But he was not quite searching; he was groping. The old spiritual beliefs had broken apart beneath his feet, and the new "natural science ideology" refused to support the artist unless he violated his heroic calling and became utilitarian. The artist had nothing to sustain him, and "at first," Rank says, he "seemed to find some support in psychoanalysis." [61] Soon, however, in less than a generation, the truth came out. Results showed that psychoanalysis was directed toward neurosis and not toward creativity, even though Freud himself was a creative type. The psychological point of view, whether in Freud's version or the other analytical psychologies derived from Freud, could provide some therapy for the artist as a neurotic; but it could not lead him to authentic creativity. As it has turned out in fact, analytic types of therapy have found the artistic type of person to be a fertile source of data that they could interpret, that is, rationalize, in terms of their theoretical formulas. The artist is, after all, by nature sensitive to his inner life and he is therefore a prolific producer of "symbols of the unconscious." "Thus," Rank says, "psycho-analysis has rather used the modern artist as an object of study than helped him to a psychological ideology of art." [62]

The failure of psychology to produce a new point of view with which the creative person can guide his life brought the situation back to where it had been when psychoanalysis first

[61] Rank, *Art and Artist, op. cit.,* p. 391.
[62] *Ibid.,* p. 391.

came along. The artist was caught at a crossroads of history without an "ideology" that could channel his creative urge. Psychoanalysis was not able to show him the way, but only added to the confusion and depleted the artist's energies still further. "Today," Rank says, "all collective means fail and the artist is thrown back on an individual psycho-therapy." [63] And this psycho-therapy is not separate from his art, but actually *is* his art."

Under the influence of the psychological point of view, the art work of the artist becomes either an act of "self-expression" or a "self-confession" unconsciously but specifically designed to rid him of his emotional tensions. The artist may actually achieve his purpose in using his art work as a form of therapy; but if he persists in it, he will in time negate his original goal altogether. Even though he may seem to "heal" himself temporarily, in the long run he harms himself much more because he has placed himself upon a path of sub-jective self-consciousness leading away from creative activity. He cuts himself off from the fundamental power that could sustain him, for he deviates from the mythological theme that underlies the artist's life and gives it its basic validity. Without his core of "mythical stuff" the artist's personality is little more than an empty shell. He becomes then the very opposite of the legendary hero who stood ready to sacrifice himself for a spiritual ideal; and without the will to sacrifice, he is also without the capacity to succeed in his life task. In direct contrast to the hero, the artist who follows the psy-choanalytical way stands ready to *use* the spiritual ideal of his art as a means of relieving his emotions, of "understand-ing" himself better, and perhaps healing himself of some subjective ills.

[63] *Ibid.,* p. 391.

When the creative person has come to this point, he is no longer creative. He is then totally without a belief in immortality in any of its ideological forms, and his will is therefore deprived of the unconscious motivation that is essential for creative work. Without a sense of immortality, the artist is cut off from life. He can experience no enduring meanings beyond those that he can "explain" rationally and psychologically, and he is left with only personal and subjective concerns. At that point, as Rank sees it, we should no longer speak of the "artist type," since the individual has lost the will to create works of objective dedication. Under the influence of psychology, the artist increasingly fits the description of the "neurotic type." No longer believing in his soul, nor in the validity of the experience of his soul, the artistic mission that could have been the meaning of his life becomes pointless. When the connection between immortality and art is severed, the creative person is cast adrift in life. All that is left to him then is his personal anxieties. The potential artist who has ended in neurosis under the guidance of psychology constructs his art work out of his fear of life, and uses it as a substitute for living. His art then displays the characteristics of the psychological attitude. Self-conscious and self-analytical, art becomes, like psychology, a way of rationalizing life and, ultimately, a means of avoiding it.

"In their extremely conscious effort to reproduce what they call the 'unconscious,'" Rank says, "modern painters and writers have followed modern psychology in attempting the impossible, namely to rationalize the irrational." [64] But if we do not seek to restrict the irrational with reasonable explanations, what else shall we do with it? Rank's answer was direct: Live it. "I have realized more and more," he wrote

[64] Rank, *Beyond Psychology, op. cit.*, p. 13.

in his last year, "that, because of the inherent nature of the human being, man has always lived beyond psychology, that is, irrationally." [65] When the artist undertakes to interpret the sources of his creative work intellectually, and when he assigns specific "reasons why" he is engaged in art, he is being untrue to the inner principle of his existence as an artist. These sources are far beyond rationality; but they are no less valid, and no less true.

At the core of his being, the artist is a hero in embryo, for the primordial hero is his prototype. To say this means simply that the driving force behind the artist's life is an unconscious striving to create an individual work that will give him immortality, just as the hero struggles for the prize that brings eternal life. Rank's conception here has much in common with C. G. Jung's theory of the archetypes. The hero as a "prototype" corresponds to a potentiality in the nature of an individual that stamps him as a particular "type," in this case the heroic or creative type. Such "types" have their basis in the deep ground of human nature of which Jung spoke as the psychoid substrate of the unconscious. Their underlying patterns of behavior are universal, and since the essence of these patterns is generically true for mankind as a species, they provide the basis of the archetypal themes of mythology that are found in all races. The point that Rank stresses, and that brings an exceedingly valuable clarification of Jung's point of view, is that these "archetypes" —or "prototypes" as Rank prefers to call them—vary with man's cultural situation. In the changing contexts of history, the figure of the hero appears in diverse forms as a deep unconscious image that is eventually expressed in the individual's life as a drive to a dedicated heroic existence

[65] *Ibid.*, p. 14.

either in warfare, or religion, or art, or as a creative individual in another field depending upon the circumstances of the time. Always the individual experiences his life in a particular historical version whose tone and limitations are set by the "ideology" of the "era," but underlying the historical forms is the "prototype" that contains beyond rationality the latent *patterns* in which the will will *tend* to be expressed in that personality.

These deep psychoid images, described in detail by Jung and worked with in principle by Rank, are the primary forces in the individual's life. They set, in the seed of the human being, the "nature" or "type" of his personality, give to each his peculiar destiny, and place each person upon his characteristic path in life. [66] The potentialities of the individual's existence are implicit in the "prototype" that is effective for each personality; and this, being made, as Rank says, of "mythical stuff," carries overtones of transcendent validity. There is, for example, in the creative type of person an "inner hero" seeking to find expression in life by means of a work of immortality; and the individual will be "healthy" or "neurotic" according to whether that image of his potentiality finds its proper channel in life. The individual can be true to his prototype, or false to it, and that is a question neither of what he believes consciously nor of what he thinks rationally, but a question of *how he lives*.

"It is not sufficient," Rank writes, "to *see* the irrational element in human life and point it out in *rational* terms.

[66] It is interesting to note in this respect that the historical conception of types that Rank developed is much closer to the spirit of Jung's theory of archetypes than the more academic theory of types in terms of "psychological functions" as thinking, feeling, etc., which Jung developed in his early years shortly after he had left Freud.

On the contrary, it is necessary actually to live it." [67] If modern man wishes to take an effectively creative step, he must go beyond the formulas with which psychology seeks to fit life into its ideology, and by which it achieves its partial therapies. He must realize that the insight into the paradoxical irrationality of man's life that comes from depth psychology is only an intellectual starting point. If we linger with it conceptually, seeking to theorize *about* it and describe its endless detail, we remain in the realm of rationalization, and have failed to take the vital step that is the ultimate meaning of our new knowledge.

Realizing this, Rank took cognizance of a fundamental weakness inherent in his own mature work. His first step beyond psychology had been an effort to understand the irrational depths of the human psyche in the perspective of history, but he recognized now that this also had involved a rationalization of material that was inherently irrational. His own study of "ideologies" had itself verged on becoming an ideology. "When I first realized," Rank wrote in the preface of *Beyond Psychology*, candidly recapitulating the phases of his development, "that people, though they may think and talk rationally—and even behave so—yet live irrationally, I thought that 'beyond' individual psychology simply meant social or collective psychology until I discovered that this too is generally conceived of in the same rational terms. Hence my recognition of the ideologies—including those determining our psychological theories—was not sufficient to complement our understanding of individual behavior because they too were stated in terms of the rational aspect of human life. In fact these ideologies more than any-

[67] Rank, *Beyond Psychology, op. cit.*, p. 14.

thing else seem to carry the whole rationalization that man needs in order to live irrationally." [68]

Rank then set out to revise his point of view once again at a fundamental level. Having gone "beyond psychology" once, he now undertook to go even beyond his own first effort. "The 'beyond' individual psychology," he said, "meant not, as I first thought, a resorting to collective ideologies as a subject of social psychology; it actually meant the irrational basis of human nature which lies beyond any psychology, individual or collective." [69] His systematic study of man's irrational behavior in history had given him an insight that pointed beyond itself, and Rank accepted its implications. He did not shrink from acknowledging that even his own most advanced depth psychology researches would need to be transcended. He undertook toward the end of his life the task of framing a new point of view based upon the culminating insight that "Man is born beyond psychology and he dies beyond it but he can *live* beyond it only through vital experience of his own—in religious terms, through revelation, conversions, or rebirth." [70]

As a result of his earlier studies, Rank was able to understand at least the outline of what such a "vital experience" involves. It takes place at a psychic level deeper than rationality, and its result is a sense of connection to life that extends beyond the present moment in all the directions of time. Immortality becomes then not merely continued individual existence, but a sense of more-than-personal participation in everlasting life. In this experience, the individual finds a "new soul," not quite literally but in essence, because he now perceives his personal existence in a new light. Rank spoke of this in the traditional religious terms of

[68] *Ibid.*, pp. 11, 12.   [69] *Ibid.*, p. 12.   [70] *Ibid.*, p. 16.

"revelation, conversion, or rebirth," but he was referring to the general pattern of spiritual transformation, and not to a specific theology. The new outlook does not come as a result of conscious or "rational" thought, but from a dark psychic source not directly accessible to the mind. It comes as of its own volition, and therefore it gives the impression of being a "revelation." It opens a vision of man's life and of its transcendent significance that brings conviction on a level that psychological rationalizations cannot reach; thus it is experienced as a "conversion." And because the new perception of reality changes the nature of life itself, the individual becomes capable of being in actuality a kind of person he could not be before. A new person with a "new soul" emerges by "rebirth"; and projecting this into the future, Rank envisages "a new type of human being" coming to the forefront of history with a "new structure of personality." [71]

The road beyond psychology leads to a point where art and religion meet, join, and transform each other. Today the creative person projects his creativity into an external "work" in art or science or business, and he lives through it instead of through his own developed personality. The modern artist *uses* his art work, either as a means of livelihood in a commercial world, or more often, following the psychological ideology, as a tool of personal therapy. Now, Rank says, if the creative person would fulfill the meaning of his life and play a heroic role in the modern world, he must forsake the use of his art work as a crutch on which to lean as he hobbles through life. He must rather learn to walk under his own spiritual power in the world, and be the one to take the lead in going beyond this "transitional psycho-therapeutic stage" in which we find ourselves at present. He must undertake a

[71] Rank, *Art and Artist, op. cit.,* pp. 391, 430.

new art work that can be nothing else than his own personal existence; and in that work he will find both the "new soul" and the intimate sense of connection to life that the modern personality requires. With a vitalizing experience of immortality as a reality enduring in all present moments and making each an Eternal Now, the modern person will open a new life for himself, as Paul did upon the road to Damascus in another age and in a different framework of beliefs.[72] Paul's encounter with transcendent reality was unique for him in the terms of his own life. The modern person of the creative type must struggle and wait until a comparable transforming experience, unique according to each individual's own life, comes to him. When it comes, if he is open to the irrational depths of his nature and recognizes it, he will be able to relive personally in the modern world the destiny of the primordial hero who is the prototype of the man whose art work is his own life.

By the long and difficult process we have described, Otto Rank took his two steps beyond psychology, going first beyond a psychology of consciousness and individualism, and then beyond a social psychology that studied the depths of history. By means of his historical depth psychology, Rank reached the irrational ground of man's existence. He saw then that the individual life is irreducible, and that there is no rational substitute for each man's experience of his own soul in the light of immortality. This was Rank's own experience in the few years immediately before he died. He hardly had time to attempt to live his vision, but his contribution lies in the integrity and the insight with which he pointed it out. The fundamental significance of Rank's work lies in his perception of the fact that *psychology leads beyond*

[72] Rank, *Beyond Psychology, op. cit.,* pp. 156-159.

itself. He understood that the role of psychology is as an intermediary by means of which the modern man can make the transition from his old spiritual beliefs to the experience of a "new soul" still to come. In this special sense, Rank's later writings represent the culmination of the classic period of depth psychology. He marked off the historical limits of the psychological view of man, and by doing so he opened larger vistas for the future in which psychology can play a new and creative role.

VIII

Growth and metamorphosis:

the emergence of the new psychology

In the course of a half a century, the old conceptions with which Freud began have been transformed into a new view of man. The change, as we have seen, has been gradual; but it has had a cumulative effect. Its net result has been the emergence of a new kind of psychology that no longer seeks to diagnose the modern man and reduce him to "normality." It attempts instead to provide a means by which the modern person can experience the larger meanings of life and participate in them with all his faculties. An awareness of man's spiritual nature has gradually replaced the materialism on which psychology was based in its analytical period. Psychology is now prepared to play a new role in western civilization. Its special knowledge is directed toward enlarging the capacities of life in modern times, thus making it psychologically possible for a revitalization to take place in the arts, in religion, and in all the fields of creative endeavor. The new psychology recognizes the fact that its function in the modern world is as a preliminary discipline. Its task is to open a road beyond itself, realizing that the creative experiences to which it leads can be *lived only beyond psychology*.

We have seen how the first enthusiasms of psychoanalysis ended in disappointment. After developing a large systematic theory, Freud came reluctantly to the conclusion that the depths of the psyche transcend rationality and that, therefore, an understanding of the unconscious is ultimately beyond the reach of analytical concepts. He tried then to deepen his concepts, especially with his theory of the superego and the id; but he had to confess in the end that even these new categories enabled him to make very little headway. Freud was aware of the fact that he had reached an impasse and that he was temperamentally unable to go beyond it. Nevertheless, because of the integrity with which he pursued his studies, his failure called attention to the area where a fundamental reorientation was needed. He himself could not achieve it, but those who had learned from him were able to bring new understanding. After they had freed themselves from many of Freud's personal preconceptions by reconstructing his theories in their own terms, Adler, Jung, and Rank attempted, in their individual ways, to break through the stalemate in Freud's thought; and each had a measure of success.

Of the three, C. G. Jung was the one who worked most directly with Freud's fundamental conception of man. In several stages, Jung steadily expanded the psychoanalytical theory of the unconscious, applying it, as Freud had begun to do, to impersonal or "collective" levels that underlie the individual personality. Extending this line of approach, Jung came at length to a conception of the "self" as the source of all the tendencies and potentialities of human nature. Working with the Freudian hypothesis of the unconscious depths, he was led to a view of man that placed the category of the "unconscious" in a more-than-psychological perspective. He realized that the very fact of human personality carries "metaphysical" overtones. Man's psychological nature suggests something transcedent of which the psyche is but a partial reflection. Across the centuries, man has been driven by an insatiable yearning to find the transcendent meaning of his life and to participate in it. Jung regarded this unconscious striving as a fundamental fact of the human spirit, so fundamental that he claimed that modern psychology is not entitled to call itself "empirical" unless it takes it into account.

At first Jung felt that his "scientific" role required him to interpret man's spiritual nature in strictly psychological terms; and he did this mostly by reducing spiritual experiences to the "archetypal" symbols of the "collective unconscious." In his last years, however, Jung found that his psychological hedge was a flimsy and artificial protection, for the psychologist cannot stand apart as an impartial observer of man's fate. He too is involved as a human being, and if he does not come to grips with the ultimate spiritual problems of life, his psychology will be nothing more than academic talk. Impelled by this awareness, by his personal need, and by his desire to enlarge the vistas of psychology, Jung struggled toward an experience of his own. Finally, in the intensely personal, quasi-religious work that he wrote at the age of 76, his commentary on God's *Answer to Job*, he went far in the direction of a metaphysical encounter with "reality" as "reality" is reflected in the Bible. But even then Jung did not overcome the intellectual habits of his analytical psychology, and this failure vitiated his religious experience.

Somewhat earlier than Jung, Alfred Adler reached a similar conclusion that man's psychological existence carries intimations of an essentially spiritual nature. Adler, however, did not amplify this view with the rich symbolical details that embellish Jung's writings. With characteristic directness, he interpreted the "metaphysical" aspect of personality as, in a sense, the cosmic equivalent of the relationship between two human beings. Adler spoke of "social feeling" as the cement that holds the universe together, and he was referring here to the inner kinship that binds all things and establishes the hidden harmonies of life. Social feeling meant to Adler the principle that links man not only to others of his species but to all creation. It was fundamentally a cosmic sense that he had in mind, but he expressed it in its specifically human application. It was a typically "extrovert" thing to do. Adler had achieved a metaphysical experience of major importance, but he limited its significance by describing it in terms of his own extroverted "style of life"; and that is the major reason why the deeper religious implications are much less obvious in Adler's work than in Jung's. Intellectually, Adler's point of view derived from Darwinian evolution, but his conception of the wholeness of the human organism eventually developed to the point where it had a great deal in common with Jung's far-reaching, cosmic as well as psychological, theory of the Self. Wholeness came to mean to Adler not only the fulfillment of the organism as a physical and psychological being, but also man's "perfectibility" as a spiritual being. It suggested a religious orientation with social applications, and Adler had begun to follow its new directions when he encountered the unhappy events of his last years.

Both Jung and Adler went to the borders of psychology and looked beyond. Each was convinced in the later period of his work that the truth about man's life lies somewhere over the edges of psychological theory. It remained, however, for Otto Rank to demonstrate that this was much more than a personal belief of theirs but an unavoidable outcome of psychoanalysis. With his historical style of study, Rank showed that all analytical types of psychology require a step beyond themselves; otherwise they remain on the treadmill of self-conscious analysis. The intellectual and interpretive side of Rank's work thus provided a perspective and a foundation for the special points of view at which Adler and Jung arrived independently. Rank established an intellectual basis for the step beyond analytical psychology, and his last writings before his untimely death were the beginnings of his effort to convert his new insights into the reality of personal experience.

After Rank, psychology enters a new period. It is not that he singlehandedly changed the direction of psychological work; for he did not. The works of the other three, Freud, Adler, and Jung are integral parts of the transformation of psychology. Rank's special significance derives from the fact that he carried the insights of the others far toward their logical conclusions, and because of this, much that was merely implicit in them becomes clear and evident from Rank's last books. With Rank, depth psychology finally became capable of understanding itself in perspective. It could see its transitional role in history, and it could perceive that the fundamental problems of psychology are intimately connected with man's search for a meaning in life. Freud had a vision of this, blurred but growing stronger in his later years. Adler and Jung saw it more sharply, each with increasing depth. Rank, however, brought the implications fully into the open where they could be faced squarely beyond all unconscious hedging.

If psychology is to fulfill the purpose inherent in its historical existence, if it is to enable the modern man to find the meaning of his life, it can do so only by guiding him to an experience that is beyond psychology. This conclusion culminates the analytical phase of depth psychology, and provides the starting point for its growth in new directions. It involves a radical reversal of the point of view with which Freud began, but it must be understood also as an outgrowth of Freud's foundational concepts. The new kind of psychology emerged because the logical consequences of psychoanalysis were considered and reconsidered first by Freud himself, then by Adler and Jung, and ultimately by Otto Rank. The important point that has reappeared throughout our study is that this progressive reconstruction of Freud's original conceptions has consistently involved an enlargement and refinement of the depth view of man. It was, in fact, the realization that the unconscious depths of man contain much more than Freud's first formulations had described that began the process which has resulted in the transformation of psychology. And now, as the end product, we have the emergence of a new kind of psychology that continues Freud's penetration into the depths of man, but in a transmuted form.

The conception underlying all Freud's work, as we have

seen, was his division of man into "conscious" and "unconscious" segments. Jung accepted the principle of this separation, even emphasizing it and concentrating much of his work on the effort to define the historical and mythological contents of the unconscious. As he pursued the distinction between consciousness and the unconscious to the deeper levels of the psyche, Jung found, however, that it was not as substantial as he had thought. Of much greater significance than the division in man was the underlying unity of the psychic organism. In his later writings, Jung thus attempted a description of this unity, interpreting it, on the one hand, in terms of man's emergence from evolution as a species, in which case he spoke of it as the *psychoid* substrate of personality; and on the other hand, as the seed of spiritual potentiality in man, which he referred to as the *Self*.

Adler never agreed with Freud that the distinction between consciousness and the unconscious has a fundamental importance. From the very beginning, he insisted on the inherent unity of the human organism which, he said, always functions as a whole since one part invariably compensates for another. The process of "compensation" that Adler described in detail was based on a conception of the "will" as a depth principle of the personality. This was not, however, comparable to Nietzsche's theory of the "will to power," as it has often been misinterpreted to be, but was simply a conception of the will unconsciously striving to overcome the inferiorities of the organism as a whole in order to maintain the ego in the face of an unfriendly environment. Adler's theory of wholeness was a conception of the functioning balance of the organism; but it was also something more. It involved a sense of wholeness emerging from the seed of the personality, an innate striving toward "perfectibility,"

and it is at this point that Adler and Jung approach each other in agreement on the emergent nature of the human spirit.

After he left Freud, Rank went along the path that Adler had taken. He also accepted the view that the division between consciousness and the unconscious is misleading since man lives as a unity; and Rank, like Adler, based his theories on the will as the integrating principle of the personality. Rank, however, interpreted the will in terms of its historical expressions and also as a primary instrument of creative and religious experience. By doing this he developed, within his own frame of reference and with his special intellectual skill, many of the insights that Adler had suggested but had left in undeveloped form. At many points we find that Rank's writings form a bridge connecting the systems of Adler and Jung, for the theoretical structure of his work is essentially an interpretation of the historical depths of the unconscious in terms of the unity of the organism and the will.

As we follow these varied lines of thought to the crossroads where they eventually meet, we arrive at a common ground that provides the conceptual basis for the new kind of psychology. Beginning with Freud's analysis of the repressed personal material, the study of the unconscious steadily deepened as Adler, Jung and then Rank penetrated the historical levels of the psyche. Their psychological investigations led them to a realization of the fundamentally spiritual nature of man, and this introduced a new dimension to their work. More important, then, than the insights they achieved intellectually was the direct contact they reached with the profound symbolism of the depths of man, the symbols in which the ultimate aspect of man's existence are reflected. As they came into touch with what is "mythically" and inherently valid in man's life, they gained an insight of larger significance than anything they had attained analytically.

They were led to an experience of the spiritual core of man's being, to the seed of personality that unfolds psychologically in each person and yet is always more than psychological. They came, in other words, to the metaphysical foundation of life that underlies psychology; and since each one experienced it in a personal way, each gave it a different name. Freud spoke of it as the superego accepting the ego, a characteristically intellectual way to describe a basic cosmic experience. Adler called it "social feeling," and through it he gained a profound and intimate connection to life. Jung referred to it as the "individuation" of the "Self," an abstract phrase to describe his effort to experience the cosmos psychologically by means of symbols. And Rank studied it as "the will to immortality," which meant to him man's inherent need to live in the light of eternity. Each of these terms involved a psychological experience, and each of them referred ultimately to a contact with a larger realm of reality in which man's psychological nature transcends itself. Individually, Freud, Adler, Jung, and Rank came to this culminating insight, and the totality of their experiences form the foundations of the new psychology.

The process of discovery that we have traced in this book leads to the paradoxical conclusion that psychological work fulfills itself only when it goes beyond psychology. The old analytical theories were caught in a psychological circle of their own creation, and it cut them off from life. To break out of that circle, we require a theory and practice that approaches the human personality with an awareness of its magnitude; and especially one that uses psychological concepts as instruments with which to develop man's spiritual and creative capacities.

It cannot be said that any one of the authors we have been discussing satisfies this criterion, but each of them contributes to its fulfillment. Considered as a whole as they have unfolded over the years, their collective lifeworks comprise the chief source of insight for the new kind of psychology. In their continuing concern with the development of basic concepts, their formulations have fertilized one another, and their joint efforts have provided the elements for a profound and varied understanding of man's psychological nature in ever-expanding contexts.

One of the most significant and valuable instances of this is the conception of wholeness with which Alfred Adler began. Working in the years around the turn of the century, Adler's early vision was limited to a conception of the human organism as a functional biological unit; but in his later years he progressed toward the view of Jan Christian Smuts that personality is the creative spiritual principle in the wholeness of man, the living seed of unfolding potentiality in human nature.[1] This conception, as we have seen, involved a major enlargement in Adler's general approach to psychology, but it did not bring him the specific knowledge he required. The irrational depths in the seed of personality were still inaccessible to him. It remained for Jung and Rank to develop the conceptual tools with which to interpret the historical forces in the modern personality and to clarify the strange though dynamic effects of the symbols that arise out of the dark mythologic levels of the psyche. With the larger understanding that their concepts provided, Jung and Rank amplified Adler's sense of the emergent wholeness of

[1] Jan Christian Smuts, *Holism and Evolution.*

man. Their psychological study of the deep unconscious made it possible to comprehend the spiritual aspects of the personality more specifically, in a much more meaningful and workable way than Adler's theories alone had made possible.

The later, advanced works of Adler, Jung, and Rank complement one another, balance one another, and give one another depth and perspective. Drawn together in terms of their ultimate conclusions, they provide the basis for a new and constructive period in psychological work. With this in mind, one of our main purposes in writing this book has been to break the ground for an eventual integration of their individual systems from the point of view of their culminating insights. This would involve a reconstruction in the foundations of depth psychology, both in its theory and practise; and should it be achieved, it would provide us with a body of hypotheses and working principles sufficient to take us far in the new directions leading beyond the analytical types of psychology. Toward that time, there are many empirical data that still need to be collected and collated with reference to the new orientation. Depth psychology is in a unique position, for at the point in the foreseeable future when it will finally establish its position as the fundamental science of man, it will do so by validating the very opposite of the materialistic view of life that was the premise of the natural sciences in a day gone by. It will then, in all likelihood, open a psychological road toward the view of the universe emerging from the new physics.

The foundation of the new kind of psychology is its conception of man as an organism of psychological depth and of spiritual magnitude. Its underlying aim is to carry out its psychological work on the unconscious levels of the personality in such a way as to open the dormant potentialities of the spirit and permit them to emerge and unfold. This means something considerably more basic than the analytical development of those capacities that the individual requires in order to adapt successfully in the modern competitive world. It involves much more, a penetration by psychological experience deep into the core of one's being, deep into the spiritual seed of life itself. The ultimate task of the new psychology is to re-establish man's *connection to life*, not superficially in terms of slogans or therapeutic stratagems, but fundamentally and actually as an evident fact of modern existence. Its task is to bring the modern person into touch with the sustaining and creative forces of life beyond all intellectual doctrines that may be preached or professed, to make these forces available to man, and to make man psychologically available to them in terms of experiences that he can learn to verify by himself, within himself. In this way, depth psychology will finally fulfill the purpose for which history called it into existence in western civilization. It will then make its destined contribution to the search for a faith beyond dogma in which the man of science is presently engaged; for of all the programs offered in our time, the new depth psychology holds the greatest promise of leading the modern man along the road of science to an experience of the meaning and the spiritual authenticity of his inner life.

Since the time when the Freudian psychology first came into vogue, many sensitive persons have felt that there must be a close kinship between the psychology of the depths of man and the problems of religion, the arts, and the creative personality in everyday life. Consequently, there have been innumerable attempts to relate depth psychology to religion and art; but for the most part these have been uneasy failures, suggesting that, despite their very good intentions, they were artificially contrived. The kind of psychology they chose to apply did not deal sympathetically with their material. Working with the analytical type of psychology, they labored under a severe handicap, for its reductive point of view was inherently out of tune with the requirements of spontaneous experience that is the core of the creative life.

Now, however, we have come beyond the analytical period in psychology. At length it is becoming possible for us to proceed with a new view of man, a new structure of thought, and new goals for our psychological work, all in harmony with the deep needs and nature of the human being. We are now much better equipped to attend to the disturbances of spirit in the modern person who has been caught in the transitions of history. While the old analytical psychology verges on death, a new psychology is coming to birth in its very midst, transmuting the old insights and using psychological tools to rebuild the modern spirit. The new psychology brings a conception of personality that nourishes and strengthens man's creative will. Finally it frees us from the chronic pessimism of the age of anxiety out of which we are now emerging. Ours is an age in which science, transforming itself in many areas from physics to psychology, is opening new spiritual vistas and extending the range of modern experience. Emergent depth psychology has a major role to play in the making of the new era, for it brings a great challenge and a great hope to modern man.

Bibliography

Reference is made to the English translation wherever possible. The original French or German version is cited only where no translation has yet been published.

I. THE MAIN WORKS OF SIGMUND FREUD

The Interpretation of Dreams. New York: Basic Books, Inc., 1955.

Psycho-pathology of Everyday Life. New York: The Macmillan Co., 1914.

Totem and Tabu. New York: W. W. Norton & Co., Inc., 1952.

The History of the Psycho-analytical Movement. Washington: Nervous and Mental Disease Publishing Company, 1917.

On Aphasia: A Critical Study. New York: International Universities Press, Inc., 1953.

Moses and Monotheism. New York: Alfred A. Knopf, Inc., 1939.

The Future of an Illusion. International Psycho-analytical Library, No. 15. London: Hogarth Press, Ltd., and the Institute of Psychoanalysis, 1949.

Leonardo Da Vinci: A Study in Psychosexuality. New York: Random House, 1947. Reprinted in Modern Library edition.

An Autobiographical Study. New York: W. W. Norton & Co., Inc., 1952.

Beyond the Pleasure Principle: The International Psycho-analytical
Library, No. 4. New York: Liveright Publishing Corp., 1950.
New Introductory Lectures on Psychoanalysis. New York: W. W.
Norton & Co., Inc., 1933.
The Ego and the Id. London: Hogarth Press, Ltd., and the Institute of
Psycho-analysis, 1949.
Civilization and Its Discontents, The International Psycho-analytical
Library, No. 17. London: Hogarth Press, Ltd., 1930.
A General Introduction to Psycho-analysis. New York: Liveright Pub-
lishing Corp., 1935.
The Problem of Anxiety. New York: W. W. Norton & Co., Inc., 1936.
Group Psychology and the Analysis of the Ego. The International
Psycho-analytical Library. London: Hogarth Press, Ltd., 1922.
The Origins of Psychoanalysis, Letters to Wilhelm Fliess, Drafts and
Notes: 1887–1902. Marie Bonaparte, Anna Freud, and Ernst
Kris (eds.). New York: Basic Books, Inc., 1954.

II. THE MAIN WORKS OF ALFRED ADLER

A Study of Organ Inferiority and Its Psychical Compensations. Wash-
ington: Nervous and Mental Disease Monograph Series, No. 24,
1917.
The Neurotic Constitution. New York: Moffat, Yard & Company,
1917.
The Practise and Theory of Individual Psychology. New York: Har-
court, Brace and Co., 1924.
Understanding Human Nature. Garden City: Garden City Publishing
Company, 1927.
Problems of Neurosis, A Book of Case Histories. Philippe Mairet (ed.).
New York: Cosmopolitan Book Company, 1930.
The Education of Children. New York: Greenberg : Publisher, 1930.
The Science of Living. New York: Greenberg : Publisher, 1939.
The Pattern of Life. W. Beran Wolfe (ed.). London: Kegan Paul,
Trench, Truebner & Co., 1931.
What Life Should Mean to You. Alan Porter (ed.). Boston: Little,
Brown and Co., 1932.
The Case of Miss R., The Interpretation of a Life Story. New York:
Greenberg : Publisher, 1929.

Social Interest: A Challenge to Mankind. London: Faber and Faber, Ltd., 1938.

(with ERNST JAHN) *Religion und Individualpsychologie, Eine Auseinandersetzung,* Vienna, 1931.

III. THE MAIN WORKS OF C. G. JUNG

Collected Papers on Analytical Psychology. Constance Long (ed.). New York: Moffat, Yard & Company, 1920.

Psychology of the Unconscious. New York: Dodd, Mead and Co., 1949. Rewritten under title *Symbole der Wandlung.* Zurich: Rascher, 1952. Translated as *Symbols of Transformation* in *The Collected Works of C. G. Jung,* Bollingen Series, No. 5. New York: Pantheon Books, Inc., 1956.

Psychological Types. New York: Harcourt, Brace and Co., 1923.

Contributions to Analytical Psychology. New York: Harcourt, Brace and Co., 1928.

Modern Man in Search of a Soul. New York: Harcourt, Brace and Co., 1933.

Psychology and Religion, The Terry Lectures. New Haven: Yale University Press, 1938.

The Intergration of the Personality. New York: Farrar and Rinehart, 1939.

Essays on Contemporary Events. London: Routledge and Kegan Paul, Ltd., 1947.

Essays on a Science of Mythology (with CARL KERENYI). Bollingen Series, No. 22. New York: Pantheon Books, Inc., 1949.

Psychology and Alchemy, Collected Works. Bollingen Series, No. 12. New York: Pantheon Books, Inc., 1953.

Two Essays on Analytical Psychology, (rev. ed.), *Collected Works.* Bollingen Series, No. 7. New York: Pantheon Books, Inc., 1953.

The Practise of Psychotherapy, Collected Works. Bollingen Series, No. 16. New York: Pantheon Books, Inc., 1954. Includes Jung's long essay on "The Psychology of Transference."

Answer to Job. London: Routledge and Kegan Paul, 1954.

The Secret of the Golden Flower (with RICHARD WILHELM). London: Kegan Paul, Trench, Truebner & Co., 1931.

The Interpretation of Nature and the Psyche (with W. PAULI). Bollingen Series, No. 48. Pantheon Books, Inc., 1955.

Aion, Untersuchungen zur Symbolgeschichte. Zurich: Rascher, 1951.
Paracelsica, Zwei Vorlesungen über den Arzt und Philosophen Theo-
   phrastus. Zurich: Rascher, 1942.
Uber Psychische Energetik und das Wesen der Traüme. Zurich:
   Rascher, 1948.
Symbolik des Geistes. Zurich: Rascher, 1948.
Gestaltungen des Unbewussten. Zurich: Rascher, 1950.

IV. THE MAIN WORKS OF OTTO RANK

The Myth of the Birth of the Hero. New York: Robert Brunner, 1952.
The Development of Psychoanalysis (with SANDOR FERENCZI). Wash-
   ington: Nervous and Mental Disease Publishing Company, 1925.
The Trauma of Birth. New York: Harcourt, Brace and Co., 1929.
Will Therapy. New York: Alfred A. Knopf, Inc., 1936.
Truth and Reality. New York: Alfred A. Knopf, Inc., 1936.
Will Therapy and *Truth and Reality* published in a one volume edi-
   tion. New York: Alfred A. Knopf, Inc., 1945.
Psychology and the Soul. Philadelphia: University of Pennsylvania
   Press, 1950.
Modern Education, A Critique of Its Fundamental Ideas. New York:
   Alfred A. Knopf, Inc., 1932.
Art and Artist, Creative Urge and Personality Development. New
   York: Alfred A. Knopf, Inc., 1932.
Beyond Psychology. Camden: Haddon Craftsmen, 1941. Posthumously
   and privately printed.

V. SUPPLEMENTARY WORKS

ADLER, GERHARD. *Entdeckung der Seele von Sigmund Freud und Alfred
   Adler zu C. G. Jung.* Zurich: Rascher, 1934.
————. *Studies in Analytical Psychology.* New York: W. W. Norton
   & Co., Inc., 1948.
ALEXANDER, FRANZ. *Fundamentals of Psychoanalysis.* New York: W.
   W. Norton & Co., Inc., 1949.

ALLERS, RUDOLPH. *The Successful Error.* New York: Sheed and Ward, 1940.

ALLPORT, GORDON. *Becoming: Basic Considerations for a Psychology Personality.* Terry Lectures. New Haven: University Press, 1955.

BAUDOUIN, CHARLES. *L'Ame et l'Action.* Geneva: Editions du Mont-Blanc, 1943.

BAYNES, H. G. *Analytical Psychology and the English Mind.* London: Methuen & Co., Ltd., 1950.

BERG, CHARLES. *Deep Analysis.* New York: W. W. Norton & Co., Inc., 1947.

BOTTOME, PHYLLIS. *Alfred Adler: A Biography.* New York: A. P. Putnam's Sons, 1939, 1946.

BRACHFELD, OLIVER. *Inferiority Feelings in the Individual and the Group.* New York: Grune and Stratton, Inc., 1951.

BRAIN, W. RUSSELL. *Mind, Perception and Science.* Oxford: Blackwell Scientific Publications, 1951; U.S.A., Springfield: Charles C Thomas, 1951.

BRILL, A. A. *Basic Principles of Psychoanalysis.* New York: Doubleday and Company, Inc., 1949.

CUSTANCE, JOHN. *Wisdom, Madness, and Folly.* London: Victor Gollancz, Ltd., 1951.

DALBIEZ, ROLAND. *Psychoanalytical Method and the Doctrine of Freud.* New York: Longmans, Green and Co., Inc., 1941.

DESOILLE, R. "Le Rêve Eveillé en Psychothérapie," Essai sur la fonction de regulation de l'inconscient collectif. Paris: Presses Universitaires de France, 1945.

DIEL, PAUL. *La Divinite, Etude Psychoanalytique.* Paris: Presses Universitaires de France, 1950.

DOLLARD, JOHN. *Criteria for the Life-History with Analyses of Six Notable Documents.* New Haven: Yale University Press, 1935; Gloucester: Peter Smith, 1949.

DREIKURS, RUDOLPH. *Fundamentals of Adlerian Psychology.* New York: Greenberg : Publisher, 1950.

ERANOS YEARBOOKS. *Spirit and Nature: Papers from the Eranos Yearbooks.* Series 1. Joseph Campbell and Olga Froebe-Kapteyn (eds.). Bollingen Series No. 30, 1. New York: Pantheon Books, Inc., 1954.

———. *The Mysteries, Papers from the Eranos Yearbooks.* Series 2. Bollingen Series No. 30, 2. New York: Pantheon Books, Inc., 1955.

GANZ, MADELAINE. *The Psychology of Alfred Adler and the Development of the Child*. London: Routledge and Kegan Paul, Ltd., 1953.

HALLIDAY, J. L. *Psychosocial Medicine, A Study of the Sick Society*. London: William Heinemann, Ltd., 1949.

HARDING, M. ESTHER. *Psychic Energy*. Bollingen Series, No. 10. New York: Pantheon Books, Inc., 1947.

———. *The Way of All Women*. New York: Longmans, Green and Co., Inc., 1933.

JONES, ERNEST. *Hamlet and Oedipus*. New York: Doubleday and Company, Inc., 1949, 1954.

———. *The Life and Work of Sigmund Freud*. Vol. I, 1856–1900, "The Formative Years and the Great Discoveries." New York: Basic Books, Inc., 1953.

———. *The Life and Work of Sigmund Freud*. Vol. II, 1901–1919, "Years of Maturity." New York: Basic Books, Inc., 1955.

———. *On the Nightmare*. International Psycho-analytical Library. London: Hogarth Press, Ltd., 1931, 1951.

KARPF, FAY B. *The Psychology and Psycho-Therapy of Otto Rank*. New York: Philosophical Library, 1953.

KRANEFELDT, W. M. *Secret Ways of the Mind*. New York: Henry Holt and Co., Inc., 1932.

KUNKLE, FRITZ. *In Search of Maturity*. New York: Charles Scribner's Sons, 1940.

LEVI, CARLO. *Of Frea and Freedom*. New York: Farrar, Straus and Young, Inc., 1950.

LUDWIG, EMIL. *Doctor Freud, An Analysis and a Warning*. New York: Hellman, Williams & Co., 1947.

MC DOUGALL, WILLIAM. *Body and Mind, A History and Defense of Animism*. London: Methuen & Co., Ltd., 1911.

———. *The Group Mind*. New York: A. P. Putnam's Sons, 1920.

———. *Outline of Abnormal Psychology*. New York: Charles Scribner's Sons, 1926.

MC NEILL, JOHN T. *A History of the Cure of Souls*. New York: Harper & Bros., 1951.

MARTIN, P. W. *Experiment in Depth*. New York: Pantheon Books, Inc., 1955.

MAY, ROLLO. *Man's Search for Himself*. New York: W. W. Norton & Co., Inc., 1953.

———. *The Meaning of Anxiety*. New York: The Ronald Press Company, 1950.

MEIER, C. A. *Antike Inkubation und Moderne Psychotherapie.* Zurich: Rascher, 1949.

MILLIN, SARAH GERTRUDE. *General Smuts.* Boston: Little, Brown and Co., 1936.

MULLAHY, PATRICK. *Oedipus—Myth and Complex.* New York: Hermitage House, Inc., 1948; New York: Evergreen Books, 1955.

MURCHISON, CARL (ed.). *History of Psychology in Autobiography.* 4 vols. Worcester: Clark University Press, 1930, 1932, 1936, 1952.

MUMFORD, LEWIS. *The Condition of Man.* New York: Harcourt, Brace and Co., 1944.

———. *The Conduct of Life.* New York: Harcourt, Brace and Co., 1951.

MURPHY, GARDNER. *Personality.* New York: Harper & Bros., 1947.

MYERSON, ABRAHAM. *Speaking of Man.* New York: Alfred A. Knopf, Inc., 1950.

NEUMANN, ERICH. *The Origins and History of Consciousness.* Bollingen Series, No. 42. New York: Pantheon Books, Inc., 1955.

ORGLER, HERTHA. *Alfred Adler, The Man and His Work.* London: C. W. Daniel Company, Ltd., 1939, 1948.

OVERSTREET, H. A. *The Enduring Quest.* Chautauqua: Chautauqua Press, 1931.

———. *The Mature Mind.* New York: W. W. Norton and Co., Inc., 1949.

PROGOFF, IRA. *Jung's Psychology and Its Social Meaning.* New York: Julian Press, Inc., 1953.

PUNER, HELEN WALKER. *Freud, His Life and His Mind.* New York: Howell, Soskin, Publishers, 1947.

REIK, THEODOR. *From Thirty Years with Freud.* New York: International Universities Press, 1949.

RICHARDS, O. W. *The Social Insects.* New York: Philosophical Library, 1953.

ROBERTS, DAVID E. *Psychotherapy and a Christian View of Man.* New York: Charles Scribner's Sons, 1950.

SACHS, HANNS. *Freud, Master and Friend.* Cambridge: Harvard University Press, 1944.

SALTER, ANDREW. *The Case Against Psychoanalysis.* New York: Henry Holt and Co., Inc., 1952.

SCHAER, HANS. *Religion and the Cure of Souls in Jung's Psychology.* Bollingen Series, No. 21. New York: Pantheon Books, Inc., 1950.

SCHNEIDER, LOUIS. *The Freudian Psychology and Veblen's Social Theory.* New York: King's Crown Press, 1948.

SINNOTT, EDMUND W. *The Biology of the Spirit*. New York: Viking Press, Inc., 1955.

SOROKIN, PITIRIM A. *Altruistic Love*. Boston: Beacon Press, 1950.

———. *The Crisis of Our Age*. New York: E. P. Dutton and Co., Inc., 1946.

———. *The Reconstruction of Humanity*. Boston: Beacon Press, 1948.

SMUTS, JAN CHRISTIAN. *Holism and Evolution*. New York: The Macmillan Co., 1926.

STEKEL, WILHELM. *Technique of Analytical Psychotherapy*. New York: Liveright Publishing Corp., 1938, 1950.

STERN, KARL. *The Third Revolution*. New York: Harcourt, Brace and Co., 1954.

THOMPSON, CLARA. *Psychoanalysis: Evolution and Development*. New York: Hermitage House, Inc., 1950.

TOYNBEE, ARNOLD. *Civilization on Trial*. New York: Oxford University Press, 1948.

TRILLING, LIONEL. *Freud and the Crisis of Our Culture*. Boston: Beacon Press, 1955.

TRUB, HANS. *Heilung aus der Begegnung*. Stuttgart: Klett Verlag, 1951.

VAN DER HOOP, J. H. *Character and the Unconscious, A Critical Exposition of the Psychology of Freud and Jung*. New York: Harcourt, Brace and Co., 1923.

VAN DER VELDT, JAMES H., and ODENWALD, ROBERT P. *Psychiatry and Catholicism*. New York: McGraw-Hill Book Co., 1952.

VEBLEN, THORSTEIN. *The Instinct of Workmanship*. New York: Viking Press, Inc., 1914, 1937.

———. *The Place of Science in Modern Civilization*. New York: Viking Press, Inc., 1919, 1942.

WAY, LEWIS. *Adler's Place in Psychology*. London: George Allen and Unwin, Ltd., 1950.

WECHSLER, I. S. *The Neurologist's Point of View*. New York: A. A. Wyn, Inc., 1950.

WELLISCH, ERICH. *Isaac and Oedipus*. London: Routledge and Kegan Paul, Ltd., 1954.

WHITE, VICTOR, O.P., *God and the Unconscious*. London: The Harvill Press, Ltd., 1952.

WICKES, FRANCES G. *The Inner World of Childhood*. New York: Appleton-Century-Crofts, Inc., 1927.

———. *The Inner World of Man*. New York: Farrar and Rinehart, 1938.

WITTELS, FRITZ. *Freud and His Times.* New York: Liveright Publishing Corp., 1931.

WORTIS, JOSEPH. *Fragments of an Analysis with Freud.* New York: Simon and Schuster, Inc., 1954.

ZILBOORG, GREGORY. *Sigmund Freud, His Exploration of the Mind of Man.* New York: Charles Scribner's Sons, 1951.

ABOUT THE AUTHOR

Both as critic of the old and as originator of new conceptions, Dr. Ira Progoff has long been in the vanguard of those who have worked toward a dynamic humanistic psychology. In his practice as therapist, in his books, as lecturer and group leader, as Bollingen Fellow, and as Director of the Institute for Research in Depth Psychology at the Graduate School of Drew University, he has conducted pioneer research and has developed major new techniques for the enlargement of human potential.

These studies have led to the founding of two significant organizations. The first is Dialogue House Associates which is devoted to using the *Intensive Journal* developed by Dr. Progoff as the basis for varied programs of personal growth in education, religion, industry, and social organization. The second is the Humanic Arts Research and Resource Center, which is devoted to developing experiential programs of advanced training for people who work in the helping and teaching professions.